VIRTUAL AESTHETICS IN ARCHITECTURE

Virtual Aesthetics in Architecture: Designing in Mixed Realities presents a curated selection of projects and texts contributed by leading international architects and designers who are using virtual reality technologies in their design process. It triggers discussion and debate on exploring the aesthetic potential and establishing its language as an expressive medium in architectural design. Although virtual reality is not new and the technology has evolved rapidly, the aesthetic potential of the medium is still emerging and there is a great deal more to explore.

The book provides a comprehensive overview of the current use of virtual reality technologies in the architectural design process. Contributions are presented in six parts, fully illustrated with over 150 images.

Recent projects presented are distributed in five themes: introduction to mixed realities; space and form; context and ambiguity; materiality and movement; body and social. Each theme includes richly illustrated essays by leading academics and practitioners, including those from Zaha Hadid Architects and MVRDV, detailing their design process using data-driven methodologies.

Virtual Aesthetics in Architecture expands the use of technology *per se* and focuses on how architecture can benefit from its aesthetic potential during the design process. A must-read for practitioners, academics, and students interested in cutting-edge digital design.

Sarah Eloy is PhD in Architecture and Assistant Professor. Eloy's main areas of research include digital technologies applied to architecture, shape grammars, virtual and augmented reality, space perception, and housing rehabilitation. She is the director of the Information Sciences, Technologies, and Architecture Research Centre (ISTAR) at Instituto Universitário de Lisboa (ISCTE-IUL), where she is also a fellow researcher. She has curated "CLOSE to cities and CLOSER to people" for the Lisbon Architecture Triennale 2013 and "Artificial Realities: Virtual as an Aesthetic Medium for Architectural Ideation" for the Lisbon Architecture Triennale 2019. She has participated in national and international research projects and published her work in several journals.

Anette Kreutzberg is Teaching Associate Professor at the Institute of Architecture and Design at the Royal Danish Academy, and a member of the Architectural Representation research and teaching unit. Kreutzberg's activities focus on the digital representation of architectural concepts, with a special interest in the Nordic daylight phenomena. Her research involves the use of immersive VR, 360° panorama photography and renderings, as well as animation and interactive media as tools to experience and evaluate daylight quality in architectural spaces.

Ioanna Symeonidou is Assistant Professor at the Department of Architecture at the University of Thessaly, specializing in digital media for design and manufacturing. She graduated from the Architecture Department of the Aristotle University of Thessaloniki and completed her postgraduate studies at the Architectural Association in London. Her PhD focuses on digital design and construction methods. Symeonidou has previously taught at the Department of Architecture at the Aristotle University of Thessaloniki, and the Graz University of Technology in Austria. She is the author of more than 40 papers published in scientific journals, books, and conference proceedings, and has participated in research projects in Greece and abroad.

VIRTUAL AESTHETICS IN ARCHITECTURE

Designing in Mixed Realities

Edited by Sara Eloy, Anette Kreutzberg, and Ioanna Symeonidou

Routledge
Taylor & Francis Group
NEW YORK AND LONDON

First published 2022
by Routledge
605 Third Avenue, New York, NY 10158

and by Routledge
2 Park Square, Milton Park, Abingdon, Oxon, OX14 4RN

Routledge is an imprint of the Taylor & Francis Group, an informa business

Library of Congress Cataloging-in-Publication Data
A catalog record for this book has been requested

ISBN: 978-1-032-02372-4 (hbk)
ISBN: 978-1-032-02373-1 (pbk)
ISBN: 978-1-003-18310-5 (ebk)

DOI: 10.4324/9781003183105

Typeset in Bembo
by Apex CoVantage, LLC

Photo of the cover by Mariana Veríssimo from the Perspectiva Virtuais project by Julien Rippinger and Arthur Lachard.

CONTENTS

PREFACE

Sara Eloy, Anette Kreutzberg, and Ioanna Symeonidou

Virtual reality and technology projects involving simulated environments have been around since the 1950s. In recent years, the interest in virtual reality (VR), augmented reality (AR), and mixed reality (MR) has been reawakened due to open-source, lower-cost, higher-quality, and easier-to-use hardware and software, now linked with game engines. In addition, the emerging social virtual reality (SVR) as well as x-reality (XR), in which ubiquitous sensors and actuator networks play a role, are being used to generate a new blend of virtual and physical realities. Together with the Internet and its potential as a cultural communication channel, these realities now are gaining a new momentum.

Virtual reality is currently used as an umbrella term to refer to other technologies similar to, but different from, an actual VR experience, and this is how we will use VR in this preface. Since these technologies are constantly evolving, new terms to describe immersive experiences will continue to emerge in the years to come.

Architectural design professionals are increasingly discovering the potential of these technologies. Architecture is no longer tied to specific geographical places but can instead be present in multiple environments and in multiple ways that extend beyond real-world experiences. The use of VR is now widespread in architecture, and the work which has been developed has focused in particular on user studies, collaborative design, building management, and design education. These studies and the associated publications are related to the benefits of VR in simulating environments, comparisons of different VR systems, new VR systems, and frameworks for designers, as well as the evaluation of collaborative practices in design and the integration of VR within schools of architecture.

Although VR as a technology is not new, its aesthetic dimension has still not been fully explored.

In October 2019, a group of leading international architects and designers who are using VR technologies in their design process gathered in Lisbon for the *Artificial Realities: Virtual as an Aesthetic Medium for Architectural Ideation* exhibition and conference, a project associated with the *Lisbon Architecture Triennale 2019*. During the course of one week, we presented and discussed the role of mixed realities and virtual aesthetics in architecture. This event paved the way for subsequent discussions that were extended to a larger number of practitioners that are now part of this book, exploring ways in which virtual technologies can enable designers to expand their creative processes and present them aesthetically.

From the "Poetics of Reason", the keynote of the *Lisbon Architecture Triennale 2019*, to the new domains of the digital in the design process, we have framed this project around the confrontation between technology and poetry, and between rationality/efficiency and aesthetics/art in relation to the virtual technologies applied to the architectural design process. The experience of the architectural space and the state of contemplation and delight in the architectonic exercise materialize through the digital throughout this book.

Virtual Aesthetics explores the ways in which mixed realities, namely VR and AR technologies, can enable designers to create immersive, aesthetically pleasing, and expressive experiences.

The book presents the work of 47 authors from 15 countries, including a curated selection of projects by leading international designers who are using VR and AR technologies in their design process. *Virtual Aesthetics* aims to stimulate discussion and debate, not only on the two keystones of VR (immersion and interaction), but mainly on exploring the potential of the aesthetic dimension of the medium and establishing its own language as an expressive medium in architectural design.

The book offers a comprehensive overview of the current use of VR in architectural design processes, both in practice and in academia. Recent projects presented here are organized into six sections: an introduction to visual aesthetics in architecture; space and form; context and ambiguity; materiality and movement; body and social; projects. Each section is fully illustrated with contributions from leading academics and practitioners detailing their design process using different methodologies.

The printed version of the *Virtual Aesthetics* book is augmented by online content that includes videos and navigable content on the VR described in the book. The reader can explore this content by following the QR-codes in the book using a mobile or desktop device.

ACKNOWLEDGEMENTS

We would like to thank all the authors in this book for their pioneering work which, in exploring new approaches in the digital world, has been inspiring the world of architecture.

We would also like to thank the colleagues, students, and staff that were involved in the book, symposium, and conference organization, namely Fábio Costa, Micaela Raposo, Joana Gouveia Alves, Luís Dias, and Nuno Pereira da Silva as well as Sheena Caldwell for her proofreading. Finally, we would like to thank Nancy Diniz for her contribution to this project.

The project *Artificial Realities: Virtual as an Aesthetic Medium for Architectural Ideation* that led to this book was funded by grant FBR_OC1_020—ISCTE from EEAGrants Portugal.

PART 1

Introduction

The Visual Aesthetics of Architecture

This introductory section of the book addresses the topic of **'Visual Aesthetics of Architecture'**, comprising five chapters in which the authors provide an overview of virtual reality (VR) and augmented reality (AR) in architecture and the aesthetic paradigm they bring to the discipline.

Henri Achten follows the developments of VR and AR from a historical point of view, providing the reader with a concise history of these technologies in architecture. He summarizes a number of important milestones from the 1950s to the present day, highlighting the wide range of applications of immersive technologies in architecture and recent developments in academic institutions and pioneering research teams around the world.

From a more philosophical point of view, Federico Ruberto offers an insight into the architectonic of VR. Ruberto discusses the border between the "virtual" and the "physical" (ideal/real) influenced by Lacanian psychoanalysis and epistemological constructivism, alluding to the metaphilosophy of François Laruelle. This contribution offers a new perspective on the real/ideal dyad through a renewed engagement with fiction.

Helmut Kinzler et al. discuss the emergence of cybernetic aesthetics present in the work of Zaha Hadid Architects. Considering the present-day speed of communication and contemporary developments in machine learning, Kinzler et al. question contemporary aesthetics, affirming that never before has our understanding of beauty been so broadly and diversely communicated, reciprocated, and challenged. They contrast the concept of the superindividual with creative collectives and the role of VR within this transition, presenting case studies that reveal the influence of cybernetic culture in architecture.

Questioning the capacity of VR for enhanced 'authenticity' of the first-person experience in architecture, Sean Pickersgill affirms that there is a fundamental tension between the different modes of decision-making in architectural design and the particular focus on phenomenal reality that VR promotes. This contribution discusses the evolution of representational technologies in architecture, from 3D models and animations to immersive experiences, speculating on the capacity of VR to highlight 'pliability and brilliance' as aspects of virtual realities.

Immersive technologies promise to reshape aspects of architectural design, as they provide an interface for visiting, experiencing, sharing, and evaluating the designs, datasets, models, and increasingly data-rich buildings that result from the design process. Dustin Schipper and Brittney Holmes offer a review of the ways in which architects engage with immersive technologies.

DOI: 10.4324/9781003183105-1

They discuss the potential of such technologies to influence the design process today and in the future, and their integration into society and the built environment as the various immersive technologies reach maturity.

Follow the QR-code to navigate through the online content of Part 1.

1

A CONCISE HISTORY OF VR/AR IN ARCHITECTURE

Henri Achten

A concise history of virtual reality (VR) and augmented Reality (AR) in architecture inevitably requires a broad brush, omitting a lot of detail and neglecting many careful considerations from past decades. A certain myopia distorts the overview, since I rely mostly on English-language publications on the topic which disregard a large portion of the work done in South America, for example, or in the French-speaking research community which I got to know through two research stays at the excellent Lab-STICC[1] in Brest, France. Another limitation concerns the sometimes surprisingly scarce documentation on sources, especially for the early days. Moreover, highlighting certain advances may give the impression that inventions and developments were isolated events. However, VR and AR were developed in a 'kettle', informed by an extremely diverse group of scientists, engineers, artists, writers, and philosophers. Thus, much as we like to celebrate the individual, milestones really are the products of their age, reflecting many different influences.

Yet another caveat concerns me, as the author of this overview. I am in no way a specialist in either field, although I did have the privilege of witnessing the work of VR pioneers Walther Roelen, Sjoerd Buma, and Jo Mantelers at my alma mater, Eindhoven University of Technology, from the early 1980s onwards (Achten et al., 1999), and later in the Design Systems group headed by Bauke de Vries (Vries et al., 2003). As a tech-enthusiast, I went to mind-blowing events such as Doors of Perception,[2] read the magazine *Wired* and my fair share of SF, and firmly believed that VRML was the future. In recent years, I had the pleasure of working with Andrew Vandemoere at KU Leuven (Nguyen et al., 2020). Hence, what follows is my understanding of the developments and what has caught my attention over the past 35 years.

At the outset, it is important to define what VR and AR are. I will use this definition as a reference point to indicate the differences when they occur, rather than as a final one. In the beginning, people did not really make rigid distinctions between the terms, as VR was considered augmented reality and vice versa, and they only developed into separate branches later.

Virtual reality can be understood as technology for an immersive perception of a digital model, in such a way that the person using it has the impression that they are inside the model.

Augmented reality can be understood as the coupling of physical objects and digital processes in such a way that any manipulation of one has a causal effect on the other.

The distinguishing feature between the two is that VR attempts to draw the individual completely inside a digital world that is remote from the real world, whereas AR is always tightly coupled with the real world.

DOI: 10.4324/9781003183105-2

The development we now understand as VR is the older of the two. For the current purposes, I will limit myself to the history that most closely resembles mainstream VR technology. Within the five basic human senses, VR predominantly focuses on sight (followed, in descending order, by sound, touch, smell, and taste). Thus, the centrepiece of any VR technology is the display. In order to experience the sensation of being *inside* the display, the projection works either by placing it very close to the eye (using a helmet or glasses) or enclosing the individual within a wide area projection on one or several large screens. Both types of projection can evoke very strong experiences of immersion, even to the extent that perceived movement inside VR actually has physical effects (nausea or problems with balance).

VR purists would draw the line here, but the tricky part in the definition of VR lies in the phrase 'sense of immersion', which is a rather flexible criterion. 'Being immersed' is not a passive act, but a human capacity. Watching a movie or reading a book can give you the feeling of 'being there', while playing with scale models can give you the sense of being in the model: the key point is that you establish some kind of emotional or anticipatory relationship. What distinguishes VR from a good book, or a great movie, is the digital aspect that is being displayed for the user (usually the virtual part of VR). The emotional or anticipatory relationship is established through real-time graphics that are shown on the display. The real-time feedback creates a strong bond between what you do (changing your viewpoint or effecting some action) and the response in the display (an immediately changed perspective or reaction). The implication is that you do not need a head-mounted display or a cave to experience immersion in VR—a simple computer screen suffices.

In a way, VR can be seen as a development in theatre and movie-making. By nature, theatre and movies present an immersive experience, on stage and on the big screen. American cinematographer Morton Heilig (1926–1997) tried to break through the boundaries of movie-making in the 1950s when he created the Sensorama Simulator.[3] It offered a comprehensive single-person 3D-movie experience, complete with sound and smell, wind, and motion. It worked with pre-recorded film, hence the narrative for each use was always the same (there were films for motor-riding, go-karting, helicopter, bicycle, and a belly dancer).[4]

What if the content is not pre-recorded but, thanks to the computer, can be generated on the spot, as the creator or user demands? Ivan Sutherland (born 1938), the famed father of today's CAD systems with his 1963 Sketchpad PhD thesis, gave a lecture at the IFIP Congress (Sutherland, 1965) entitled *The Ultimate Display*. The final section reflected on the lasting dream of Virtual Reality, as a real substitute for reality:

> The ultimate display would, of course, be a room within which the computer can control the existence of matter. A chair displayed in such a room would be good enough to sit in. Handcuffs displayed in such a room would be confining, and a bullet displayed in such a room would be fatal. With appropriate programming such a display could literally be the Wonderland into which Alice walked.
>
> *(Sutherland, 1965, p. 508)*

As a side note, a chair, handcuffs, and plenty of bullets are specifically emphasized visual elements in Morpheus' interrogation scene and Neo's subsequent rescue in the 1999 film *The Matrix*: in a sense, the film deals with the ultimate display Sutherland had described 34 years earlier.

Three years later, the same Ivan Sutherland presented a working prototype for a stereoscopic head-mounted display (Sutherland, 1968). The head-mounted display (HMD hereafter) projects a separate digital image for each eye, thus offering depth information. The position and orientation of the HMD was measured by an arm attached to the ceiling and linked to the HMD (aptly nicknamed the Sword of Damocles). By immediately tracking the user's head position and orientation, the computer would generate an updated 3D view of the model displayed in the HMD. It must be noted that, for this system to work, everything had to be invented by Sutherland and his team. Apart from the displays and the measuring of head position and orientation, especially hidden line removal, clipping of elements outside the viewing space, and perspective drawing, needed to be fast enough to support real-time graphics.

The world of ideas, inventions, and research condensed around the term 'virtual reality' when it was first coined in 1987 by Jaron Lanier (born 1960) (no definite source for this claim can be found). Earlier, Myron Krueger had characterized his work as "artificial reality" (Krueger, 1983), but this term did not catch on. The importance of the term was that it acquired an identity outside the community of people involved in the research, leading to increasing awareness and the spread of the research to areas had not previously used VR.

The term 'augmented reality' was first used by Thomas Caudell in his work for Boeing where, as part of their work, the HMD (called a *HUDset*) was taken out of the laboratory and into the aircraft assembly hall. HUD, or Head-Up Display, refers to the technology in airplanes which overlays information for the pilot on an area in front of his eyes (hence, the pilot can keep his/her *head up* rather than looking down at the controls). Caudell's HUDset would overlay projected information required for tasks such as formboard wiring, connector assembly, composite cloth layup, and maintenance/assembly onto the workers' screen (Caudell and Mizell, 1992). Whereas a VR HMD only needs to track relative movement and head orientation, the HUDset must also match information on the correct location in the real world in the user's view, which is a much more complicated task.

Before looking at architecture, a number of milestones are summarized next, using a slightly adapted list taken from Mazuryk and Gervautz (1996, pp. 2–3):

- Sensorama (1950–1961). Morton Heilig.
- The Ultimate Display (1965). Ivan Sutherland.
- Head-Mounted Display (1968). Ivan Sutherland.
- Grope (1971). Frederick Brooks and team: haptic display with force feedback (Brooks et al., 1990).
- Videoplace (1975). Myron Krueger: live captured video image of a person interacting with virtual objects (Krueger et al., 1985).
- VCASS (1982). Thomas Furness, Visually Coupled Airborne Systems Simulator (Furness and Kocian, 1986).
- VIVED (1984). Virtual Environment Display System. NASA Ames Research Center (McGreevy, 1991).
- VPL Research (1985). VPL (Virtual Programming Languages) Research, founded by Jaron Lanier in 1984, one of the first companies to develop and sell VR products.
- UNC Walkthrough Project (1986). Frederick Brooks and team: a VR environment for architectural walk-throughs (Brooks, 1986).
- BOOM (1989). Fakespace Labs. Commercial stereoscopic high-resolution VR viewer mounted on an arm.
- Virtual Wind Tunnel (early 1990s). NASA Ames Research Center (Bryson and Levit, 1991).
- CAVE (1992). CAVE Automatic Virtual Environment: surround multi-screen projection of a virtual environment (Cruz-Neira et al., 1992).
- Augmented Reality (1992). Thomas Caudell (Caudell and Mizell, 1992).

Returning to architecture, the combination of VR and architecture makes a lot of sense. In 1974, Donald Greenberg had already stated in *Scientific American* (cited from Brooks, 1986, p. 10):

> For architects the ability to simulate motion is highly useful. . . . To obtain a deeper understanding of architectural space it is necessary to move through the space, experiencing new views and discovering the sequence of complex spatial relations.

In the way described by Greenberg, VR has been applied most in architecture as a presentation tool. Although lacking the figures or research for this, I would say that this is also the most successful commercial application of VR in architecture—using "commercial" in the sense of VR moving out of academia to make its own living.

From among many excellent examples, I would highlight three milestones in the application of VR in architecture:

1. Digital city models, for example Glasgow (Maver, 1987). This project was an attempt to model the 6-km^2 centre of Glasgow in a way that enabled the computer to generate on-the-fly perspective views inside the model (at the time, a delay time of 4s was reported for the whole model). Digital city models have culminated in the world-encompassing Google Earth application.
2. Sculptor, developed by David Kurmann at ETH Zürich (Kurmann, 1995). Sculptor offered modelling and manipulation actions inside a VR environment. It kept the actions of the user as simple and direct as possible, without reverting to traditional GUI elements such as 2D input boxes and sliders. Everything was of the 'grab' and 'do something' type. Collision detection and gravity gave the objects physical behaviour which the user understands intuitively.
3. Hyve-3D, being developed by Tomás Dorta at the University of Montreal (Dorta et al., 2016) since the early 2000s. Hyve-3D is a projected virtual environment for sketch and ideation support in architecture. The large projection allows a number of people, both co-located and dispersed in online teams, to take part in the design process.

Despite the promises and potential of VR for architecture, it should be noted that VR never became a standard part of the regular architect's toolkit. Its level of adaptation is far removed from the everyday CAD stations and rendering software that have found their way into almost every office in the world. For a long time, the prohibitive high price of the equipment, sensitivity of the hardware, and specialized software outside mainstream architecture programs were the main cause of this. In the past decade, this changed quite dramatically: reliable and cheap headsets such as the Oculus Rift (introduced in 2012), easy workflows enabled by real-time rendering game engines such as Unity (released in 2005) and Unreal Engine (original 1998, Version 3 from 2004 onwards and free release of Software Development Kit in 2009), and regular computers that can handle modest to advanced models have made the technology much more accessible. Hopefully, these advantages will provide enough momentum for VR to deploy its full potential in the architect's office.

AR, as stated in the introduction, purposefully links physical and digital objects together. I can only partly summarize what has caught my eye concerning works and people I have encountered in recent decades. Personally, I think it helps to consider AR as a subset of the later term "ubiquitous computing" introduced by Mark Weiser (1991). Ubiquitous computing places computing everywhere (embedded in all kinds of physical objects), while AR specifically looks at the causal relationship between the two. In essence, however, they are very closely related, as they increasingly merge the digital and physical worlds.

At TU/Eindhoven, the Design Systems Group was expanding the work on VR to incorporate it as a design tool: AR was the next logical step. From around 2002, we collaborated with Matthias Rauterberg, Jean-Bernard Martens from the Industrial Design Department, and Jarke van Wijk from the Department of Mathematics and Computer Science on various PhD projects and prototypes. One of the first AR systems that I encountered was Built-IT, developed by Matthias Rauterberg at ETH Zürich (Rauterberg et al., 1998). It featured a desk working area with top projection, for example of a building layout, and vertical projection with a 3D view of the layout. By moving special markers on the table, objects could be manipulated in the digital environment.

At the same time, Ianus Keller was working on his PhD project prototype Cabinet at the Department of Industrial Design at TU Delft (Keller, 2005). Cabinet was an image-processing tool. It had a desktop with top-down projection and a camera looking at the desk. Digital images could be projected onto the desk and manipulated directly (using move, rotate, overlay, etc.). A new image was captured simply by putting a magazine or book on the desk, open at the page to be captured, so that the camera could collect and add the image to the database. Although it was meant for industrial designers, Cabinet struck me as an elegant tool for architects as well.

The Arthur system, developed at the Bartlett by Alan Penn and his team (Penn et al., 2004), combined see-through glasses and manipulation markers to enable architects to work on virtual models, while also allowing a design team to work together, with each member having equal access to the model.

As in Caudell's original AR work, the real challenge in AR lies in getting the devices out in the field and making the digital model match the real world. Although I am sure people were working on this earlier, one of the first architecture projects that struck me in this respect was produced by Peter Anders and Werner Lonsing (2005). In their work, they use captured location information and digital information to create overlays of single digital images. Using the C-Navi system, Lertlakkhanakul and team aimed to create outdoor time-based visualization (Lertlakkhanakul et al., 2005). GPS technology and markers have proved an important means of matching the digital model to the real world. Later research, such as the work by Miyake et al. (2017), then aimed to get rid of the markers, using a technique called SLAM: Simultaneous Localization and Mapping. This technique blends an internal model of the position with information from cameras to infer the correct location.

AR has moved out of the laboratory as a commercial product with varying degrees of success, including Google Glass (introduced in 2013, essentially terminated in 2019) and Microsoft HoloLens (introduced in 2016). As far as I can tell, HoloLens has still not taken off as a commercial success. In academia, the technology is used to advance further research projects. Finally, with the BloomShell experiments (Song, 2020) we are returning to Caudell's initial vision, using HoloLens and AR to instruct craftsmen in how to assemble complex structures.

Conclusion

VR and AR truly are fields that have developed through visions and dreams of what may be and tremendous efforts by the most varied group of people to turn these visions and dreams into reality. It was, and still is, a privilege to witness this development. As both fields mature, we can see how scientists, artists, architects, and engineers are developing a distinct aesthetics and experience that is quite different from all other modes of representation that we use today. This is something that will grow through intensive debate within our disciplines. I am confident that the chapters in this book will, in time, be part of this narrative of imagination and new aesthetics.

Notes

1. LAB-STICC, Available at: www.labsticc.fr/en/index/ (Accessed: 23 November 2020)
2. Thackara, Available at: http://thackara.com/notopic/doors-of-perception-portfolio/ (Accessed: 23 November 2020)
3. US Patent 1961, 3,050,870: Sensorama Simulator. M.L. Heilig. Aug. 28, 1962.
4. Techradar, Available at: www.techradar.com/news/wearables/forgotten-genius-the-man-who-made-a-working-vr-machine-in-1957–1318253 (Accessed: 22 November 2020).

References

Achten, H. et al. (1999) 'Virtual Reality in the Design Studio: The Eindhoven Perspective', in Brown, A., Knight, M., and Berridge, P. (eds.) *Proceedings of the 17th International eCAADe Conference*. Liverpool: University of Liverpool, pp. 169–177.

Anders, P. and Lonsing, W. (2005) 'AmbiViewer: A Tool for Creating Architectural Mixed Reality', *Proceedings of the 2005 Annual Conference of the Association for Computer Aided Design in Architecture*, Savannah, Georgia, pp. 104–113.

Brooks, F. P. Jr. (1986) 'Walkthrough: A Dynamic Graphics System for Simulating Virtual Buildings', *Interactive 3D Graphics*. New York: Association for Computing Machinery, pp. 9–21.

Brooks, F. P. Jr. et al. (1990) 'Project GROPE: Haptic Displays for Scientific Visualization', *Computer Graphics*, 24(4), pp. 177–185.

Bryson, S. and Levit, C. (1991) 'The Virtual Windtunnel: An Environment for the Exploration of Three-Dimensional Unsteady Flows', *RNR Technical Report RNR-92-013*.

Caudell, T. P. and Mizell, D. W. (1992) 'Augmented Reality: An Application of Heads-Up Display Technology to Manual Manufacturing Processes', *Proceedings of the Twenty-Fifth Hawaii International Conference on System Sciences*, Vol. 2. Kauai, HI, USA, pp. 659–669. doi: 10.1109/HICSS.1992.183317.

Cruz-Neira, C. et al. (1992) 'The CAVE: Audio Visual Experience Automatic Virtual Environment', *Communications of the ACM*, 35(6), pp. 65–72.

Dorta, T., Kinayoglu, G. and Boudhraâ, S. (2016) 'A New Representational Ecosystem for Design Teaching in the Studio', *Design Studies*, 47, pp. 164–186.

Furness, T. A. and Kocian, D. F. (1986) 'Putting Humans into Virtual Space', in *Proceedings of Conference Aerospace Simulation II*, Vol. 16, pp. 214–230.

Keller, I. (2005) *For Inspiration Only: Designer Interaction With Informal Collections of Visual Material*. PhD Thesis. Delft, NL: TU Delft.

Krueger, M. W. (1983) *Artificial Reality*. Boston, MA: Addison-Wesley.

Krueger, M. W., Gionfriddo, Th., and Hinrichsen, K. (1985) 'VIDEOPLACE: An Artificial Reality', *ACM SIGCHI Bulletin*, pp. 35–40.

Kurmann, D. (1995) 'Sculptor: A Tool for Intuitive Architectural Design', in Tan, M. and The, R. (eds.) *The Global Design Studio: Proceedings of the Sixth International Conference on Computer-Aided Architectural Design Futures*. Centre for Advanced Studies in Architecture. Singapore: National University of Singapore, pp. 323–330.

Lertlakkhanakul, J. et al. (2005) 'Using the Mobile Augmented Reality Techniques for Construction Management', in *Proceedings of the 10th International Conference on Computer Aided Architectural Design Research in Asia*, Vol. 2. New Delhi, India, pp. 396–403.

Maver, T. (1987) 'Modelling the Cityscape with Geometry Engines', *Computer-Aided Design*, 19(4), pp. 193–197.

Mazuryk, T. and Gervautz, M. (1996) 'Virtual Reality-History, Applications, Technology and Future', *Technical Report TR-186-2-96-06*. Vienna, Austria: Vienna University of Technology.

McGreevy, M. W. (1991) 'The Virtual Environment Display System', *National Aeronautics and Space Administration, Technology 2000*, 1, pp. 3–9.

Miyake, M. et al. (2017) 'Outdoor Markerless Augmented Reality', in Janssen, P., Loh, P., Raonic, A., and Schnabel, M. A. (eds.) *Protocols, Flows and Glitches, Proceedings of the 22nd International Conference of the Association for Computer-Aided Architectural Design Research in Asia (CAADRIA) 2017*, Hong Kong, pp. 95–105.

Nguyen, B. V. D. et al. (2020) 'How to Explore the Architectural Qualities of Interactive Architecture: Virtual or Physical or Both?', in Werner, L. and Koering, D. (eds.) *Anthropologic: Architecture and Fabrication in the Cognitive Age: Proceedings of the 38th eCAADe Conference*, Vol. 2. Berlin, Germany: TU Berlin, pp. 219–231.

Penn, A. et al. (2004) 'Augmented Reality Meeting Table: A Novel Multi-User Interface for Architectural Design', in Van Leeuwen, J. P. and Timmermans, H. J. P. (eds.) *Recent Advances in Design & Decision Support Systems in Architecture and Urban Planning*. Dordrecht: Kluwer Academic Publishers, pp. 213–231. ISBN: 1-4020-2408-8.

Rauterberg, M. et al. (1998) 'BUILD-IT: A Planning Tool for Construction and Design', *CHI 98 Conference Summary on Human Factors in Computing Systems*. doi: 10.1145/286498.286657.

Song, Y. (2020) 'BloomShell: Augmented Reality for the Assembly and Real-Time Modification of Complex Curved Structure', in Werner, L. and Koering, D. (eds.) *Anthropologic: Architecture and Fabrication in the Cognitive Age: Proceedings of the 38th eCAADe Conference*, Vol. 1. Berlin, Germany: TU Berlin, pp. 345–354.

Sutherland, I. (1965) 'The Ultimate Display', *Proceedings of IFIP Congress*. London: Macmillan and Co., pp. 506–508.

Sutherland, I. (1968) 'A Head-Mounted Three Dimensional Display', *Fall Joint Computer Conference 1968*. New York: Association for Computing Machinery, pp. 757–764.

Vries, B. de et al. (2003) 'The Tangible Interface: Experiments as an Integral Part of a Research Strategy', *International Journal of Architectural Computing*, 1(2), pp. 133–152.

Weiser, M. (1991, September) 'The Computer for the 21st Century', *Scientific American*, pp. 94–104.

2

MODELS AND FICTIONS

The Archi-tectonic of Virtual Reality

Federico Ruberto

[Virtual | Reality]

What is (*real*) reality? A speculative definition of real-ity may see it as the hybrid model constituted by *multiplicities* of models (and sub-models), a non-totalizable set of material and digital events, the time-space in which signifiers and signifieds are entangled, where beings and places are entities constructed by the medium of technics. This text addresses what is 'real/virtual' from a wide and *generic* (Laruelle, 2012) point of view, bypassing the technical particularities of the previous terms in order to define the shared core characteristics of the *model* in which they are emerging. The 'Real' as a model is the variable admixture of two dichotomies, physical/virtual and analogue/digital, which should be rearranged in four recombinable structures: physical (external nature); virtual-physical (internal nature, ideas); analogue-physical-digital (hardware infrastructure, apparatuses for capture and re-production); digital-virtual (logical mediums of presentation, language, and software). For sake of clarity, all forms of digitalization and idealization, whether purely virtual or augmented, will be categorized under the heading of virtual reality (VR).

Reality is, to some extent, always already *implicitly* virtual: it is an open set driven and concretized by processes of virtualization. VR is a paradigmatic event that *explicitly* structurally transforms the very *sense of reality (virtual realism)*, which could help us understand the implicit layers-mechanism of base reality, enabling the emergence of new forms of *subjects-objects-concepts* (Figure 2.1).

To understand virtual-reality as active part of reality, one must conceptualize reality at large as a layered system, a metastasis of matter and signs, of *virtual* events enmeshed in real time with physical encounters. As Thomas Metzinger speculated (2018), what if *deep* virtual events/environments reiteratively update themselves (through machine learning and real-time sensor acquisition) using

> the same computational principles of top-down processing, statistical estimation, prediction error minimization, hierarchical Bayesian inference, and predictive control many theoreticians now believe to be operative in the brain itself? Would this change the user's phenomenology in any interesting way, for example its fine-grained temporal dynamics?

When actualized, this last description will explicitly render what we mean by *deep* virtual reality. Design should commit to define presentational modes in virtual reality, utilizing software

DOI: 10.4324/9781003183105-3

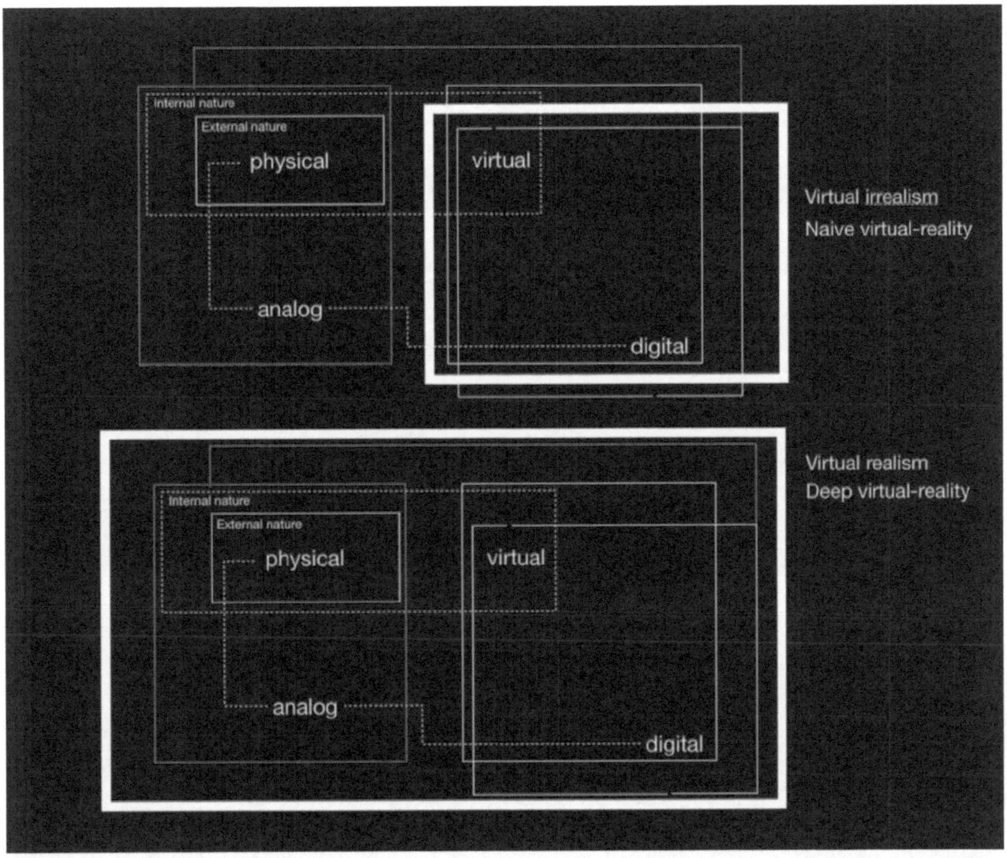

FIGURE 2.1 "Virtual realms"

Source: Federico Ruberto, 2019

and devices (game engines and ocular devices), not to represent facts but to test *queer* narratives capable of critically dissecting reality and of grafting onto it, of enabling, new forms of perception and communication. The deep hybridization of experience is not only changing how we *see things in space* but changing *things and spaces themselves*—the narration of sequences and experiences, and of events that could unfold by intersecting different space-times, alterable on the fly given that their causal core and rules of transformation could be remodelled *ad hoc*, according to communal principles (rather than individual desires) (Figures 2.2 and 2.3).

Models, of Bodies and Ideas

What is the difference between virtual topoi and those of dreams and hallucination? Is the virtual real, or a simulacrum of the real? What is an *object* in the virtual: does it have the same weight as a thought-white-unicorn? Does it exist or *subsist* the real? What is the metaphysical space of a fictional entity? Does an emotion triggered in the virtual existentially weigh on the subject as *real*? What ethical principles must be adopted when experiencing the world as a concatenation of physical/virtual bundled experiences? These are questions stemming from an ontological divide. The divide instantiated by the question "*what is real?*" is as old as philosophy itself, reiterated ad infinitum, it keeps problematizing the *mind-body* relation. VR and physical reality are problematically linked in a similar way to exterior physical states and internal mental

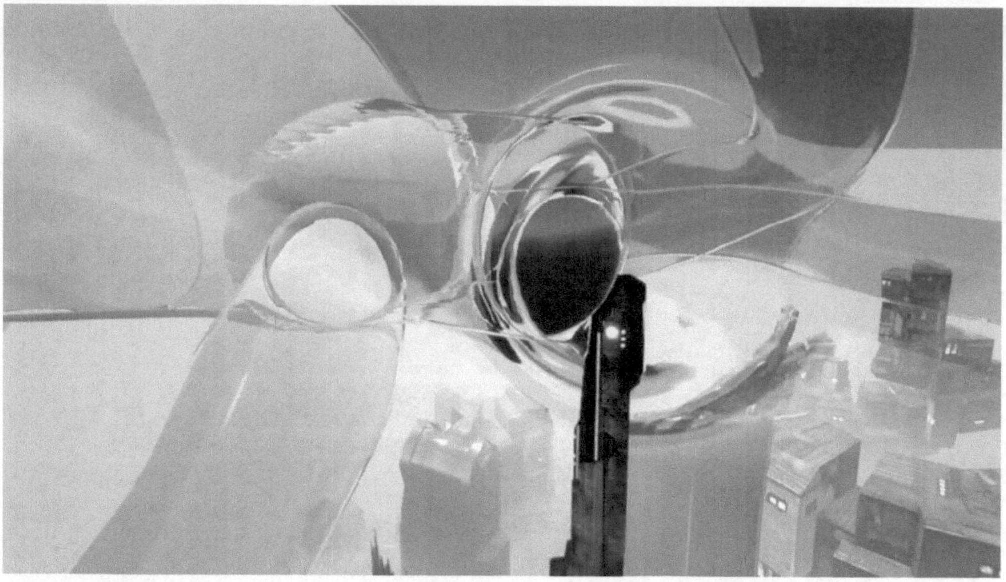

FIGURE 2.2 "The Digital Archive"

Source: Benedict Tan, Singapore University of Technology and Design—ASD—2019

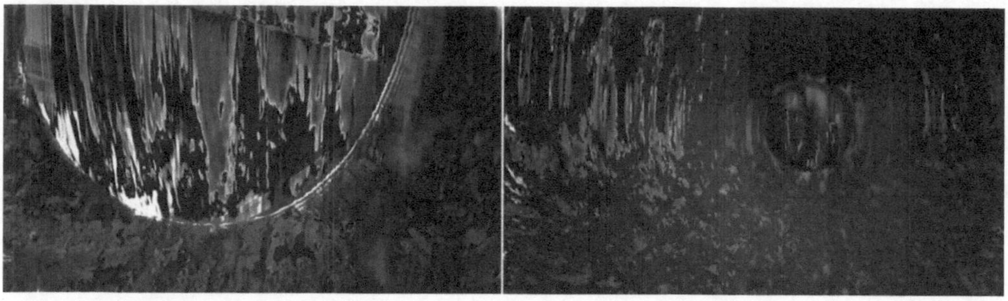

FIGURE 2.3 "The Digital Archive"

Source: Benedict Tan, Singapore University of Technology and Design—ASD—2019

states. The question that must be asked is whether reality lies within the physical, or whether the physical is a consequence of the virtual. Is the mind enmeshed in the physical, or does it create a personal and solipsistic illusion (virtual filter) to overlay the physical? Plato's *allegory of the cave* instated this dichotomy at the dawn of thought: an *internal* world of appearances—the projections in the cave—and an *outside* in which appearances are dissolved by the presence of light, where the real-reality is apprehended. Are we in such a *cave*, needing to find a way to escape from it, or is the cave all there is: a *model* that is reconstructed by the deployment of new languages, experiences, and experiments, the communal, intersubjective outputting of new models? With the help of virtual-augmented reality, philosophy of mind and neuroscientists are exploring the *real* as electrical signals interpreted by the brain, testing the limits of what characterizes the experience of the *self*. *Virtual embodiment* researchers test the limit of *one-self*, not by dislocating the body in space (as in video games) but by dislocating it in space and time by creating a *distancing* between what the individual feels and what they think. Experiments generally test the de-synchronization of two or more senses by embodying the subject in an avatar to activate in the brain some form of estrangement from the *model* of one-self. As reported by Joshua

Rothman (2019), experimenters stimulate a series of virtual and physical events, attempting, for example, to make the subject feel the presence of a lost limb, or to transposition the subject in another person/figure (someone that has emotionally charged their past, or perhaps mistreated the subject). Other experiments recreate a self-driven psychoanalytic session in which a subject is alternately embodied in both the analyst and the analysand (Rothman, 2019). VR-AR could help us question the form of presence and experience by testing the limits of cognition and perception, in order to see the "transparent model of the self" (Metzinger, 2017). Virtual reality, Metzinger states, "is the best technological metaphor for conscious experience we currently have" (2018). What is then *reality* given that is filtered by perceptual-cognitive models? What is it that constitutes the base reality of a body enmeshed and experiencing space-time, synthesizing the *given* by filtering subconsciously by invisible meta-structures, by ideas?

As various psychoanalytical approaches have proposed, supplementing the physical with *ideas* (symbolic virtual constructs in narratives) constitutes the core of being human, as the essential alienating ability to abstract (plan-project) events-qua-signs in time-spaces that have some form of independence from the immanent physical materiality of the body. Planning a reality involves constructing counterfactuals through which the supposedly most common *reality* can be tested and modified. Slavoj Žižek (2017) asks whether reality is not, in fact, a kind of plot constituted subjectively by growing and filling in the gap of experience. He states that

> we look at reality and interact with it through the fantasy frame of the digital screen, and this intermediary frame supplements reality with virtual elements which sustain our desire to participate in the game. . . . [A]t its most basic, ideology is the primordial version of augmented reality.

What, then, is the *real* and true core of reality? For us, it is a transfinite model, the actual assemblage of shared signs—an unstable ontological *void* manipulated by ideological filters—which constitutes the actual totality of the given set of phenomena as they are read-translated-rewritten, signs codified and encrypted in a plot always transcending itself in time. It is a transcendental virtual model that actualizes in-as an immanent actuality. *Real, the a-priori*, is the structure that intrinsically pervades actuality and is formed by it: the ever-changing model of models, a scaffolding dwelling on change, contingency, instability, transformation. Since the birth of language—since the phantasmatic birth of man—real-ity, in itself, has been augmented. *Concepts* and *objects* exist in a materially-semantically determined co-relation. A model is the most fitting shared structure of sense and meaning capable of explaining and covering, silently and only for a specific lapse of time, the totality of *phenomena*. A model is a structure that coherently organizes the multiple sets of signs that make up what we call actuality: it is the map and the territory, the invisible medium for reading and living within the common, the shared history (histories) of the *world*. As Marshal McLuhan famously stated, ultimately "the medium is the m(e)(a)ssage" (1964, 1967): everything is communicated, forming a medium-process-model that is not solely the passive conveyor of such signs, but the predetermining structure *massaging* the very existence of events qua signs. Is the model (physically) real then, or is it imaginary? The *model* for us is a shared construct, not a filter applied to the *true*, but the truth-of-the-generic, that that actually is built upon the *generic*—which is not pure void, but the a-priori voided constituency of things, that should allow meaning to be mapped and discussed by a community of agents imbricated in ideological and material constructs. The *generic*: the ontological and ethical necessity that a-priori there is nothing but a state of featureless co-belonging.

Hence, is the model imaginary and constructed, or is it the only *real* structure in-itself? A model is both; it is a metaphysical-ideological construct. *Real-ity* is material and imaginary; it is the supplementation-augmentation of materials by layers of signs organized by *us* within a community of other agents. Its coherency and solidity are imbricated in the life of a community—which today supposedly, given the global reach of communications, may (possibly!) be as extensive as the *world* itself. Plato's *cave*—if there is one at all—is so re-doubled: one implicit (internal) and defined by our processing-sensing apparatus and one (external) explicitly feeding in/on it. Hence the importance of VR, as it offers us the possibility of explicitly testing such a *cave* (or communal model made of local models) by asking what the *true/real* core of reality is: is it purely *exterior* to the subject, or is it *internally* re-meshed by the subject? What is really *true* is a sort of metaphor (Nietzsche, in Kaufmann, 1976, pp. 46–47), but not quite. It is not either reason in-itself or illusion; what is real is a meaningfully operative construct (Arendt, 1981). Meaning, however, gets in the digital constantly refracted; thus to counter the intense plural-singularization of reality and splintering of consensus reality, we will need to consolidate models that can still belong to each other and create virtual narratives that still retain the common desire to co-belong (Figure 2.4).

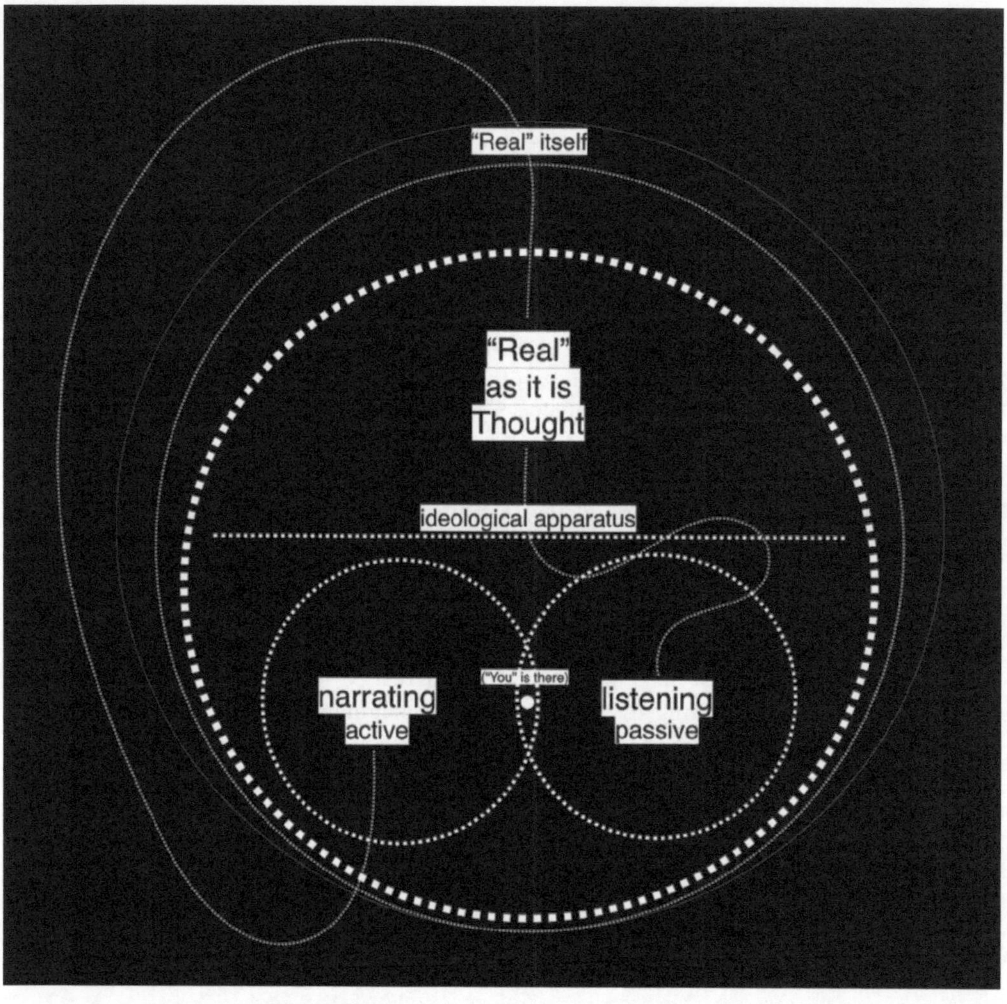

FIGURE 2.4 "Fiction and narration"

Source: Federico Ruberto—2019

Writing Wor(l)ds

Virtual-augmented reality explicitly revolutionizes the process of storytelling by blurring the boundaries between the oneiric-subconscious-hallucinated and the conscious. Hybrid content could be present in real time already manipulated. The new virtual model—namely the integrated infrastructure composed of devices, sensors for capture, databanks, cloud-based machine-learning algorithms and rendering engines—will allow for truly hybrid environments synchronously deploying digital and physical *encounters*. The collapse of traditional (pre-modern, modern, and postmodern) narratives will be instantiated by a network holding multiple stories: multi-linear and potentially non-causal series. The semiotic base through which we phenomenologically read transformation and figure in space and time will be radically transformed; signs will be mediated and reconstructed in ungraspable fractions of seconds, filtered/augmented/censored/promoted by algorithms. Experiences will be integrative translations directed by machine-learning—acquiring through sensors different realities and different times. The deep hybridization of reality will be total, a total diffraction and refraction of signs as foreseen by James Graham Ballard.

Given the form of such an emerging fractured reality, one question emerges concerning design, space, and experience: to what extent and in what way will deep virtually augmented plots affect the way of thinking sequences in architectural terms, namely series traditionally conceived of as *one* spatio-temporal structure (narrative)? In what ways will architectural models influence this emerging reality? The collapse of *form* and *content* (the linearity of traditional narratives) and the increasing augmentation of experiences in real time will force a radical transformation of the potential of an architectural *object*. The medium-model we will be operating in will be synthetic, with digital mechanisms shaping experiences in real time and vice versa, resulting in a weird, orchestrated synchronicity between two sets of events: physical and ideal. The physical world (unmediated depth) will need to be constantly re-fused with digital sets. Reality will be deeply hybrid, implying a *depth* composed of physical events integrated with digital ones: translations and filtering operations, complex interferences between devices of capture and agents' actions, apparatuses wired to real-time feedback loops driven by machine-learning algorithms, interpolations of signs and actions outputting reality (realities) whilst re-adjusting it, continuous processes of alteration reiteratively feeding from syntheses of *latent-spaces*, statistical categorization, and evaluation of *meaning*, the quantification of the meaning of experience. What we will call *reality* will need to be a designed *actuality* of meta-narratives, parallel plays comprising both physical and digital constructs.

Writing the connection between the concrete and the imaginary (ideological) is the space of architecture, a space created by acts of writing. As with writing, architecture requires the integration of abstract models and concrete materials: it is a machine that works by crafting *narratives-plots-stories*, namely models. Without succumbing to computational totalities, in challenging the *transparency* of the subject to discover new forms of subjectivity, we will have to design new stories (and hence worlds) without losing the possibility of *this world*: remaining faithful to a *generic* base, a voided ontology committed solely to the ethical commonality of all forms, all forms of living on this planet and beyond. There is no set formula for designing these new narration machines, although we will certainly learn how to critically invent new boundaries between facts and fiction by analysing how radical forms of cinema—Chris Marker's docu-fictions, Michael Snow's time dilations, Stan Brackage's material montages, or even Khrzhanovsky's recent life-cinematic performance *DAU*—keep challenging our preconceived ideas of space and time with cunning intelligence, questioning the boundaries of the *subject* and the *object* at the same time. Rather than producing new solitary objects, we will need to architecturally challenge the 'given' to create space-times in which new forms of subjects and new forms of community could be emancipated without being commodified. Design(ed) spatial stories will be operations that involve *queering* the physical with the digital and the digital with the physical, genders with genders, and categories with categories. In such operations, new words and new worlds—new subjects—could be invented, or serendipitously founded. As designers, what shall we become? *Meta-modern* strategists, trans-media storytellers, *world-builders* that manipulate geometries and events, confronting the multi-dimensionality of the world by delivering meta-worlds that can emancipate themselves from totalitarian closures. And so, in this new post-digital milieu, we swing between the sphere and the labyrinth, between construction/ruination and figure/disfigurement. Design will be a novel form of both: actions resisting and emancipating entropy; noise. Through design, we should create the topology of the labyrinth making itself spherical: a metamorphosis through noise, empowered—by diverging from the *given* as it becomes dissipated—to open up new reality. The architect will draw the lines of *inception* (Nolan, 2010), the play enacted by both oneiric (virtual-ideal) and physical happenings—killing and crafting minotaurs to re-create the meaning of space, and with it the reality of new myths. We will not only need to model spaces, but stories to emancipate-emanate new senses, as sensation gets broken apart by the incremental systemic need for quantification, valuation, and numerical control. We need to be writing new hybrid topologies, signs carrying new myths that must be narrated not for self-complacent consumption but for Others, for the self-combustion of one-self. We must produce *meaning*, craft narratives, and give non-strictly numerical sense to what otherwise will sensually have none. Through game engines, we could produce trans-media narrations, platforming heterogenous sets of signs in an architectonic that moves deeper than sequential time, interlacing events unfolding in physical and virtual times. We will design by having to understand pathologies of deep-space, problematizing them through a peculiar type of spatial psychoanalysis, perhaps something Gaston Bachelard had in mind and called "topoanalysis" (1958). We must design space(s)-time(s) by committing neither to a pure external reality nor a purely internal one, perhaps moving towards a kind of intersubjective "surrationalism" (Bachelard, 1935), with models oscillating between rational and irrational drives. It is because we worry about the relentless march towards a future in which we will be sold our "psychopathologies as games" (Ballard, 1998) that we will understand how space-time(s) are never purely physical—and that the narratives that hold these together must be constructed not to be sold but to understand and counter the rampant radical commodification of the living.

Fiction and Hyper-Spectral Models

We must build stories and narrate buildings that transcend the pure linear causality of the here and now by radiating a spectral aesthetics, outputting flashes of a sublime and alien subject in the manner of the new-digital, new-weird work of video artist Rick Farin. He writes that his "Cathedrals" (2019), an exemplary work of critical reconstruction of the future with a powerfully hybrid aesthetics, is built with "locations [that] have been infected by a neural-net generated virus. . . . Trained on religious iconography and images of microchips, they have produced digital dioramas in which one can revere the symbiotic relationship between technology, thought and nature". His work does not irremediably abandon the given world, but it engages from unfamiliar angles. The process of world(s) construction through the inventions of hybrid objects-events-stories involves a dose of mythopoeia, the creation of signs that transcend the here and now to *occupy*, for a brief lapse of time, a fictional heaven, to expose the oneiric idiosyncrasies of thought, of thoughts that forget their bare commonality by being buried under the factual materialities of the world; to unveil once more the world as a power set in motion deeper than its sum of materialities (as J. L. Borges, J. R. R. Tolkien, H. P. Lovecraft, F. Kafka, have intuited).

As Tolkien wrote in *On Fairy-Stories* (1947, p. 3), "mythology is not a disease at all, though it may, like all human things, become diseased". The meta-project requires a re-engagement with mytho-poietic fiction, the critical apparatus of science fiction. This is imperative; as Ursula Le Guin put it, "*hard times are coming*"—what we need most is "the voices of writers who can see alternatives to how we live now . . . writers who can remember freedom—poets, visionaries—realists of a larger reality" (2014). Fiction, Rancière writes (2010, p. 141),

> is not a term that designates the imaginary as opposed to the real; it involves the re-framing of the 'real', or the framing of a dissensus. Fiction is a way . . . of building new relationships between reality and appearance, the individual and the collective.

Fiction is the enablement of "emancipated signs", "events" of divergence that potentially refolds in new convergences. The possibility of fiction is not found in the *mirror* but within the *real*—when politically driven and not serving as a means of sedation/commodification, fiction is the instantiation of "dissensus", "hollowing out that 'real' and multiplying it in a polemical way. . . . It is a practice that invents new trajectories between what can be seen, what can be said and what can be done" (p. 149).

In short, critical fictions must be developed in *hyper-spectral depth*, topoi of agents and spaces augmented in real time by layers of information that can be fed, manipulated, and transformed on demand. A continuous alteration of the physical must be imagined where augmentation and immersion are deployed not for consumption but as tools for emancipation. In hyper-spectral models, sight-sound-touch-taste-smell could be wired to machine-learning apparatuses that blend layers of physical reality with layers of virtual reality, not to enhance what Jean Baudrillard called the "hyperreal" (1988, pp. 166–184), but to craft the realm of *experience* as a multi-model of interferences, where fictions and facts are virtually in critical co-relation. Hyper-spectral models must be designed to coexist, leading to new communities that retain their singularity whilst responding to the commune that is the *world*. Hyper-spectral architectonics must be designed on the ethical principle that the *world* is the finite material system (with limited capacities and potential havocs that must be taken care of communally), a multi-text to be written on the transfinite multiplicity of the uni-verse—where, ontologically speaking, the uni-verse is a generic *condition-without-features*, without specific *forms* and *characters*. Hyper-spectral models must challenge the *grammatological*, *archetypical* sediments of reality, questioning facts and fictions, writing the text that determines new *forms* of existence, springing out of (whilst remaining immanently in) the "generic-real" (Laruelle,2012), swerving from the *void beyond reason* and breaking through because of the desire to be other, diving into the domain of inscription whilst inventing new realms of signification, of self-alienation, dictating new conditions of reality, of forms to exist. It is a leap and a form that must pre-emptively embed its essential fragility within itself and, with delicate precision, the possibility of its presence and absence, to leave the space-and-time necessary for (the) other(s), to be. From this base, models must be built to contest the structures of the *given*. *Real* is the synthetic verse, the generic and transparent model through which the common set with all the models of *reality* could be played out. There is no metaphysical difference between *real* and *reality*, as the two are co-constituted; their difference is, in fact, determined a posteriori, epistemologically, by models holding consistently intuitive actions, by leaps, and sometimes leaps of faith. What we call *reality* is the explicit model made up of the many stories that compose it, what we call *real in-itself* is the implicit one, the *less-than-zero* state that cannot be lived through language. We must design realities that are held together by an ethical stance tattooed onto the *generic-real, the emptied ontological body*—realities built by ontologically-ethically summoning a communal real(m), the reality to come (Figures 2.5–2.7).

FIGURE 2.5 "The Digital Archive"

Source: Lucas Ngiam, Singapore University of Technology and Design—ASD—2019

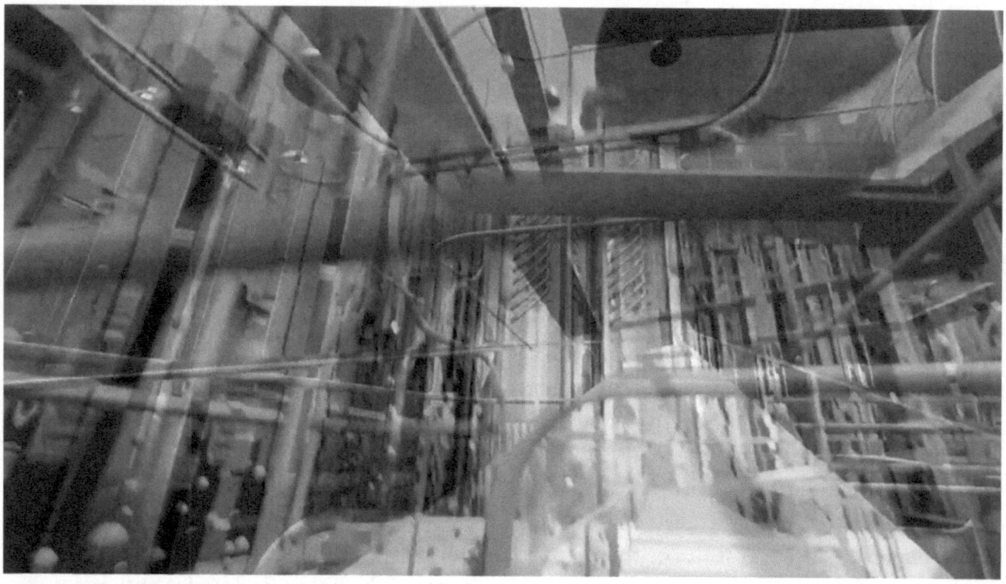

FIGURE 2.6 "The Digital Archive"

Source: Ran Chen, Singapore University of Technology and Design—ASD—2019

This text is nothing but a preliminary call for a communal myth underlying the stories of the world: one without transcendent materiality, figure, and features; one without god, nature, and self; one with myriad signs remoulding the materialities of the world. Hyper-spectral models, even when detached from the material world, must keep the *generic* as their genetic conditioning, the meta-fact that ontologically *we* are nothing but a generic-commonality that must write

FIGURE 2.7 "The Digital Archive"
Source: Paris Lau, Singapore University of Technology and Design—ASD—2019

it-self (the multiplicities of selves) out. To de-sign (already) means writing hyper-spectral congregations, calling up new models, inventing realities that can interfere with physical processes; increasingly it will require creating-twisting-augmenting databanks, engaging and influencing machine-learning operators, maybe becoming a new type of operator, a game-maker and game-changer, a generic-anonymous hacker, as "you are a gamer whether you like it or not, now that we all live in a gamespace that is everywhere and nowhere" (Wark, 2007, p. 2). We will need to write spaces and times remembering what Chris Marker stated (1983): "we do not remember, we rewrite memory much as history is rewritten. How can one remember thirst?" Therefore, let us design new communal forms and diagrams to write the sensual verses of the past and those of the future, adding them together, making the multiplicity of the *generic* uni-verse, becoming the "true alchemists" that Antonin Artaud (1958, pp. 49–51) dreamt of, designing "the transgression of the ordinary limits of art and speech, in order to realize actively, that is to say magically, in real terms, a kind of total creation in which man must reassume his place between dream and events" (p. 93).

References

Arendt, H. (1981) *The Life of the Mind*, Vol. 1–2. Edited by McCarthy, M. New York: Mariner Books.

Artaud, A. (1938 [1958]) *The Theater and Its Double*. Translated by Caroline Richards, M. New York: Grove Press.

Bachelard, G. (1935 [1989]) 'Surrationalism', translated by Levy, J. in Rosemont, F. (ed.) *Arsenal: Surrealist Subversion*, Vol. 4. Chicago: Black Swan Press.

Bachelard, G. (1958) *La poétique de l'espace*. Paris: Presses Universitaires de France.

Ballard, J. G. (1998) *Theatre of Cruelty*, interview by Jean-Paul Coillard, in Disturb ezine. Available at: www.jgballard.ca/media/1998_disturb_magazine.html (Accessed: 1 September 2019).

Baudrillard, J. (1988) *Selected Writings*. Edited by Poster, M. Palo Alto, CA: Stanford University Press.

Farin, R. (2019) *Cathedrals*, VR Film for NOWNESS. Premiered at Royal Academy London as Part of "Invisible Landscapes".

Kaufmann, W. (ed./trans.) (1976) *The Portable Nietzsche*. London: Penguin Books.
Laruelle, F. (2012, November 17) *The Generic Orientation of Non-Standard Aesthetics*. Lecture at University of Minnesota, Weisman Art Museum. Available at: https://performancephilosophy.ning.com/profiles/blogs/the-generic-orientation-of-non-standard-aesthetics-by-f-laruelle (Accessed: 1 September 2019).
Le Guin, U. K. (2014) *Speech Given at the National Book Awards*. Available at: www.newyorker.com/books/page-turner/national-book-awards-ursula-le-guin (Accessed: 1 September 2019).
McLuhan, M. (1964) *Understanding Media: The Extensions of Man*. Berkeley: Ginko Press.
McLuhan, M. (1967) *The Medium Is the Massage: An Inventory of Effects*. Berkeley: Ginko Press.
Metzinger, T. (2017) *The Question of Will* (lecture). Available at: www.youtube.com/watch?v=WzpFSo-Qlpuw (Accessed: 1 September 2019).
Metzinger, T. (2018) 'Why Is Virtual Reality Interesting for Philosophers?', *Frontiers in Robotics and AI*. https://doi.org/10.3389/frobt.2018.00101 (Accessed: 1 September 2019).
Nolan, C. (2010) *Inception*. Legendary Pictures and Syncopy, USA and UK.
Rancière, J. (2010) *Dissensus: On Politics and Aesthetics*. Translated by Corcoran, S. London and New York: Continuum.
Rothman, J. (2019) *Are We Already Living in Virtual Reality*. Available at: www.newyorker.com/magazine/2018/04/02/are-we-already-living-in-virtual-reality (Accessed: 1 September 2019).
Tolkien, J. R. R. (1947) *On Fairy-Stories*. Available at: http://heritagepodcast.com/wp-content/uploads/Tolkien-On-Fairy-Stories-subcreation.pdf (Accessed: 1 September 2019).
Wark, M. (2007) *Gamer Theory*. Cambridge and London: Harvard University Press.
Žižek, S. (2017) *Ideology Is the Original Augmented Reality*. Available at: http://mitp.nautil.us/feature/271/ideology-is-the-original-augmented-reality (Accessed: 1 September 2019).

3

CYBERNETIC AESTHETICS

Helmut Kinzler, Daria Zolotareva, and Risa Tadauchi

Introduction

The advance of computerized communication technology and its permeation into every aspect of society and business have opened our eyes to the central role of communication within the recursive nature of cultural production. Today's speed of communication—whereby new ideas and concepts are traded with the immediate presence of collective evaluation and feedback—has eliminated the notion of the avant-garde, an elite place for a group of enlightened forerunners who previously shaped and anticipated our understanding of beauty and aesthetics. In addition, machine learning, and the accumulated scientific data of our modern history offer an alternative means of evaluating cultural processes that lies *outside* the human visionary and have thus played a role in the decline of the iconic, charismatic human author. Our cultural interfaces, i.e. the channels through which our cultural inputs are transmitted, have also been altered tremendously. Aesthetics—our principles relating to our shared understanding of beauty—have never before been so broadly and diversely communicated, reciprocated, and challenged.

The most recent recognizable shift within architecture has been the emergence of the creative collective, following the collapse of the solipsistic creator, thus rebranding architectural practice towards the amicable and seemingly principled nature of architectural collectives. The prominence of these groups may indicate a new-found recognition of the relationship between architectural authors and their post-structuralist audiences, whilst also acknowledging the authors' vital ideological dependence on these audiences.

However, these new author-collectives and their *participatory design* have little in common with the collective initiatives of the 1970s. Whereas the latter embodied revolutionary ambitions for society as a whole and incorporated an experimental openness towards their results and economic successes, the new collectivism operates commercially within existing, often dystopian, societal and economic rules. Another phenomenon implying deep socio-cultural and economic change is the reduced role and budgets of public institutions, which until now had performed a mandated role as the benefactors and patrons of art and culture. It is public-private partnerships and private commercial institutions, relying on different imperatives to their state-funded predecessors, that are now engaging with the creation of architectural briefs and projects. One qualitative difference here is the adherence to an immediate economic focus, with a reduced target

DOI: 10.4324/9781003183105-4

audience and a break with the immediate, wider mandate of cultural patronage—mirroring the restricted and short-term nature of these new institutions' creations.

For us, the present situation is the result of two conditions. On the one hand, there is the latency and impermeability created by the existing societal and cultural paradigm, while on the other hand a completely new troupe of individuals are emerging, enabled by technology's entry into the cultural discourse. In order to support liberal individualism and diversity of expression for the emerging societies and cultures, a new shared language must be created. On the part of the collective, this requires a platform that can embed and accept this language, and both sustain and incorporate change. The outdated systemic societal structures, with their slow internal responsiveness, must overcome the digital divide and yield to a more reliable, faster, and articulate solution that offers accessibility and inclusiveness for dynamic global audiences, as vast levels of information are contained within this discourse.

It is necessary for us to examine the conceptualization of the individual at the smallest unit of our culture and society and to explore the history of the individual. To discuss how the individual changes when in contact with information technology, ZHVR has introduced the idea of creating a new interface through virtual reality, promoting a platform in which this interface is used to serve creativity and society. The first case study, *Spatial Matrix Prototype 01*, showcases the individual's existence within data-space. The second case study, *Project Correl*, explores collective change and the impact of technology on a cultural level, prototyping an *informatted* collective culture: a culture created through information systems.

The Superindividual

Dame Zaha Hadid's unique design language was the result of her distinctive, individualistic, and emphatic approach. Influenced by humanist thought, she strived to further and expand the possibilities of architecture through a creative process based on a deep knowledge and critique of architectural convention. Through her persona and lifestyle, Hadid embodied her own idea of what it means to be a space-maker, living completely immersed in her work through fashion, furniture, and product. For us, Zaha represents the prototypical superindividual, formulating the blueprint for a re-envisioned, updated concept of the individual; a force for moving our definition of 'the self' beyond the reductionist materialism that has developed slowly over recent centuries and has been justified until now.

At the dawn of our modern society were the empiricists and theoreticians of the Renaissance and the early scientists and philosophers of the Enlightenment era, who implicitly assumed that the biological body defined the individual. Political philosopher C. B. MacPherson (1962) proposed that the individual's internal conception was seen as *possessive* in nature, with the human as the owner of their own capacity and independence, "owing nothing to society for them". The individual, however, is far from clear cut in terms of economic and societal dependency. MacPherson infers that the "state of nature", which Thomas Hobbes and John Locke claimed this *unpossessed* individual possessed, was a retrospective creation of the market economy.

From the mid-20th century, the idea of the individual as an un-disenfranchisable entity clearly no longer functions amid the shift from materialist to information-based societies and economies. The postmodern literary critic N. Katherine Hayles (1999, p. 3) states that "the posthuman subject is an amalgam, a collection of heterogeneous components, a material-informational entity whose boundaries undergo continuous construction and reconstruction". The *informatted* society, given information-technology's impact on the individual, is challenging the natural perception and formation of the individual more than any previous human-made technology.

Neuroscience and Cognition

Recent insights into how humans construct unique versions of their reality, drawn from the medical sciences and from cybernetics itself, show that the structuralist belief of a shared, broad system of meaning has been invalidated forever.

The contemporary German philosopher Thomas Metzinger, who has devoted his research to the exploration of cognition, defines human cognition as a cyclical, iterative process. Metzinger (2003, pp. 210–211) proposes that human consciousness produces a model of itself (the Phenomenal Self Model), while also maintaining a self-held, contextual, and relational model of the outside world (the Phenomenal Model of Intentionality Relation), and iterates between these two models in a continual, permanent cycle, comparing the modelled reality with the self's experiences and knowledge. Within this, our consciousness adjusts these models whenever any discrepancy becomes apparent and does so as often as is needed to maintain continuity of experience. One important point here is the level of cognitive information and the type of information that this process embodies. No longer can logical thought, nor a focus on externalized knowledge and data formation, sustain the holistic understanding of the self. Humans rely on knowledge gathered through the body, including through reflexes and muscle memory, which relates to the human's physical, experiential space.

This model suggests that no shared reality exists. Instead, each individual continuously and dynamically constructs their own model with their own cognitive construct of reality. The complete model of the human entity is therefore an assemblage in a continual flux (termed *malleability* within philosophy, sociology, and engineering) of construction and reconstruction. The human being is, essentially, an open system.

Adding Information Technology

With the introduction of computation into the immediate context of the reality-generation process and with the latest results of technological evolution widely adopted in our everyday lives, the *informatted* individual is no longer tied to a specific physical location, instead gaining an awareness that is spread across multiple placements. This construct of reality blurs with a feed gathered from the augmentation system.

Nancy Katherine Hayles (2017, p. 27) states that in this new era of technological augmentation and with the externalization of the human cognitive process

> [the] new unconsciousness differs from the psychoanalytic unconsciousness of Lacan and Freud in that it is in continuous and easy communication with consciousness. In this view, the psychoanalytic unconsciousness might be considered as a subset of the new unconscious, formed when some kind of trauma intervenes to disrupt communication and wall off that portion of the psyche from direct conscious access.

The main conclusion stemming from this argument is that the *old model* of the absolute individual, within structuralist and matter economics, is irretrievably lost. Seeing the potential and role of individualization within the new technological sphere, our emerging cultural and formative system is still under development and is severely constrained by the fledgling infrastructure. In order to mitigate this and help establish a new form of liberal individualism, we must find new ways to construct and coexist in realities that are *natural* to our internal processes. We must allow individual process and expression to become emancipated in relation to new technology and to the collective human-made environment. If unfiltered technological access can be provided in a pluralistic, non-structuralist way, it will enable the formation of the *superindividual.*

Introducing VR to Assist the Formation of the Superindividual

As an enhanced form of human-machine interaction, VR now has a far more extensive application and has been widely adopted by architects and the general population. According to the German research firm Statista, the global VR hardware market is expected to grow to 43.5 million VR and AR headsets by 2025. The philosopher Philip Zhai formulates one key conclusion: VR, as a practical means to access information and the data-sphere, is valid. Zhai (1998, p. 38) shows that, logically, VR experience is identical to physical-reality experience because both rely on the same 'wetware' physiological equipment. This is not only determined by the physiological means, but is tied to the human biological reference system that forms human cognition. On the basis of this equation, VR is the optimal way for humans to interact within the information sphere, connecting human cognitive facilities with information systems.

However, further groundwork is required to turn VR into a valid individualistic toolkit. The virtual realm must be defined and constructed to a) exist as a worldwide, permanent infrastructure and b) perform in a way that serves the superindividual. In order to realize proper VR re-embodiment, we must first achieve feedback and responsiveness within VR, and VR must inherit a basic rule-matrix that allows us to interact with it in a meaningful way. This applies in particular to the collective culture aspect, where actions must have repercussions visible to other users in order for cultural exchange to become possible. This system also needs to accumulate the changes and impressions left by previous users—much like footprints or other terraforming events such as erosion and molecular reaction.

Research into the Virtual Void (Spatial Matrix Prototype 01)

In 2018, ZHVR piloted research into the fundamental constitution of virtual reality space, to investigate how this space may differ from physical reality space on an ontological level. Entitled *Spatial Matrix Prototype 01*, this conceptual research project was exhibited as part of the *Zaha Hadid Architects: Evolution* exhibition inside TheGallery venue at the Arts University Bournemouth (Figures 3.1–3.3). The research focuses on the structure required to generate a responsive spatial system for superindividual human experience within VR space.

In order to advance the discussion, we must first acknowledge that VR, as a human-made construct, requires a specific system and rule-set to enable any human presence. The *Spatial Matrix Prototype 01* explores this new locale by introducing a theoretical model for an infradata system, offering a substrate for the experiential machine-space-interface reality. All programmed functions are rooted in this infradata system and together respond and adapt to agent inputs and presences, changing dynamically over time. The virtual reality space never simply mirrors the physical, but actively co-constructs the experience.

All events and functions experienced inside VR space are a construct that originates within the human mind. Prior to the creation of any such system, all we have is a void. Ideally, both the system and its users have constant access to all root-level information, including information on all the decisions responsible for the evolution of the construct. All individuals with open and free access to this machine space are superindividual, which leads to the next question: how does the superindividual collective equate to the larger phenomenon of culture and society?

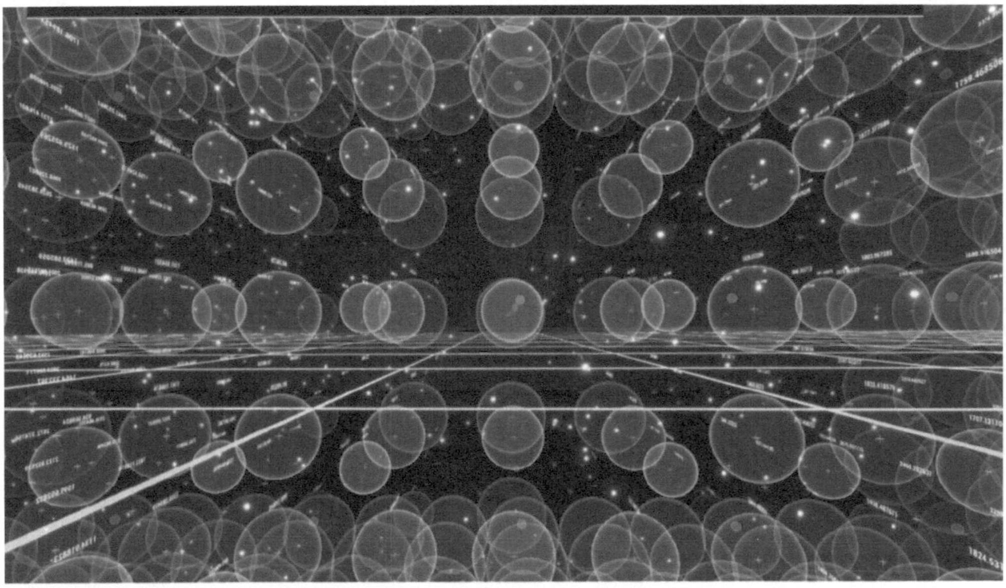

FIGURE 3.1 Spatial Matrix Prototype 01: Fundamental Research in Virtual Spatiality (2018)

Source: Evolution exhibition, TheGallery, Arts University Bournemouth, UK

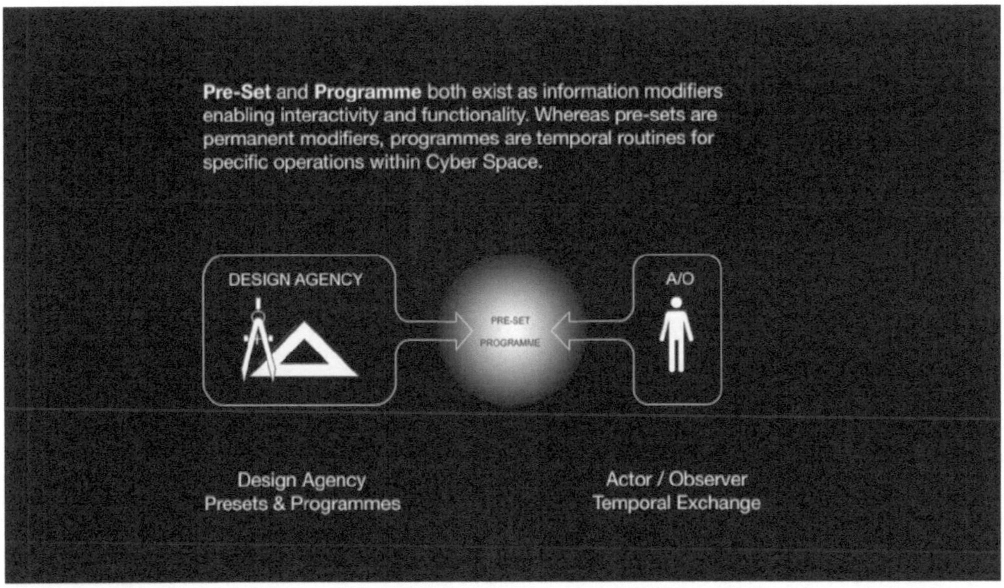

FIGURE 3.2 Human Interaction in Cybernetic Architecture: Spatial Matrix Prototype 01: Fundamental Research in Virtual Spatiality (2018)

Source: Zaha Hadid Architects: Evolution exhibition, TheGallery, Arts University Bournemouth, UK

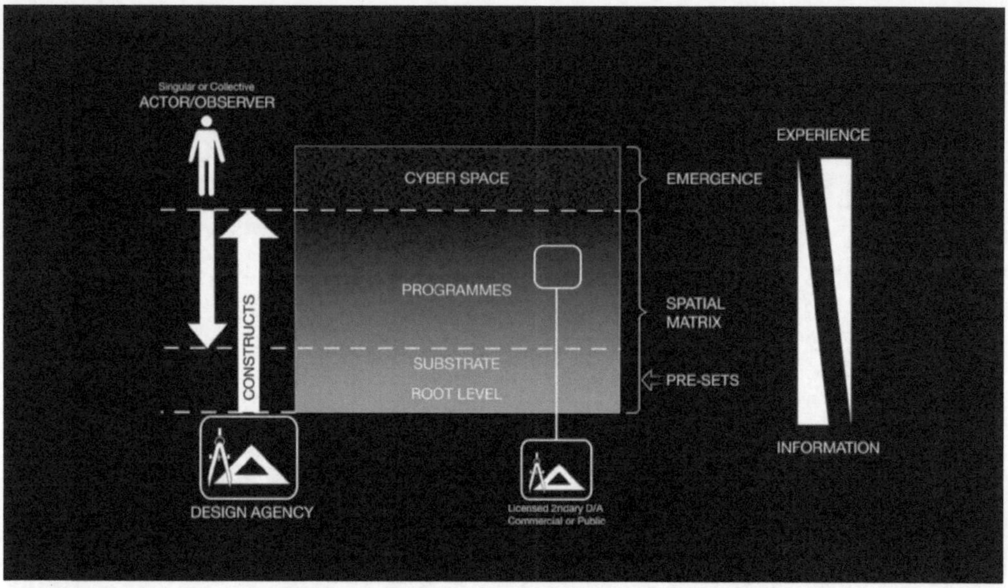

FIGURE 3.3 Physical and Digital Spatial Layers in Cybernetic Architecture: Spatial Matrix Prototype 01: Fundamental Research in Virtual Spatiality (2018)

Source: Zaha Hadid Architects: Evolution exhibition, TheGallery, Arts University Bournemouth, UK

Cybernetic Culture and Architecture

The notion of culture as a multifaceted, dynamic phenomenon has gained importance in recent years, while structuralism no longer predominates. Global mass communication technology concurrently offers a faster and much higher level of personal individual input and throughput within such dynamic cultural entities. The individual is synthetically connected to several layers and bodies of culture, independent of physical location and time.

While we see a clear acceleration to real-time commentary and evaluation, with a re- or dislocation of cultural discourse within the anthropocene, several other disciplines, including the social sciences and neurosciences, affirm that the human species depends far more on collective networks and value-sharing than was previously assumed. Cybernetic culture, however, is in its infancy; individuals lack the fundamental access and platform for a deeper, qualitative human cultural endeavour.

Architecture depends on the existence of the cultural platform as much as it provides for it, and therefore it must be mandatory for the architecture to facilitate the emergence of cybernetic culture. Contemporary architecture has entered the cybernetic era with a tentative, stylistic answer that is insufficient for the fundamental changes occurring in our human environment. Impeded by an outdated toolkit and ideology—like all late-20th-century institutions—it must reformulate the authoring process at its very core to find answers to the demands of cybernetic culture.

Culture, stemming from the Latin *cultura*, refers to a system of values that are evaluated, adopted, and coveted within a collective. In the 1950s, under the leadership of Norbert Wiener, cybernetics became a stand-alone scientific discipline aimed at investigating all areas of information, communication, and artificial intelligence. Wiener (1948) defined cybernetics as "the scientific study of control and communication in the animal and the machine", in a book of the same title which laid the foundations for artificial intelligence, reliable communications, and neuroscience. Further research by cognitive biologists Humberto Maturana and Francisco

J. Varela during the 1960s and 1970s established the term 'autopoiesis' for the self-organization of organisms (Maturana and Varela, 1972, p. 73), leading to a critical milestone in how human organization and realization are interpreted. Starting in the 1970s, Niklas Luhmann applied this theory to the realm of anthropology and sociology and proposed that autopoietic societies develop structures with embedded collective functions, including those intended for political, judicial, and cultural systems. Luhmann's societal *System Theory* has since been widely accepted to describe and critique contemporary conditions within postmodern cultures.

Culture: Progression Into the Cybernetic Paradigm

These institutions now seem at odds with the accelerated levels of individual throughput and are stifled by the economic nature and unresponsiveness of their own systems. Having founded Toronto's Institute for Culture and Technology in 1963, Marshall McLuhan refers to channels that are not open enough to convey the message fully. "The medium is the message", McLuhan wrote (2001, p. 6), stressing the importance of the *means* of communication. The global information channels needed for spatial and architectural information processes are entirely non-existent, and the formation of consistent discourse therefore requires the creation of an entire information platform.

A further problem preventing the required radical changes lies in certain intrinsic aspects of the architectural system. Separate and highly specialized architectural co-authors are needed to enable the full spectrum of architectural performance, but these authors remain isolated due to technological and ideological barriers. In order to connect the existing architectural production system to the emergent cybernetic superstructure and cultural spheres, the entire architectural ecosystem must holistically converge. From this, a new understanding of design will be able to address the challenges of cybernetic societies, closely related to design as a discipline.

From Simulation to Reality

Jean Baudrillard's description of resistance to the simulacra and the fear of obscuring or deflecting from *the real* (Baudrillard, 1981, p. 2) both hinder this transformation and perpetuate a current misconception of the work done by architects and through cultural processes in general. Despite the risk of Baudrillard's envisaged "catastrophe of meaning", it seems necessary to embrace the need for simulation with all manner of human information-manipulation, as part of the realization process. Our approach to the threshold of a collectively experienceable, hyper-nonconformist reality inside the simulation is the topic at the core of current cultural and technological development.

Analogous to most modern cultural systems, the process that enables modern architectural practice is acquired specialization and technique, the pre-envisioning of spaces: selling the idea of space to future owners while guiding the selection, optimization, and economization processes and controlling the realization of the solution. Simulations are therefore the very reason for the existence of the architectural discipline and underlie the philosophical and scientific paradigms that influence professional production, its technique, and the resulting aesthetics.

Peter Mörtenböck (2001, p. 17) highlights the impact of the 14th-century (re)discovery of central perspective under Brunelleschi. This artistic technique enabled early architectural designers to construct spatial compositions in simulated first-person view and, by incorporating a novel 'outside' location in the formulation of the construct, also determined and established the placement of the subject and viewer within the simulated space. In Mörtenböck's view, the reason for central perspective dominance in modern visual culture is its colonization of knowledge and its supervision by an external operator, at the price of separating subject from object.

From the mid-1990s to the early 2000s, computerization in architecture involved migration from the manual to the digital, starting with two-dimensional drafting software (CAD) that emulated the physical and manual processes of information drafting and issuing. The previously mentioned separation of the subject was continued and amplified by the infinitely scaleable, reconfigurable nature of this disembodied digital information. The design industry's subsequent embrace of 3D-modeling software replaced physical model making with the introduction of much higher levels of geometric complexity, refinement, and variation. Today, submissions that offer complex 3D building information models, complete with hypertext information and creation history, are standard within most architectural processes and deliverables.

This digitalization of architectural technique also borrowed heavily from the entertainment industries, with animation and visual-effects software, from film and the visual arts, which are now entering the design-presentation process to facilitate high-definition visualization. During the first two decades of the 21st century, early parametricism appeared in the form of aerospace engineering software that had been repurposed for architectural design. With parametric tools and programming—producing a computerized model that responds to digitized design criteria, i.e. parameters—in the hands of designers, the architectural design process took on completely new aspects, while the computer also facilitated the automation of complex analytical and design tasks, allowing for greater iteration and new form-finding.

While some architectural design subsets were already familiar with dynamic, digital spatial simulations and the associated software (such as software for functional design, logistic design, and specialist engineering), the latest arrival in the architectural toolkit has been physics engines, from game development. With these world-simulation capabilities, the architect can place designs in a holistic, dynamic space, simulating the behaviour and movement of artificial agents inside the projected environment. Lighting, acoustic quality, and other spatial criteria all form part of this new toolset.

Only with the introduction of immersive virtual reality, with real-time interaction and content creation, can we enable direct 'contact' between the designer and subject, a synthetic dissolution of the 'fourth wall' between the human and the machine-contained construct. When we add a collective function by immersing multiple human participants (designers and recipients) in the digital simulation and solution-finding process, we begin to see the possibility for a widely accessible, commensurable spatial design platform and, with this, a deeper form of cybernetic culture. The initial apparent welcoming of a loss of artistic control must be negotiated in terms of the immediate benefit of greater democratic value in the design, which is gained through wider exposure during the development stages.

With this emergence of cybernetic culture, architecture could be viewed with revised notions of completeness, persistence, authorship, and use. Projects will be able to exist and trans-navigate through these different forms of reality. ZHVR's experimental *Project Correl* stages a prototypical scenario for this cultural process and architectural development.

Cultural Production (Project Correl 1.0)

Project Correl is an interactive and collaborative multi-presence VR sculpting experience designed by the ZHVR Group. The project was launched in 2019 at the University Museum of Contemporary Art (MUAC) in Mexico City, where it formed part of the exhibition *Zaha Hadid: Design as Second Nature*. The platform ran continuously for three months and attracted over 2,500 creators who collaboratively placed more than 20,000 components (Figures 3.4–3.6). Each sculpting session involved four people, working as a group.

The project's construction involves five constituents: (1) the users; (2) the hardware, including VR headsets with full-scale user-tracking and networked computers; (3) the custom-built

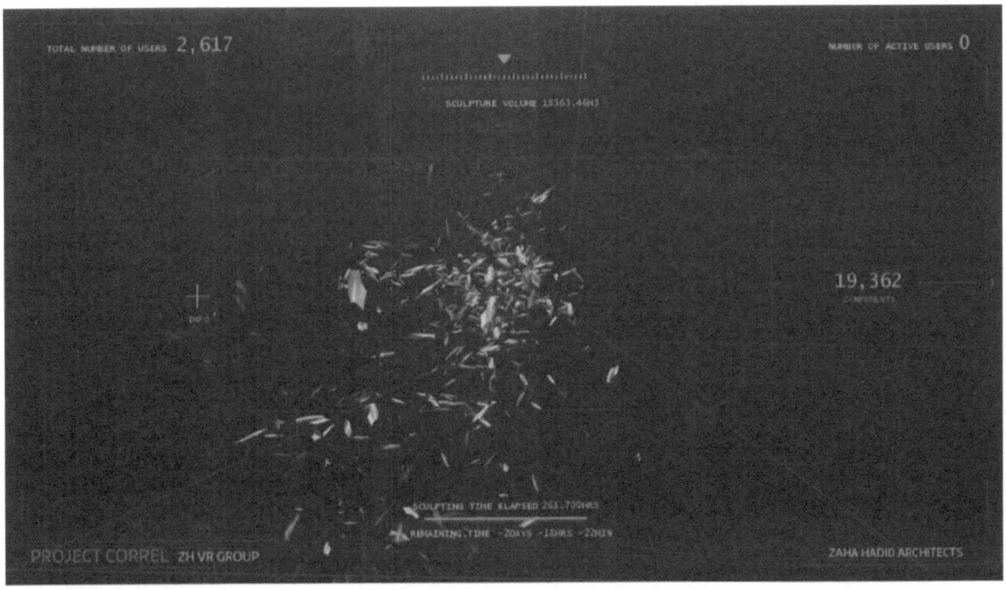

FIGURE 3.4 TimeStamp:18h22m23s05MAY2019: Project CORREL (2019)

Source: Zaha Hadid Architects: Design as Second Nature exhibition, Museo Universitario Arte Contemporáneo (MUAC), Mexico

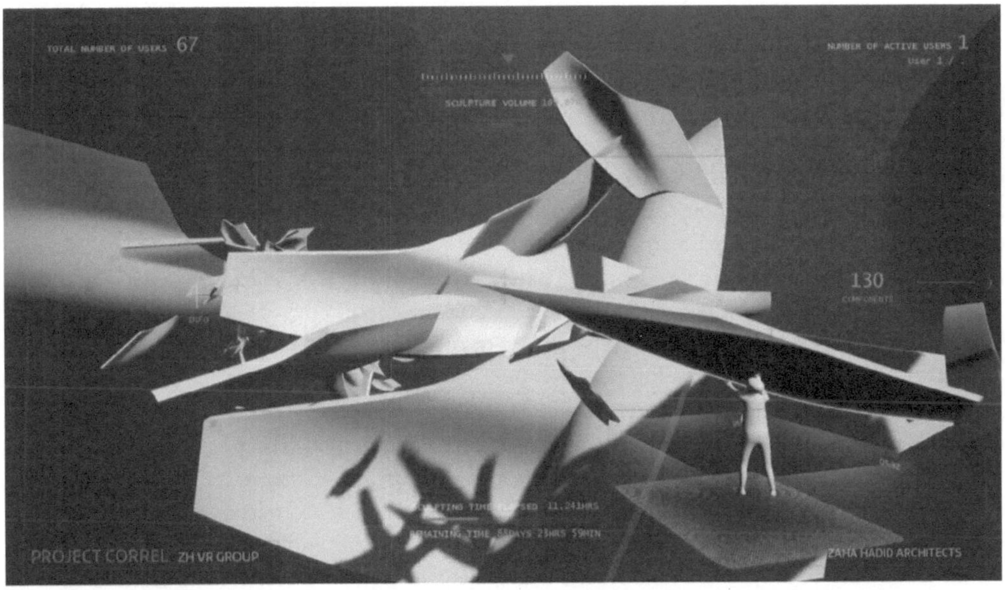

FIGURE 3.5 Multi Presence VR experience: Project CORREL (2019)

Source: Zaha Hadid Architects: Design as Second Nature exhibition, Museo Universitario Arte Contemporáneo (MUAC), Mexico

FIGURE 3.6 Multi Presence VR experience: Project CORREL (2019)

Source: Zaha Hadid Architects: Design as Second Nature exhibition, Museo Universitario Arte Contemporáneo (MUAC), Mexico

software package, including avatars, the User Interface, the designed space, and the data structure; (4) the 'user preset data' and the 'emerging data' which interact inside the virtual space; (5) the characterized, materialized, 'authorized data' which is formed into a scaled physical model of the virtual experience using rapid prototyping technology.

In addition to the five previously listed constituents, *Project Correl* examines three data categories. The first data category is the user preset data, which is collected upon entering the virtual space and includes the user's height, language, and name. The second data category is the emerging data, which is authored by the users inside the virtual space and requires an immediate response to the user's input: the component locations, rotations, and scales together make up the user's decision-making patterns, while the placement timestamps are also recorded. Finally, the third data category is the authorized data, which is recorded in snapshot at a selected date and time and then materialized using rapid prototyping technology for display alongside the virtual reality experience, as a physical outcome of the project.

Throughout the project development, sequential prototyping and testing was necessary as part of designing the data collection routines and streamlining the user experience. This prototyping and testing was extended to cover system performance, plus the prediction and correction of errors within functions, user navigation and comfort studies, and the ergonomic aspects of interactivity. An avatar, representing the user's self within VR, was also required, to help bring the user's cognitive awareness into the virtual-reality space and help them identify the self from others (Figure 3.5). Additionally, the avatar helps users to experience the relative scale of their components and better understand the shape of the collective construct.

Project Correl proves that we can design in an entirely unique, collective way and that we can manifest, import, and export the emerging result out of the digital realm, in this instance through a scale model (Figures 3.7 and 3.8). In the most basic terms, *Project Correl* demonstrates the capacity of human designer-builders to create and interchange information spanning both realities.

FIGURE 3.7 Materialization of the VR experience (rapid prototyping technology): Project CORREL (2019)

Source: Zaha Hadid Architects: Design as Second Nature exhibition, Museo Universitario Arte Contemporáneo (MUAC), Mexico

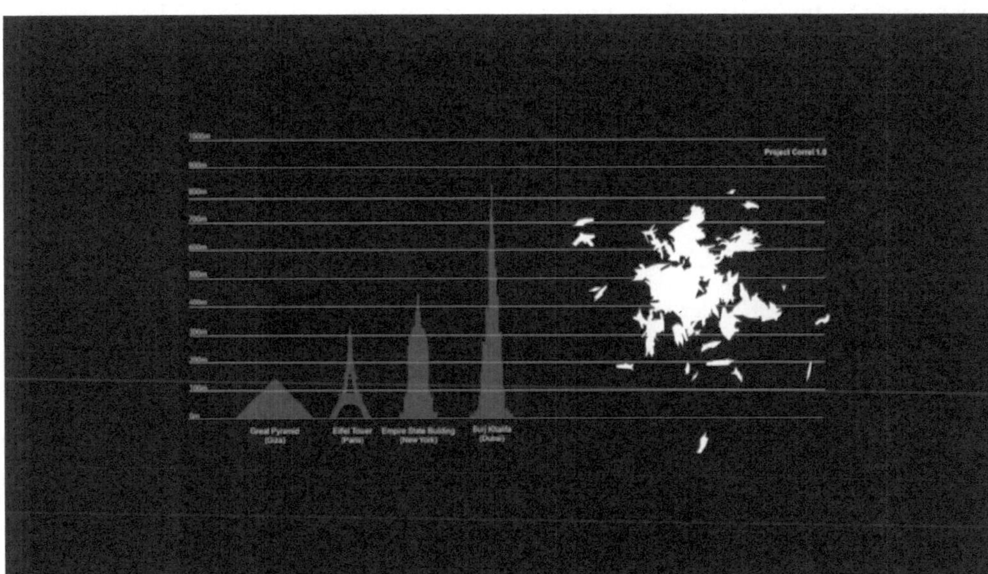

FIGURE 3.8 Scale of the Collaborative Sculpting Experience: Project CORREL (2019)

Source: Zaha Hadid Architects: Design as Second Nature exhibition, Museo Universitario Arte Contemporáneo (MUAC), Mexico

Summary and Conclusion

Paradigm changes affect how we perceive beauty. The inception of cybernetics, under Norbert Wiener in the 1950s, laid the foundations for a reinterpretation of the individual and for the organization of human communication with artificial systems. What started as a purely scientific endeavour, promoting the possible creation of artificial life and organisms, began to influence how we regard our traditional roles and conditions within human culture. With media such as science fiction and, later, computer gaming and social media, our human contact with digital communication and artificial space was no longer restricted to the specialist entities that required these technological resources (such as the military, economic, and scientific communities) and started to form part of a broader, popular culture.

At this stage, however, we are still only experiencing the beginning of this cultural and technological change. As described, the technological means and the predominant mindsets, societal functions, and cultural techniques are all lacking the capacity to integrate or even allow such discourse. It is important for architecture to adapt to the technology and open up architectural discourse to the new paradigm of authoring in order to enable the development of cybernetic spatial concepts. The aforementioned experiential, immersive machine interface will help initiate an intensified, revived connection with audiences and cultural proprietors, creating a wider architectural mandate and meaning.

Cybernetic architecture and its aesthetic concepts must transform, through real-time co-authoring and extensive inclusion of user-audiences within the cultural production, to become an open system whose primary characteristic is adaptiveness. The discipline's prevailing formative dialectic will be replaced with emergent or evolutionary principles.

ZHVR's experience with *Project Correl* shows that all who gain access to this platform and gain control and an ability to author, will engage and contribute inside the collective space. A high level of intuitiveness and playfulness will advance user participation and early engagement. Tapping into this collective energy, a new form of consensus will democratize the design process.

With these changes, a new set of informed participants will formulate space in multiple realities, using a new set of aesthetic principles.

Note

The Zaha Hadid Virtual Reality (ZHVR) Group—part of Zaha Hadid Architects (ZHA)—was established by Helmut Kinzler in 2015, with the aim of understanding the full implications of virtual reality (VR) in the architectural complex, while also developing a relevant skill-set within ZHA's practice.

Zaha Hadid Architects is a global architectural studio that brings together over 400 employees from more than 50 countries. Founded by the late Dame Zaha Hadid in 1979, the office is known for its highly innovative and industry-advancing design approach, with Hadid receiving both the 2004 Pritzker Architecture Prize and the 2016 RIBA Gold Medal in recognition of ZHA's outstanding contribution to the discipline.

Acknowledgements

ZHVR would like to thank our collaborators: Epic Games, HP Virtual Reality Solutions, NVIDIA and HTC VIVE, the University Museum of Contemporary Art in Mexico City (MUAC), The-Gallery at the Arts University Bournemouth, and Zaha Hadid Design, and Luke Fox for copy editing and proofing.

References

Baudrillard, J. (1981 [1994]) *Simulacra and Simulation*. Michigan: The University of Michigan Press.
Hayles, N. K. (1999) 'How We Became Posthuman: Virtual Bodies', in *Cybernetics, Literature and Informatics*. Chicago: University of Chicago Press.
Hayles, N. K. (2017) *Unthought: The Power of the Cognitive Nonconscious*. Chicago: University of Chicago Press.
Macpherson, C. B. (1962 [2011]) *Possessive Individualism: Hobbes to Locke*. Oxford: Oxford University Press.
Maturana, H. R. and Varela, F. J. (1972) *Autopoiesis and Cognition*. Dordrecht, Netherlands: D Reidel Publishing Company.
McLuhan, M. (2001) *Understanding Media: The Extensions of Man*. Abingdon: Routledge Classics.
Metzinger, T. (2003) *Being No One: The Self-Model Theory of Subjectivity*. Cambridge, MA: MIT Press.
Mörtenböck, P. (2001) *Die Virtuelle Dimension: Architektur, Subjektivität und Cyberspace*. Vienna: Böhlau Verlag.
Wiener, N. (1948) *Cybernetics, the Scientific Study of Control and Communication in the Animal and the Machine*. Cambridge, MA: MIT Press.
Zhai, P. (1998) *Get Real*. Maryland: Rowman & Littlefield.

4

WISH YOU WERE HERE

Virtual Reality and Architecture

Sean Pickersgill

Introduction

The relationship between architectural design and the tools with which it is realized is a well-considered field of enquiry. In recent decades, seminal texts such as Robin Evans' *The Projective Cast* (1995), Alberto Pérez-Gómez and Louise Pelletier's *Architectural Representation and the Perspective Hinge* (2000), and Greg Lynn's *Animate Form* (Lynn, 1999) have each investigated clear morphological relationships between patterns of design thinking and the role played by representational tools in shaping design outcomes. For Evans, Pérez-Gómez, and Pelletier, the relationship between architecture and its methods for projecting geometric variations played a clear role in determining the exploratory arc of form and meaning. Lynn, writing at the advent of the digital age, recognized that the inherent reproducibility and incremental variety afforded by parametric digital design had created an entirely new paradigm driven by the temporal and mutable qualities of 3D media.

A recent book summarizing the use of virtual reality (VR) within architecture and the built environment noted, naturally enough, that there were clear developmental opportunities within VR capabilities to enhance the communicative relationship between architect, design team consultants, and clients (Whyte and Nikolić, 2018). Unsurprisingly, it found that the efficiency of the process was determined by the degree to which data management and problem-solving logistics were positively managed within the platform. BIM software clearly assists in this respect, but the question remains as to the nature of qualitative judgements in this area.

There is an inverse relationship between the volume of parametric data that needs to be correctly organized within the decision chain of an AEC (Architecture, Engineering, Construction) design team, and the time available for discretionary decision-making that may in some sense be deemed 'aesthetic'. Hence, at the pragmatic level of building design, documentation, and construction, BIM software and the attendant capabilities for 3D visualization make value-management decisions more 'visible', but arguably do not make the challenge of designing more phenomenally rich and aesthetically pleasing environments any easier.

Skills

It can be contended that the challenge involved in understanding this situation and properly managing current digital design practices rests on a number of methodological principles. Architects/designers need to:

DOI: 10.4324/9781003183105-5

1. have a clear idea of the nature of the material conditions of their designs;
2. have the capability to understand and manage levels of abstraction within the visualization process;
3. have the ability to properly manage the material and lighting conditions of visualization software;
4. understand the relationship between construction processes within the modelling/simulation stage and the ultimate/final construction stage.

More specifically, in the current ecology of 3D visualization software, architects and designers need to:

1. Understand the interoperability between documentation platforms such as Revit and ArchiCad, and visualization environments such as 3DS and Enscape, Lumion and Twinmotion;
2. Have the capacity and commitment to ensure material and lighting fidelity is understood and incorporated into the design process;
3. Have the capability to shift modelled environments between documentation (Revit), animation/still (3DS) (Figure 4.1) and game (UE4) applications.

In order to explain and explore these evolving skills and attributes, it is worth considering how the evolution of representation software has entailed and encouraged a different type of architectural practice.

FIGURE 4.1 RAH Ideas Competition Entry, Space Laboratory and Dominique Perrault Architects, 2017.

An Evolving Technology

Based on the assumption that the process of decision-making in architectural design can cover the full range of macro *parti* sketches drawn by hand to micro-immersive impressions in fully rendered scenes, it is worthwhile identifying and isolating some of the key stages in which the various platforms, ultimately including VR, are especially effective.

1. From Simple Modelling to Rendered Still Image or Camera Animation

   In a scenario in which a design is modelled simply within a non-parametric environment such as SketchUp or 3DS, the decision chain rests largely on the What You See Is What You Get (WYSIWYG) metric. Images are produced for the purpose of creating an impression of an environment dictated by the 3D characteristics of the application (Figure 4.2) and determined by the capacity for 'realistic' rendering of the outcome, dependent upon rendering software and user capacity.

2. Parametric Modelling to Rendered Still Image or Camera Animation

   This is similar to the previous example but incorporates the modelling capacity of parametric software such as Revit or ArchiCad, in which the application is capable of producing metrically accurate geometries that align with documentation standards, and also may sit within an image production pipeline that allows for similarly realistic still images in third-party rendering applications, such as VRay, Lumion, Enscape, and Twinmotion. In this instance, design development changes within the documentation process can be quickly updated and tested for their visual qualities while retaining data integrity.

FIGURE 4.2 Student lounge project, UniSA, 2019

3. 3D Modelling to Immersive Environment (Non-Game Engine)

   In this scenario, modelling is undertaken within either a simple or parametric modelling environment and is then tested within a low-complexity immersive environment such as those native to metric environments like the Revit and SketchUp 'Walk' tools and the ArchiCad 'Explore' tool. The fundamental ontological shift is towards an immersive camera that is able to approximate a first-person perspective and allow for a real-time negotiation of the geometry of the environment, although lighting and material qualities are inherently limited by the capacities of the user to employ the program effectively, and the capacity of the program to deliver complex and realistic lighting conditions (Figure 4.3).

4. 3D Modelling to Immersive Environments (Game Engine)

   In this scenario, the data pipeline is more complex, depending on the 3D modelling environment chosen to create geometry in general. In structural terms, game engines prefer to treat all surfaces as the sole material presence within the view frustum. Previously, one of the barriers to integrating high-resolution modelling and rendering environments with parametric applications has been the interoperability between them, in the case of Revit and 3DS for example. Whereas 3DS has the capacity to acquire the geometrical and material data from Revit and effectively suppress the 'internal' geometries/layers of composite walls to allow for rendering, Revit is unable to acquire geometry from 3DS in an intuitive manner or assign parametric material data to imported geometries.

5. Immersive VR Environments

   In this final scenario, data acquired from the previous modelling processes is tested via a critical decision-making process that allows clients and designers to test the immersivity of the design through the metric of anthropometric proximities. In addition, ambient qualities of lighting and material richness may be created to better approximate the phenomenal vividness of an environment (Figure 4.4).

FIGURE 4.3 Kanmantoo mine lookout, Space Laboratory, 2018

FIGURE 4.4 A bridge too far: Kangaroo Island, South Australia, Space Laboratory, 2018

Output Ecologies

However, while simple walk-through or rendering environments could perform in a real-time fashion to allow for intuitive switching between accurate parametric modelling and immersive 3D experience (Figure 4.5), the question regarding the best mode of decision-making to ensure a better design output still remains. Until recently, the render quality of the industry leaders, Enscape, Twinmotion, and Lumion, was compromised by the hardware capacities of video cards to reproduce realistic real-time environments. The consequence of this limitation is that the balance between realistic rendering and the immersivity provided by game engine

FIGURE 4.5 OnSite Immersive Construction Experience, UniSA, 2015

software meant that architectural environments tended to remove detail in order to enhance performance.

Current adaptations of game engine software architecture, led by Lumion, Twinmotion, and Enscape, have continued to improve the nexus between immersive environments and parametric functionality. In effect, this now allows two areas, namely realistic rendering and immersive experience, generally considered peripheral to architectural design and documentation, to be incorporated into both the internal design development phase and external presentations to clients and stakeholders. The development of VR technology has also changed to adapt the screen clarity of game engine software to the production of environments that emulate a bi-focal experience. Although the 'telepresence' of conventional game-based experiences via a monitor or screen remains the general standard, the development of VR has raised more pressing questions regarding the degree of 'presentness' (telepresence) a person experiences within an environment.

Deciding and Doing

Ultimately, the key issue is the relationship between the form of representation employed within architectural practice and the decision-making process for design improvement which is made self-evident by the process. The effectiveness with which architects can view a 'real-world' emplacement of a design decision is central to the design development and imagination process. One of the essential aspects of architectural design education and practice is the understanding that designing is a conjecture based on a possible formal arrangement of material and space, and that design tools serve the purpose of testing propositions visually.

However, it can also be argued that the process of virtualization directed towards a realistic presentation of an environment, with all of the indexical content this entails, also ultimately distracts the designer from the core components of the design process which they must manage. If the weather and lighting effects of a rendered scene are sufficiently engaging and pictorially stimulating, it is reasonable to assume that an architect may be as susceptible to the poetics of an image as someone unfamiliar with, or unskilled in, the design process. The considerable industry dedicated to 'artist's representations' of unremarkable and poorly designed buildings bears witness to this.

Narrative

At question is the instrumental value of diagrams versus images, given that diagrams accept and employ a level of abstraction conventionalized by their role as an intermediary expression of a process, and images employ their degree of (sur)reality as part of a narrative. One of the less understood aspects of architectural representation is the question of narrative and how an architectural project exists not just as the outcome of a set of economic and technological parameters but is always placed and explained as a consequence of various narrative structures. Borrowing from film theory, architecture is considered by those external to its production as the *mise-en-scene* of the actions and events of life, whether real or fictional. It is generally understood that figural and representative forms of expression generally derive their aesthetic authority from the degree to which they contextualize the actions and decisions of actors/agents within a setting, and that the degree of intellectual freedom associated with this suspension of disbelief is a core aspect of the plausibility of a narrative (Figure 4.6).

Phenomenal Experience

For this reason, the use of VR as an extension of a trajectory of increasing phenomenal realism within architectural representation does not simply entail it becoming accessible to non-architects,

FIGURE 4.6 The story of the city: Adelaide, Space Laboratory, 2019

FIGURE 4.7 Sirius Building VR project, Space Laboratory, 2019

but is also an acknowledgement that architects are designing and bringing into effect more than the structure itself. In *The Seven Basic Plots*, Christopher Booker (Booker, 2004) summarizes a version of narrative archetypes which, it is argued, infiltrate all types of human communication, not just those directed towards fiction. In all forms of communicative interaction in which behaviour, judgement, and outcomes are presented, narrative plots play a role in explaining events. Architecture, in particular forms of architectural expression that draw on possible narrative contexts, is also involved in demonstrating value and authenticity.

Hence, VR is yet another means of enhancing the desire for architecture to move from a solely diagrammatic practice to one in which the core aspects of phenomenal experience are incorporated into the experience (Figure 4.7). As David Seamon, in his chapter on Architecture and Phenomenology states:

> Phenomenological concepts like lifeworld, natural attitude, intentionality, body-subject, environmental embodiment, place, and atmosphere identify integral constituents of any human experience, whether of the past, present, or future; whether real or virtual. Human beings are always already immersed in their worlds, even if that immersion becomes virtual.
>
> *(Seamon, 2018, p. 12)*

Conclusion: Pliability, Brilliance

Seamon ultimately criticizes trends within VR because it does not deliver what it attempts to do. Referring to Albert Borgmann's analysis, he points out that it delivers an unnatural pliability to the world through its ability to simulate experiences that are inherently 'improvements' on the real, and that the 'brilliance' of this experience is at odds with a necessary reconciliation with the world as it is (Borgmann, 1992). Our world is ultimately one that 'encumbers and confines' us within a number of existential realities and it is not desirable to separate these from life, however intoxicating the proposition is.

However, what Seamon, and perhaps Borgmann, do not address is the role that this technology is playing in developing new environments in which forms of human communication and experience are evolving and new types of economic activity, both monetary and social, are taking place. While figures regarding the scale of the computer game industry, valued at US$134.8bn in 2018, are now well known, the web-based streaming platform Twitch[1] provides a platform for game-based interactions in which practically all of the broadcasters interact with a viewing community while playing solo or participatory games (Twitch Statistics).

So how does VR technology intersect with the problem of authentic immersivity and the appetite for mediated digital experience? Whereas VR-based chatrooms such as VR Chat and Sansar employ low-resolution 3D VR environments as spatialized locations for social interaction, much as Second Life did in the 2000s, their current limitations concerning immersive authenticity are driven by server-side Netcode logistics and user-side hardware performance. The game industry capably serves a form of architectural immersivity that optimizes the use of PC- and console-based platforms, but the next step will involve the seamless integration of VR on a commercial level.

Each of these environments utilizes the same general environmental 'architecture'—a game engine–based software that is built and made to be lived in, the same software architecture that lies behind the turn to phenomenal realism within architectural VR, and perhaps a new reality for architectural practice. In many respects, Seamon is correct in identifying pliability and brilliance as key determinants in the uptake of VR as an architectural design tool, but it can be argued that the appetite for mediated experience in gaming and social VR means that the future is inevitable rather than encumbered.

Note

1. Available at: www.twitch.com

References

Booker, C. (2004) *The Seven Basic Plots.* New York: Continuum.

Borgmann, A. (1992) *Crossing the Postmodern Divide.* Chicago: University of Chicago Press.

Evans, R. (1995) *The Projective Cast: Architecture and Its Three Geometries.* Cambridge, MA: MIT Press.

Lynn, G. (1999) *Animate Form.* New York: Princeton Architectural Press.

Pérez-Gómez, A. and Pelletier, L. (2000) *Architectural Representation and the Perspective Hinge.* Cambridge, MA: MIT Press.

Seamon, D. (2018) 'Architecture and Phenomenology', in *Routledge Companion to Architectural History.* London: Routledge.

Twitch Statistics. Available at: https://twitchtracker.com/statistics (Accessed: 17 September 2019).

Whyte, J. and Nikolić, D. (2018) *Virtual Reality and the Built Environment.* London: Routledge.

5

HOW ARCHITECTS ARE USING IMMERSIVE TECHNOLOGY TODAY, AND PROJECTIONS FOR THE FUTURE

Dustin Schipper and Brittney Holmes

Introduction and Context

It has been almost 40 years since architects began designing and documenting with computers, sparking what has been referred to as the "digital turn" in architecture. Recently it has been proposed that architecture is experiencing a second digital turn, epitomized by the transition from small to big data, empowered by increases in computing capabilities and data storage (Carpo, 2017). These same forces are leading to a renaissance in immersive technologies: visualization platforms for immersive experiences such as virtual reality (VR), augmented reality (AR), and mixed reality (MR). VR headsets can now be found in offices, retail environments, and living rooms, and AR has moved from phone games to industrial fabrication (Bottani and Vignali, 2019) and high-end consumer goods such as cars (Torbet, 2019). The market research company Gartner, which has been tracking immersive technology for many years, removed VR from its Hype Cycle of Emerging Technologies in 2018, signalling their belief that the technology had reached a "plateau of productivity", with AR and MR following closely behind (Panetta, 2018).

Immersive Technologies in Architecture Today

This chapter defines VR as a fully immersive digital and stereoscopic visual experience. For purposes of clarity, all other immersive visualizations on Milgram's Reality-Virtuality Continuum (Milgram et al., 1994), ranging from AR to VR, are simply referred to as 'MR'. VR is built on principles of stereoscopy, tacitly understood since at least the Renaissance (Brewster, 1856) and formalized in the early 19th century with the invention of the first stereoscope (Wheatstone, 1838). There were early demonstrations of immersive technologies throughout the 20th century, but the commercial development of VR began in earnest in around 1988 through a partnership between VPL and Autodesk (Chesher, 2003). Enthusiasm waned in the late '90s and early 2000s as the technology struggled to fulfil its initial promise, although recent computational advances are driving a resurgence of immersive technology, and a spate of experimentation in the architectural profession.

One key difference between immersive media and typical architectural representations is the sense of *presence* they convey. While the exact definition of presence is still a matter for some debate among researchers (Grabarczyk and Pokropski, 2016), there are commonly agreed

DOI: 10.4324/9781003183105-6

criteria for measuring it quantitatively. These criteria are a set of 29 questions organized into four categories of user experience: Control Factors, Sensory Factors, Distraction Factors, and Realism Factors (Witmer and Singer, 1998). Presence is what makes immersive technologies so compelling and is likely to have been a driving force behind architecture's recent push to incorporate VR and MR into design practices. An architect's clients are rarely trained to perceive spatial experiences from 2D representations such as plans and axons, whereas immersive technologies provide a substantially improved means of communicating the experience of unbuilt designs.

VR tools marketed to architects have evolved from niche products requiring serious technical knowledge, to software at least as approachable to the average designer as any commodity rendering platform. MR architectural tools are still uncommon in current practices, as reflected in the Gartner Hype Cycle for Emerging Technologies (Panetta, 2018), which places AR in the "Trough of Disillusionment" (interest is waning as experiments deliver poor results) (Gartner, 2019), with MR even further behind it. Gartner estimates each as being 5 to 10 years away from reaching a "Plateau of Productivity" (mainstream adoption beginning in earnest) (Gartner, 2019). Despite losing some initial hype, the wealth of MR tools for software developers provides the necessary resources for technical experimentation and prototyping by firms with computational capabilities and the ability to invest time in learning new technologies and methods.

Architecture firms are capitalizing on the increased accessibility of immersive technologies by conducting tests and experiments, developing proof-of-concept prototypes they are often eager to share publicly and present at conferences. Some prototypical workflows are fragile one-offs, while others are very robust and implemented throughout a firm. Architects publicizing their R+D work are rarely forthcoming about its viability for handling the complexity of actual projects, or ability to be deployed in a typical design team. Despite prototype scalability, architecture firm development work can act as a roadmap for how the industry would like to use immersive technology in the future. Figure 5.1 lists many common and well publicized immersive technology applications and prototypes from the AEC industry and where these use cases fit into the typical US project lifecycle. Table 5.1 defines the different immersive techniques and explains their proposed value for the design process.

Immersion Today and Current Development Trends

Virtual Reality

While architects were experimenting with immersive technology, it was also evolving rapidly in other industries. The recent consumer VR renaissance was primarily driven by the video game industry. Filmmakers are also embracing immersion and the new opportunities it presents for narrative creation and world building. The same technologies that enable architects to prototype new immersive practices are also advancing volumetric filmmaking techniques through a range of products and services designed to meet the needs of users ranging from hobbyists to studio filmmakers (George, 2017). These industries are responsible for massive increases in the quantity and quality of immersive content available to those with the necessary hardware to view it. There is even a high-end entertainment market emerging through VR parlours and event spaces such as the VOID (The VOID, 2019). Beyond entertainment, VR is being used as a training tool for high-stakes skills. These include jobsite safety training, flight simulation, and surgery simulation. VR is also being used in medicine to treat pain and assist with rehabilitation. The professional applications of VR are best suited to circumstances in which users should be separated from reality and completely immersed in an artificial reality. The near future of

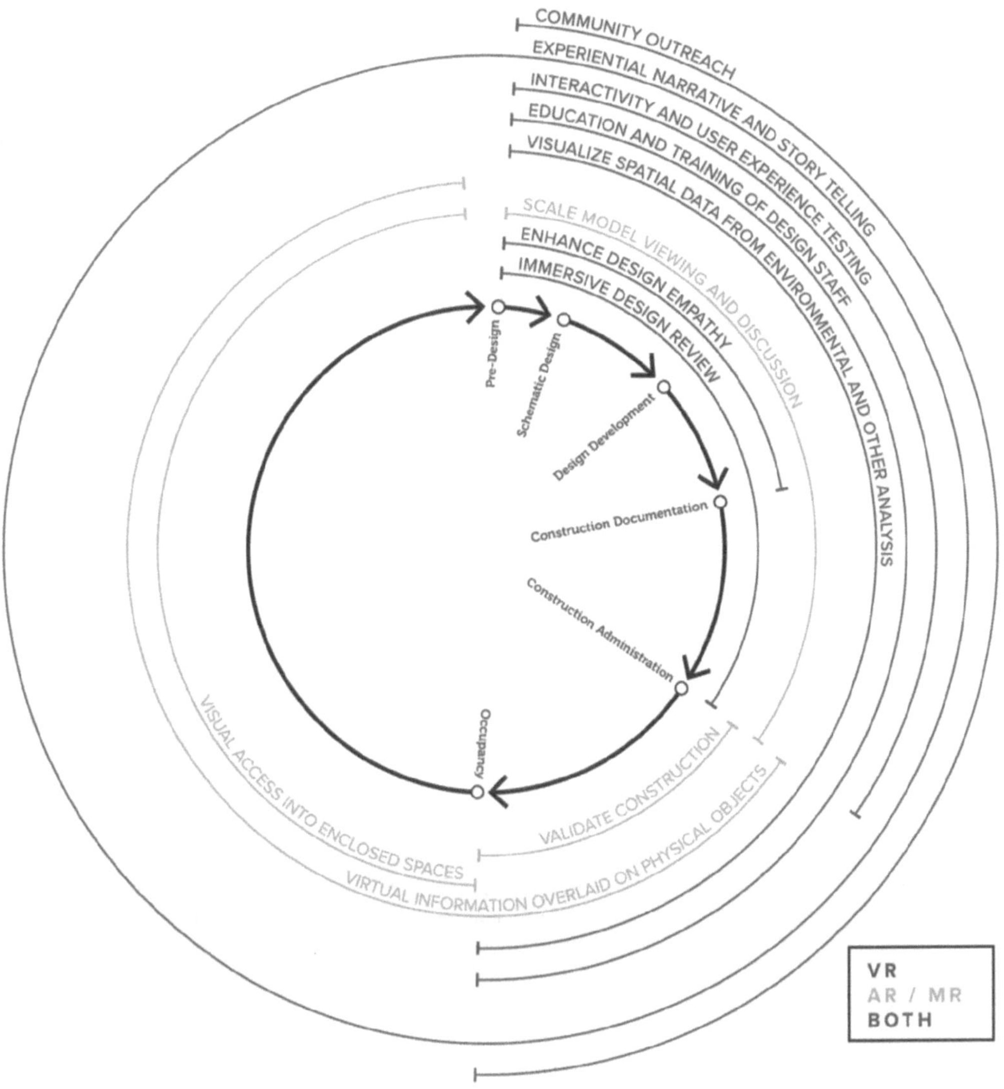

FIGURE 5.1 Demonstrated uses of immersive technology—mapped along the US architecture project lifecycle

VR will be rooted in narrative and simulation, since it is able to create experiences that can convincingly approximate physical reality and can transport viewers to compelling new realities.

Mixed Reality

Like VR, MR also has a strong presence in the entertainment sector, with a track record of phone games making innovative use of its capabilities. It has also been demonstrated in high-end entertainment and cultural applications, such as museum exhibits that come alive when viewed through a screen, or as complimentary experience enhancements for theme parks (Figueroa, 2019). Unlike VR, MR is best suited to applications in which users must remain fully aware of their immediate surroundings but benefit from layers of visual information that would otherwise be difficult to access. Some demonstrated professional applications include

TABLE 5.1

Use Type		*Description*	*Value Proposition*
Immersive Design Review	VR	Visualize and review designs like traditional design review using 2D media and physical models. This can be collaborative or individual, and is a very accessible form of immersive experience	This type of visualization allows users to experience space at a 1:1 scale as though they are in the environment. This enables reviewers to have a better sense of the design, proportions, and materiality than a 2D visualization could provide
Enhance Designer Empathy	VR	Software or physical equipment can be used to simulate the physical presence of a user group different than the design team working on the project	This experience helps designers to make better and more empathetic decisions based on a facility's end users' needs
Scale Model Viewing and Discussion	MR	Models can be viewed through screens or headsets by one or multiple people on a table in the same fashion as a physical model	This experience is like using 3D models in design review, but has the potential to be less expensive and require less additional work to create assets for the presentation
Validate Construction	MR	Visualizing digital 3D models at 1:1 scale geo-referenced with a site for point of comparison. This is most commonly demonstrated by contractors, but has the potential to be used for construction administration or on-site design review	This allows for a more rigorous comparison of design to construction, clearly illustrating where dimensions or elements are out of place from their designed conditions
Visual Access Into Enclosed Spaces	MR	Laser scans and photogrammetry can be used to generate 3D models of as built conditions and these can be geo-referenced and visualized on top of the finished construction	This allows for the creation of 3D record drawings which can be used to create future as built models, or can be used by contractors who need to know what is inside of closed conditions and would prefer to avoid opening them
Virtual Information Guiding Physical Activity	MR	Like Validating Construction, but in this approach the model is used as a guide for the construction teams working on the project	This allows designers to communicate 3D information directly to the contractors' workers. This is particularly advantageous in complex built conditions such as HVAC assemblies and curvilinear forms

Use Type		*Description*	*Value Proposition*
Visualize Spatial Data From Environmental and Other Analysis	Both	Environmental and other types of data can be overlaid on real environments or virtual environments to visualize design impacts on measurable attributes of the space	Visualizing analytical data at the scale of an occupant allows the design team to understand the data within the context of a user's perspective and from their point of view
Education and Training	Both	Interactive simulations can be created to train designers or contractors on the construction process and proper safety procedures	Training environments of this kind do not require the same equipment or set-up, and are able to simulate riskier situations than real-life simulations can
Interactivity and User Experience Testing	Both	Interactivity can be built into visualizations to allow user groups to test functional characteristics of a space, or explore designed interactive functions of the building	In user group settings, this can replace the expensive and abstract process of hosting user group sessions in 'mocked up' spaces, and can give users a much better sense of how a flexible or interactive space will function than a stationary experience is able to provide
Experiential Narrative and Storytelling	Both	Narrative elements such as sound, text, or change over time enable designs to communicate beyond just their spatial characteristics	This type of visualization takes extensive planning and storyboarding, but can communicate an experience of place more completely and convincingly than a static render is able to
Community Outreach	Both	Distributing experiences to large groups of people and community members who may not have been identified in the typical project stakeholder process	This allows people to be exposed to designs for projects with high political stakes early in the process, and can generate good will, support, and design feedback while changes are still possible

navigation overlays for cities and facilities, merchandise with embedded marketing materials, and live data overlays for industrial maintenance and assembly. While the development of MR still lags behind VR, it has more profound implications for the way people will experience and relate to their physical environments. As intelligence designed into physical objects increases, the physical environment will become rich with data that is difficult to access or visualize. MR will directly benefit from this situation, providing a window into the invisible information saturating the built environment.

Volumetric Displays

The dark horse of immersive technology is volumetric (holographic) display. There are two common types of volumetric displays on the market today: front-viewed and tabletop (Kim et al., 2019). While contemporary holograms limit the perception of depth to screen space, a recent experimental breakthrough allowed volumetric light to exist in the same physical space as the viewer. This points to a not-so-distant future in which virtual objects may share space with physical objects (Smalley et al., 2018). While these technologies are still not as polished or commercially viable as VR and MR, they should be watched closely as they have serious potential to change the relationship between the physical and the virtual, and to reshape the landscape of immersive technology.

Conclusions and Projections for the Future

This chapter focuses on how immersive technology is already impacting architectural practice in all phases of the project lifecycle, both as a visualization platform and an analytical tool. While the authors looked primarily at large architecture firms providing conventional design services, the minimal up-front cost of testing and developing immersive methods means that firms of any scale and specialization can find ways to begin exploring this evolving ecosystem of tools and techniques. Immersive technology can be a critical component of a company's research and development agenda, and firms will continue to push the cutting edge of immersive practice in architectural design. It is vital that they continue to invest adequately in the development of immersive technology as, despite the ease of creating simple VR visualizations, slight deviations from standard techniques can require substantial commitments in terms of time, energy, and expertise.

Looking to the future, the next level of artificial reality will be to augment people's skills and senses through experience and interaction (Carmigniani and Furht, 2011), and, as designers, it is our responsibility to carefully consider and manage these technologies as they become integrated into conventional building systems. Deploying strategies for immersion, interactivity, and adventure at the building scale will allow designs to engage with occupant expectations and add new levels of experience to the individual's perception of space, thus heightening wayfinding, branding and historical context, and making the invisible visible.

It is also important to consider that advances taking place in immersive technology are happening in parallel to changes in the amount of intelligence designed into buildings. Current trends related to Internet of Things devices, smart building control systems, digital twins and smart city infrastructure promise to significantly increase the availability of spatial data. Simultaneous advances in using machine learning and neural networks for cleaning, organizing, and analysing data hold promise for converting the unwieldly big data of the built environment into meaningful information ready for visualization with VR and MR. As the hidden patterns of everyday life are brought to the surface of our perception and visualized life in real space, there could be substantial urban, social, and societal impacts. This could spark changes in behaviour both for the better and the worse, and fundamentally shift the rhythm of everyday life.

Artificial realities are poised to break through the plane of the headset, phone, or screen and begin bleeding into the physical world around us. This will have profound impacts on broad categories of life and activity including learning, healing, socializing, designing, building, and how people generally understand the world around them. As these changes take place, architects who have invested in understanding and working with immersive technologies will be well positioned to design environments that can harness the experiential potential of combining the real with the artificial. This blurring of realities promises to deliver a future in which physical and digital sensory experiences can be overlaid and complementary. If this happens, a whole new design discipline would open up to architects who have dedicated time and energy to exploring these early days of consumer immersive technologies, providing opportunities for new design services, and forever changing the nature of space.

References

Bottani, E. and Vignali, G. (2019) 'Augmented Reality Technology in the Manufacturing Industry: A Review of the Last Decade', *IISE Transactions*, pp. 284–310.

Brewster, D. (1856) *The Stereoscope: Its History, Theory, and Construction*. London: John Murray.

Carmigniani, J. and Furht, B. (2011) 'Augmented Reality: An Overview', in *Handbook of Augmented Reality*. New York: Springer-Verlag, p. 41.

Carpo, M. (2017) *The Second Digital Turn: Design Beyond Intelligence*. Cambridge, MA: MIT Press.

Chesher, C. (2003) 'Colonizing Virtual Reality: Construction of the Discourse of Virtual Reality', *Cultronix*, 1(1), pp. 1–27.

Figueroa, J. (2019) *Disney Releases More Details about Star Wars: Galaxy's Edge Interactive Games in Play Disney Parks App*. Available at: https://wdwnt.com/2019/05/disney-releases-more-details-about-star-wars-galaxys-edge-interactive-games-in-play-disney-parks-app/ (Accessed: 27 June 2019).

Gartner (2019) *Gartner Hype Cycle*. Available at: www.gartner.com/en/research/methodologies/gartner-hype-cycle (Accessed: 25 June 2019).

George, J. (2017) *The Brief History of Volumetric Filmmaking*. Available at: https://medium.com/volumetric-filmmaking/the-brief-history-of-volumetric-filmmaking-32b3569c6831 (Accessed: 25 June 2019).

Grabarczyk, P. and Pokropski, M. (2016) 'Perception of Affordances and Experience of Presence in Virtual Reality', *Avant*, 7(2), pp. 25–44.

Kim, J. et al. (2019) 'Electronic Tabletop Holographic Display: Design, Implementation, and Evaluation', *Applied Sciences*, 9(705).

Milgram, P. et al. (1994) 'Augmented Reality: A Class of Displays on the Reality-Virtuality Continuum', *Telemanipulator and Telepresence Technologies*, pp. 282–292.

Panetta, K. (2018) *5 Trends Emerge in the Gartner Hype Cycle for Emerging Technologies, 2018*. Available at: www.gartner.com/smarterwithgartner/5-trends-emerge-in-gartner-hype-cycle-for-emerging-technologies-2018/ (Accessed: 25 June 2019).

Smalley, D. E. et al. (2018) 'A Photophoretic-Trap Volumetric Display', *Nature*, 553, 486–490.

Torbet, G. (2019) *Augmented Reality Navigation Overlays Direction Information Onto the Road*. Available at: www.digitaltrends.com/cars/ar-navgation-hyundai-wayray-ces-2019/ (Accessed: 25 June 2019).

The VOID (2019) *VOID*. Available at: www.thevoid.com/ (Accessed: 25 June 2019).

Wheatstone, C. (1838) 'Contributions to the Physiology of Vision: Part the First: On Some Remarkable, and Hitherto Unobserved, Phenomena of Binocular Vision', *Philosophical Transactions of the Royal Society of London*, pp. 371–394.

Witmer, B. G. and Singer, M. J. (1998) 'Measuring Presence in Virtual Environments: A Presence Questionnaire', *U.S. Army Research Institute for the Behavioral and Social Sciences*, 7(3), pp. 225–240.

PART 2
Space and Form

The second section includes four contributions which present work related to designing and representing architectural ideas of **'Space and Form'** using augmented reality (AR) and virtual reality (VR). These contributions combine digital space with physical space on various scales through the use of AR and VR tools, and present design, evaluation, and communication methods and techniques.

Elena Pérez Guembe and Rosana Rubio Hernández introduce a sensitive use of technology that supports and encourages environmental and social sustainability. They propose a multi-sensorial zoo experience, establishing architectural pavilions as a display medium, the use of gloves as an interactive device, and an information network providing live transmissions to and from many places at the same time.

The three chapters which follow focus on the initial architectural design phase and relate to design ideation, evaluation, and reflection on architectural space and form using AR and VR.

Mehmet Emin Bayraktar and Gülen Çağdaş propose an AR-based mobile environment for sketching in three-dimensional space in the early design phase. The initial design which is produced can be transferred to other environments for further development and refinement.

In the next chapter, Anette Kreutzberg demonstrates how 360° panoramas photographed within a physical scale model lit with daylight can create an immersive bodily experience when viewed in VR, which is suitable for evaluating daylight distribution in architectural space.

Turan Akman and Ming Tang discuss blending digital and physical realities to create new types of spatial qualities and experiences. They propose supplementing and enhancing existing architectural features with AR. In the design phase, they suggest using a VR walk-through for evaluation purposes and to collect quantifiable data on the spatial effects of the AR additions.

Follow the QR-code to navigate through the online content of Part 2.

DOI: 10.4324/9781003183105-7

6

RECONCEPTUALIZING ZOOS THROUGH *MILLE-OEILLE*

A Posthuman Techno-Architecture to Sustain a Human/Non-Human/Culture Continuum

Elena Pérez Guembe and Rosana Rubio Hernández

Introduction

The COVID-19 pandemic has once again shown that humans exist in a continuum with other species and nature, and also revealed the violence of our human-animal interaction and the nature of human interference, which has become an environmental and social problem on a global scale. Thinking beyond anthropocentrism has become an historical imperative, together with the way in which we conceptualize and create architecture: "ideologies are practices settled in our artefactual surroundings" (Broncano, 2020, p. 98).

Zoos, as well as natural history museums and other 19th-century Western cultural institutions, have traditionally been the strongholds of taxidermic specimens, colonization, and classification systems for more than questionable exhibitions associated with knowledge production, entertainment, and educational activities. We are now facing the need to decolonize historical narratives and unidirectional, lineal forms of thought, as well as the 'universalization' of knowledge produced by Western culture, constructed on the basis of excluding all kinds of "sexualized, racialized and naturalized 'others'" that were not recognized as part of humanity and therefore were not considered subjects of knowledge (Braidotti, 2013, p. 27). The idea of 'this man of reason' underlying these built environments is rooted in a mind-body divide which has been crucial to Western thought since the Enlightenment and which most cultures on Earth do not share (Descola, 2009, 2013; Viveiros de Castro, 2015). This has created a sense of exceptionalism in relation to other species and bodies, including nature, which regards them as endless resources to be exploited. The scale of devastation in recent times urgently requires new ways of thinking and new ethical commitments.

Situated at the point of tension between the convergence of the Fourth Industrial Revolution and the Sixth Great Extinction, *Mille-oeille*, a speculative techno-architecture alternative to the traditional zoo, aims to move beyond anthropocentrism, sharing a 'vital materialism' sensitivity (Deleuze and Guattari, 1994) within the posthuman condition.

The key question in this post-anthropocentric approach, which also "enlists science and technology studies, new media and digital culture, environmentalism and earth sciences, biogenetics, neuroscience and robotics, evolutionary theory, critical legal theory, primatology, animal rights, and science fiction" (Braidotti, 2013, p. 57), concerns how we can architecturally reconceptualize the idea of a zoo that supports the human and non-human continuum and is therefore ethically in keeping our times.

DOI: 10.4324/9781003183105-8

Methodology

In order to address this question, we applied a research-through-design method, a "designerly inquiry focused on the making of an artefact with the intended goal of societal change" (Roggema, 2017, p. 3). *Mille-oeille* was originally conceptualized in 2007 to rethink the obsolescence of zoos and was graphically revised in 2018, when it was presented at the 16th Venice Biennale International Architecture Exhibition (European Cultural Centre, 2018). *Mille-oeille* is a symbiotic techno-architectural pavilion coexisting with its environment, whose name is derived from the French *mille-feuille* cake and the noun *oeil*, meaning 'eye' in English. In other words, it offers a 'thousand layers' of data and information from the local environment and other ecosystems across the planet, casting a 'thousand eyes' onto the world to collect the information that *Mille-oeille* receives and displays. It incorporates innovative technologies, including augmented reality (AR) and climate simulation, embedded in a multi-layered smart envelope that offers a unique form of engagement with natural phenomena whilst supporting energy conservation. An empirical scientific method was therefore applied to design the material, using an iterative process of prototyping and testing. Since new forms of thinking and being in the world may need to be expressed by other types of materialities, Coloured Liquid Crystal (CLC) was prototyped in parallel with the architectural proposal to resolve and express the qualities and potential of a new aesthetic and sustainable paradigms for this specific project. Consequently, the environmental and social sustainability concerns underlying the research are addressed on both the material and the building scales. In addition, the review of the scientific literature and the analysis of case studies provide a concrete theoretical framework that validates *Mille-oeille* as a coherent response with potential for realization.

Mille-oeille Precedents and State of the Art

Zoo design evolved considerably in the previous century, from paying little attention to animal habitats to mimicking original ecosystems. Although these technical improvements have advantages in terms of ensuring a better environment for animals, the major issue of keeping living beings in captivity remains one of the last relics of the modern era. In order to respond to such a fundamental question, the concept which geographer Gail Davies terms the 'electronic zoo' comes into play:

> an emerging form of animal display . . . as informational patterns in multi-dimensional electronic spaces . . . [where] digital imaging, the internet and virtual reality take their place alongside more established technologies such as film, photography and television. These offer new ways of conceiving of and portraying natural history, and introduce the possibility of different relationships between human and animal experiences.
>
> *(Davies, 2000, p. 244)*

The 'electronic zoo' model has already been partially or fully implemented in various ways. On the one hand, traditional zoos are increasingly making use of new technologies to display and represent animals or to enhance the physical experience through digitalization. Technology-based interventions include education and entertainment materials based on gamification, virtual navigation, mobile learning applications, digital content systems, and AR (Wißotzki and Wichmann, 2019), the latter system having been identified in studies as optimal in terms of not detracting from the physical space, as other technologies do (Karlsson et al., 2010; Kelling and Kelling, 2014; Perry et al., 2008). In addition, new technologies have been implemented to assist and explore animal-computer interaction (Webber et al., 2017).

On the other hand, completely virtual solutions are gaining attention. For example, the pioneering *Wildscreen at Bristol*, planned as part of the UK Millennium Projects, combined in-place accessible IMAX cinema and an Internet-accessible database on endangered species in the world, namely the *Wildscreen ARKive* (2003). State-of-the-art AR technology is being applied in zoos and other programmes involving animals for entertainment or education. One example of this is the German Roncalli Circus (Miley, 2019), which used Optoma ZU850 laser projectors to provide a 32-metre-wide arena with a depth of 5 metres and 360-degree visibility for the entire audience. Another similar AR application, used for educational purposes, featured in the programme *Who Do You Think You Really Are*? and presented at the Natural History Museum in London (2011), enabled the audience to watch and engage with life-size dinosaurs and other extinct creatures roaming around the museum.

Although the main achievement of electronic zoos has been to avoid keeping animals in captivity, we recognize that the model has still inherited controversies from the traditional zoo, such as unidirectional narratives and taxonomical perspectives. Moreover, it poses a variety of new challenges, such as privileging the visual over the multi-sensorial experience or excessive disengagement with nature.

Searching for inspiration in other models not related to human-animal interaction, we looked back to 1960s immersive and multi-sensory spatial designs in which artists and architects worked together to explore 'radical juxtapositions' (Sontag, 2009). The so-called *Movie-Drome*, conceived by the experimental filmmaker and media artist Stan VanDerBeek, is relevant to this research. The experiment consisted of an immersive experience involving a mixture of light, sound, photographs, and news performed in real time at a geodesic dome built in the north of New York state. The artist intended his installation to be a planetary experience that would run simultaneously in other *Movie-Dromes* which could potentially be scattered around the world (Sutton, 2003). The multiple, simultaneous multimedia information was identified by Colomina (2001) as a 'new form of distracted perception': a different way of generating and perceiving reality far removed from bounded narratives, which is generative in itself and intrinsically aimed at planetary communication.

Mille-oeille builds on these precedents, aiming to generate innovation by critically adopting, mixing, transforming, and improving them in conceptual, aesthetic, and technological terms.

A Posthuman Techno-Architecture to Sustain the Human/Non-Human/ Culture Continuum

How do we resolve the important socio-cultural dimension associated with actually visiting a zoo as a relevant part of this experience (Sickler and Fraser, 2009), from the perspective of creating a just setting for all human and non-human entities? How can architecture use technology wisely to provide a relevant experience, without keeping living beings in captivity or losing sight of its research, educational, and entertainment purposes, thus supporting a human/ non-human continuum?

Mille-oeille is installed in 'encapsulated' habitats (Sloterdijk, 2016), all unique in terms of the way humans, free or domesticated animals, and nature have established reciprocal relationships, in reserves, veterinary farms, animal therapy centres, or national parks, for example. All these instances constitute being 'atmospheric spheres of existence', 'bubble-worlds', or a 'foaming together', whilst remaining existentially apart (*ibidem*): they are all unique places and different paradises in which coexistence between animals and humans has been deeply cultivated over time.

Multiple *Mille-oeille* pavilions could be distributed throughout the globe, 'foaming' a vast information network. They would receive images, data, and objects from scientific expeditions and experts around the globe. Cameras used by scientists in the field are the pavilions' eyes onto the world. The images they record are transmitted and projected in real time using holographic-based AR, which is considered an ideal solution for providing 3D visuals (although it still needs to be perfected) (He et al., 2019). The appearance of the pavilions changes according to the number of projections occurring at the same time. The transparency level of their interior membrane fluctuates to accommodate incoming transmissions, and, when viewed from the outside, the darkening of the envelope informs visitors in the surrounding park when a projection is taking place. The exhibition is organized by selecting one meridian of the globe and the expeditions taking place there. This allows the visitor to experience multiple ecosystems and different environmental conditions.

Morphologically and programmatically, *Mille-oeille* consists of a flattened spherical exoskeleton in which local animals can nest, thus creating other ecosystems in symbiosis with the building. The interior contains concentric rings of interconnected spheres decreasing in diameter from the biggest, at the centre of the pavilion, where AR holographic images and environmental conditions are recreated and multi-sensorial experiences take place, to the smaller 'bubbles' on the periphery where visitors can consult a detailed database. Between both regions, visitors pass through a section containing objects brought back from expeditions that can be studied. They enter *Mille-oeille* from the centre, where the exoskeleton stands, and can wander towards the periphery. This periplus within the pavilion provides an 'augmentation' experience: "a palimpsest-like process of overlapping information" (Gheorghiu and Stefan, 2014, p. 257). The skin of *Mille-oeille's* inner volume is a multi-layered responsive envelope that changes its transparency, tincture, and coloration dynamically, modulating the natural light coming in for optimal holographic projection-based AR and visualization in response to different transitory conditions. It can filter both visible and thermal radiation to avoid energy loss. Together, the exoskeleton and the metamorphic envelope create a moiré effect, functioning like the peripheral nervous system of a cephalopod to create dynamically controlled fading, iridescence, and pulsations with a behavioural plasticity that responds to different stimuli, such as the amount of visual information it receives, programmatic requirements, and weather conditions.

Mille-oeille not only proposes a sensitive use of technology but also reformulates architecture from a phenomenological point of view in terms of form, materiality, and spatial perception, including the aesthetic potential of AR. In order to enhance seamless perceptual depth via the spatial layering of the building, it avoids the use of headsets, screens, or other obtrusive devices, instead proposing gloves as an interactive device, together with holographic projection-based AR, similar to the Roncalli Circus technology. Experts agree that viewing interfaces have to be flexible and robust and the tracking system moving around the audience has to be reliable for AR systems to be successful in this kind of environment (Barry et al., 2012). However, in our view, in order to create the most effective illusion, the way in which the AR is woven into the physical space is extremely important. Therefore, *Mille-oeille* is more of an architectural interface with transitory qualities which is able to express the different conditions that affect it (Figure 6.1). (For more information about *Mille-oeille's* technical aspects, see Pérez-Guembe and Rubio-Hernández, 2021).

Discussion: *Mille-oeille* and a Garden of Earthly Delights

In *Mille-oeille,* the environment, technology, AR, new media, and the arts are choreographed through a bio-techno-architecture, following a human-animal-nature-culture continuum principle that understands life as a holistic collaboration of symbiotic relationships (Margulis and Sagan, 1995). It stresses the phenomenological experience, the embedded and the embodied,

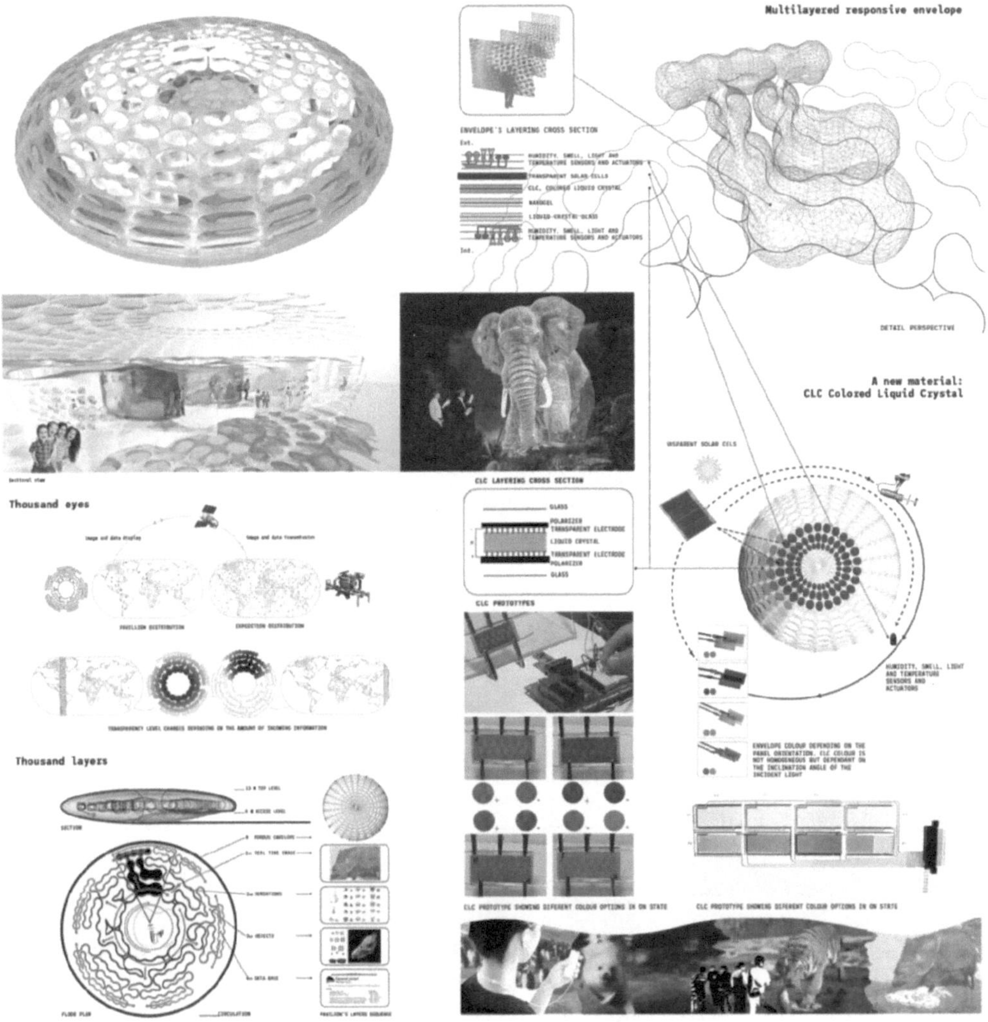

FIGURE 6.1 *Mille-oeille:* how it works and what it is made of.

supporting active visitor engagement with knowledge creation and educational and entertainment goals. It moves beyond unidirectional views, gathering information from expeditions and studies of animals rather than the animals themselves. It avoids any overemphasis of the visual over other senses or excessive disengagement from nature, placing the interconnected pavilions in varied ecosystems, 'diverse paradises' or 'Gardens of Earthly Delights', and allowing them to generate others. This kind of techno-cephalopod with architectural features and a morphing skin, positioned and connected throughout the globe, advances spatio-temporal concepts in architecture such as simultaneity and ubiquity, and the multi-temporal and multi-scalar, "merging the cyberspace with the physical space", and creating "a knowledge-intensive society", as in the Society 5.0 paradigm (Deguchi et al., 2020, pp. 6, 15), which advances the Fourth Industrial Revolution (*ibidem*). In addition, the CLC design with AR premises for image adequacy, site-specific and site-augmentative possibilities, together with the artistic and aesthetic potential and magic which both elements bring together, imply a provocative and poetic approach to

FIGURE 6.2 *Mille-oeille* in an exuberant Garden of Earthly Delights.

scientific content. *Mille-oeille* aims to serve as a technological apparatus "far more complex and generative than the prosthetic, mechanical extension that modernity had made of it" (Braidotti, 2013, p. 83). This project actively aims "to reinvent subjectivity, actualizing a relational self that functions in a nature-culture continuum and is technologically mediated" (*ibidem*). The vitality of this bond is based on the fact that we are all entities sharing the planet (Figure 6.2).

Acknowledgement

We thank Mme Giraud for allowing us to add in this collage in Figure 6.2 Moebius' characters, such as Arzach and Stel and Atan from the 'World of Edena', which not only belong to a 'diverse paradise' but to our cultural heritage. In memory of Luis Guembe and Jean Giraud for an open, exuberant, and diverse world made by all and for all.

References

Barry, A. et al. (2012) 'Augmented Reality in a Public Space: The Natural History Museum, London', *Computer*, 45, pp. 42–47.

Braidotti, R. (2013) *The Posthuman*. Oxford, UK: Polity Press.

Broncano, F. (2020) *Espacios de intimidad y cultura material*. Madrid, Spain: Ediciones Cátedra.

Colomina, B. (2001) 'Enclosed by Images', *Grey Room*, 2, pp. 6–29.

Davies, G. (2000) 'Virtual Animals in Electronic Zoos: The Changing Geographies of Animal Capture and Display', in Philo, C. and Wilbert, C. (eds.) *Animal Spaces, Beastly Places*. Abingdon, UK: Routledge, pp. 243–265.

Deguchi, A. et al. (2020) 'What Is Society 5.0?', in Hitachi-U (ed.) *Society 5.0: A People-Centric Super-Smart Society*. Singapore: Springer Singapore Pte. Limited, pp. 8–40.

Deleuze, G. and Guattari, F. (1994) *What Is Philosophy?* New York: Columbia University Press.

Descola, P. (2009) 'Human Natures', *Social Anthropology*, 17(2), pp. 145–157.

Descola, P. (2013) *Beyond Nature and Culture*. Chicago: University of Chicago Press.

European Cultural Centre (ed.) (2018) *Time, Space, Existence*. Venice: GAA Foundation-European Cultural Centre.

Gheorghiu, D. and Stefan, L. (2014) 'Augmenting the Archaeological Record with Art: The Time Maps Project', in Geroimenko, V. (ed.) *Augmented Reality Art: From and Emerging Technology to a Novel Creative Medium*. Basel, Switzerland: Springer International Publishing, pp. 255–276.

He, Z., Sui, X., Jin, G., and Cao, L. (2019) 'Progress in Virtual Reality and Augmented Reality Based on Holographic Display', *Applied Optics*, 58, pp. A74–A81.

Karlsson, J., ur Réhman, S., and Li, H. (2010) 'Augmented Reality to Enhance Visitors Experience in a Digital Zoo', *Proceedings of the 9th International Conference on mobile and ubiquitous multimedia, 2010-12-01*. Limassol, Cyprus: ACM, pp. 1–4.

Kelling, N. and Kelling, A. (2014) 'Zooar: Zoo Based Augmented Reality Signage', *Proceedings of the Human Factors and Ergonomics Society Annual Meeting 2014-09*, 58(1), pp. 1099–1103, SAGE publications.

Margulis, L. and Sagan, D. (1995) *What Is Life?* Berkeley: University of California Press.

Miley, J. (2019) 'German Circus Replaces Animals with Stunning Holograms', *Interesting Engineering*. Available at: https://interestingengineering.com/german-circus-replaces-animals-with-stunning-holograms (Accessed: 1 June 2019).

Natural History Museum, London (2011) *Who Do You Think You Really Are?* Available at: www.youtube.com/watch?v=A_3bQsO4nFA (Accessed: 1 June 2019).

Pérez-Guembe, E. and Rubio-Hernández, R. (2021) 'Mille-Oeille: An Architectural Response to Zoo's Obsolescence in Post-Anthropocentric Times', in Melendez, F. et al. (eds.) *Data, Matter, Design: Strategies in Computational Design*. Abingdon, UK: Routledge, pp. 259–266.

Perry, J. et al. (2008) 'AR Gone Wild: Two Approaches to Using Augmented Reality Learning Games in Zoos', in Kanselaar, G. et al. (eds.) *International Perspectives in the Learning Sciences: Cre8ing a Learning World: Proceedings of the Eighth International Conference for the Learning Sciences-ICLS 2008*, Vol. 3. Utrecht, The Netherlands: International Society of the Learning Sciences, pp. 322–329.

Roggema, R. 2017 'Research by Design: Proposition for a Methodological Approach', *Urban Science*, 1(1), pp. 1–19.

Sickler, J. and Fraser, J. (2009) 'Enjoyment in Zoos', *Leisure Studies*, 28, pp. 313–331.

Sloterdijk, P. (2016) *Foams: Spheres Volume III: Plural Spherology*. Semiotext(e). Cambridge, MA: MIT Press.

Sontag, S. (2009) 'Happenings: An Art of Radical Juxtaposition', in *Susan Sontag, against Interpretation and Other Essays*. UK: Penguin Classics, pp. 263–274.

Sutton, G. (2003) 'Stan VanDerBeek's Movie-Drome: Networking the Subject', in Shaw, J. and Weibel, P. (eds.) *Future Cinema: The Cinematic Imaginary after Film*. Cambridge, MA: MIT Press.

Viveiros de Castro, E. (2015) *The Relative Native: Essays on Indigenous Conceptual Worlds*. Chicago, IL: HAU Press.

Webber, S. et al. (2017) 'Interactive Technology and Human-Animal Encounters at the Zoo', *International Journal of Human Computer Studies*, 98, pp. 150–168.

Wißotzki, M. and Wichmann, J. (2019) '"Analyze & Focus Your Intention" as the First Step for Applying the Digital Innovation and Transformation Process in Zoos', *Complex Systems Informatics and Modelling*, 20, pp. 89–105.

Wildscreen Arkive (2003) Available at: www.wildscreen.org/arkive-closure/ (Accessed: 1 June 2019).

7

AN AUGMENTED REALITY-BASED MOBILE ENVIRONMENT FOR THE EARLY ARCHITECTURAL DESIGN STAGE

Mehmet Emin Bayraktar and Gülen Çağdaş

Introduction

Today's technological developments are changing the architect's workspace. Design studies are adapting to this change, and the design process is becoming more efficient. Nevertheless, increasing productivity in architectural design is a many-sided problem. Transferring and developing ideas between different media is useful, but tools should be more than information-carrying environments: they should help architects to improve their design at every stage of the process.

Representations produced by architects are not just the output of thoughts. In the early design phase, representations are created to form a basis for developing ideas. According to Goldschmidt (2003, p. 78), "one reads off the sketch more information than was invested in its making". While sketching, vague ideas are represented in a medium and transformed incrementally. This phenomenon, which is encountered when sketching, should also be present in the digital tools we use for early design. However, a great deal of the computer-aided drawing software used today does not allow for this type of behaviour, or else limits it to some extent.

Open-ended studies support the designer in a creative way and play an important role in early design. The purpose of this research is to offer a medium that can be used to illustrate ideas while maintaining their vague nature, as in a sketching exercise. Hence, an application has been developed which can be used anywhere, as it is available at any time via the user's mobile device. It has been created using the programming platform Unity 3D.

Literature Review

Augmented reality is created by making virtual additions to a video stream and displaying them both in the same environment. It presents an experience of the virtual and the real world at the same time. The mixed reality concept is defined by Milgram et al. (1994) as the reality–virtuality line. The real environment and the virtual environment blend together on different scales, while augmented reality and augmented virtuality take place in the middle.

There are relevant studies in the digital design tool area on innovative technique, augmented or virtual reality connection, multi-user capability, and the creativity-oriented approach. *Bridging the Gap* proposes a hybrid analogue and digital workplace for the early design stage and tries

DOI: 10.4324/9781003183105-9

to close the gap between the real and the virtual world (Schubert et al., 2011). The model that the designer makes in the virtual environment is reflected onto a surface by a projection device. The pieces of the physical model are placed on the surface and scanned instantly with the help of a depth camera, and the model is then processed into the simulation as if it were in the digital space. *Augmented Reality Sandbox* also proposes a hybrid workplace. It consists of a sandbox, a depth sensor camera, and a projection device. The goal is to study physical and digital information together, at the same time and in the same environment. Physical changes made to the sandbox are reflected in the topographical information projected onto the surface (Reed et al., 2014). In addition, Fitmaurice, Ishii, and Buxton have proposed a tangible desktop environment in which various types of physical objects interact with the digital environment (1995).

There are also examples of augmented reality drawing applications currently in use, namely programs that provide the opportunity to draw with a virtual pen. *Just a Line* is an ArCore platform-based, collaborative 3D drawing application (Just a Line, 2019) which enables one or more people to draw in three-dimensional space. PaintAR is another 3D drawing application based on the Google ArCore augmented reality platform (PaintAR—3D Augmented Reality Drawing, 2019), with which users can record their drawing history and share it with other people. However, although it is possible to find these types of drawing applications, which can be used for making 'doodles in the air', given the growing interest in AR research, it is not usually possible to transfer drawings to other design tools in order to develop the ideas further.

A Mobile Environment Proposal for the Early Architectural Design Stage

In order to test the mobile design environment, the topic of high-rise buildings was selected, as these types of buildings show morphological variations along their height. Thirty buildings were picked to form a collection that shows the early design of the buildings created by different architects. In compiling this list, the fact that the samples vary in form and have different façade characteristics was taken into consideration (Bayraktar, 2019). It was also helpful if the project's early sketches or models were available since this provides more insight data. Later, these projects were shown to the users of the mobile application that featured in the testing.

Proposed Application

The objective was to support productivity in the early design stage by using devices such as the mobile phone and tablet, which people can carry with them at any time. Unity 3D game engine software was used for the development of the model. Unity 3D works with object-based C# programming language support. Although it has a game-oriented approach, it is suitable for this kind of research, as loading applications into mobile devices is straightforward.[1]

The Google ArCore plug-in was used for the augmented reality link required for the mobile application proposed in the paper. Thanks to the ArCore library,[2] the real-world and virtual world connection is now possible without the use of a printed marker/QR-code. This advance helps AR applications to run with greater freedom and cover more space in the physical world.

After installation, the application is started on the mobile device. The user points the device towards any surface, the surface detection script within the ArCore starts, and the software processes the image through the camera, detects flat surfaces, and creates reference points for the virtual environment.

There are three main creation methods: sketching in 3D space, 3D matrix generation, and virtual model making can be selected to start with. In the first option, sketches can be made in 3D space as if the user were holding a virtual pen. By pressing the sketch button on the screen,

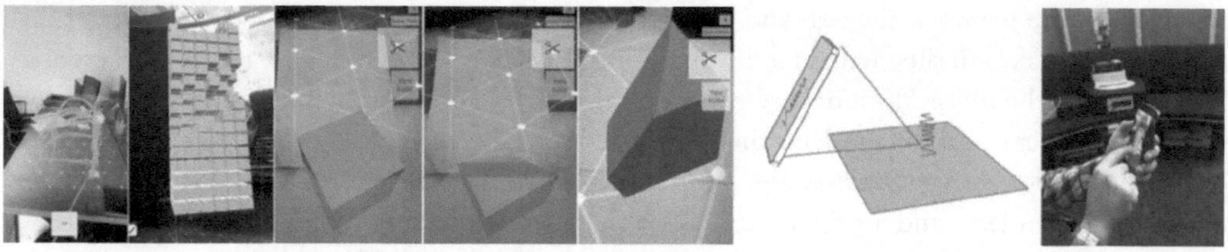

FIGURE 7.1 Different interfaces describing the mobile application: (1) a 3D sketch drawn with the pencil, (2) a model created using the 3D matrix method, (3) a model created using the virtual modelling tools (cutting process), (4) a diagram indicating the location of the virtual pen, (5) a user drawing in 3D space.

lines are drawn by moving the device in the air. In the second method, a 3D matrix is generated with smaller cubes, associated with the user width, length, and height input. For example, a three-dimensional matrix of 20 x 20 x 50 units can be produced: the user can then touch these and delete or add cubes in the area of interest. In the third method, a volume is created with width, length, and height values. The user can then either deform the mass by touching the object or cut it in the desired area using the cut button. Following this, the cut parts can be moved by touching objects, and multiple masses can be added. The user manipulates the model until it reaches the final form. These actions can be seen in Figure 7.1.

Mobile Application User Interface

The screen is mostly empty when opened for the first time, and the entire background is the real world. Architects can use either an empty table, a printed layout plan, or a real model for the surface. After selecting one of the three methods, there is a centring key to reset the position so that the model can be repositioned, and a restart button to reset everything. Sliding bars are available to adjust the width, length, and height of the model. There is a mass create and cut button, and objects are moved by touching and dragging. The non-essential elements on screen, such as the buttons, cut plane, and ground colour, can be hidden.

Examples of Use

The application was introduced to a group of architects. They were asked to try to reproduce one of the buildings from the list of high-rise buildings, and the whole experiment was recorded on the mobile phone screen. It is helpful if they think their decision process out loud, so that different actions can be isolated for further analysis during the main events. For example, one user may define design activities such as: "Move 1—I am creating a big mass that will define the boundaries of my building. Move 2—I am putting my object in front of me. 3—I am scaling and moving it again. 4—I am cutting the corner where I want an incline at the front. 5—I am adding another mass to support my ground floor connection idea. 6—I will define an entrance". These types of statements make the analysis clearer. At the very end, they responded to a 10-question survey. So far, users have been asked for general comments on the application, such as ease or difficulty, coming up with new ideas during the process, being able to model fast in comparison to their everyday modelling software, and effectiveness in terms of output of ideas.

Some experiment results are shown in Figure 7.2. While the three-dimensional sketch technique allows for more free drawing methods, other methods have features similar to solid modelling activities.

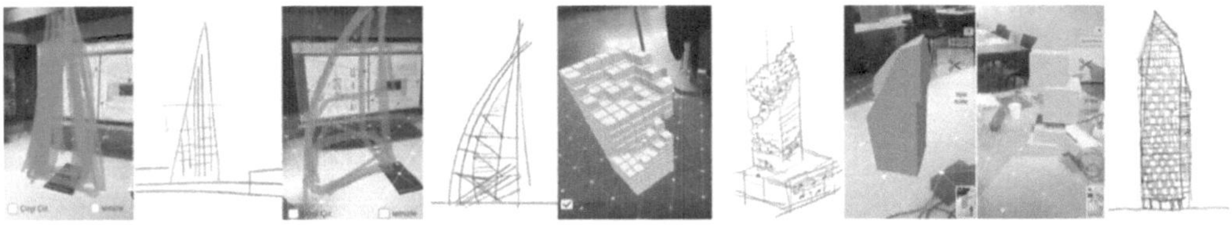

FIGURE 7.2 Samples of work produced with the mobile application

FIGURE 7.3 3D-printed models produced using the mobile application

At this stage in the study, solid models can be exported to other software as closed 3D polygons. Virtual pen drawings can also be exported, but consist of 2D planes following a path in 3D space, so extra work is needed for 3D printing: for example, architects can use the 3D sketch below the main design in another type of modelling software. Models can be directly edited or used as a supporting mass study for the project. Figure 7.3 shows some unaltered results that were 3D printed directly. The prints are the outputs of the virtual model making method. Objects are cut and deformed by pushing and moving them around. The first two examples were produced by pushing in the faces of a tall piece, and the last was formed from multiple objects cut and stacked on top of each other.

Different activities within sessions are explained in a timeline chart. In Figure 7.4, a virtual modelling process is divided into 20 consecutive steps, such as add, move, slice, rotate, scale, and remove operations. In this particular example, we can see that one person used only three operations to form a building. These charts will help to create a dataset about building modelling studies in this context. By using this information, modelling approaches between multiple sessions can be compared to each other.

Conclusion

This mobile tool has been tested by a group of architects. The questionnaire was helpful in terms of gathering initial comments. A second evaluation with precise questions and a numbered scale will help the assessment of the research. The application can be transformed into a design environment that responds to different design problems. It can support working with different scales, since markerless augmented reality is not bound to a particular surface. This means that it is possible to view and modify full-scale buildings on site.

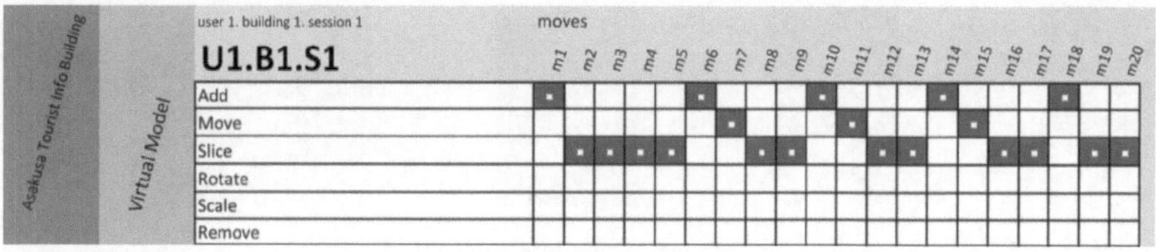

FIGURE 7.4 User actions are shown in a timeline chart for one modelling study

The design which is produced can be transferred to other environments. The solid models can be exported in the OBJ file format as a solid model for modelling programs such as Sketchup, 3Ds Max, etc. Sketch drawings need to be transformed into solid objects for 3D printing. In addition, drawings can be exported as curves for parametric software in theory, although further study is needed in order to implement this approach. Afterwards, the design process can continue in another application. Cooperative study can also be added in the future for multiple user participation.

Notes

1. Unity, Available at: www.unity3d.com (Accessed: 15 September 2019)
2. *ArCore*, Available at: https://developers.google.com/ar/ (Accessed: 15 September 2019)

References

Bayraktar, M. *High-Rise Buildings Collection-ARresearch*. Available at: https://my.archdaily.com/@mehmet-bayraktar/folders/high-rise-buildings-collection-arresearch (Accessed: 15 September 2019).

Eisenbruch, N. *PaintAR*. Available at: https://play.google.com/store/apps/details?id=com.NoahAR.PaintAR (Accessed: 15 September 2019).

Fitzmaurice, G. W. et al. (1995) 'Bricks: Laying the Foundations for Graspable User Interfaces', *CHI*, Vol. 95. New York: ACM Press, pp. 442–449.

Goldschmidt, G. (2003) 'The Backtalk of Self-Generated Sketches', *Design Issues*, 19(1), pp. 72–88.

Google Creative Lab. *Just a Line*. Available at: https://experiments.withgoogle.com/justaline (Accessed: 15 September 2019).

Milgram, P. et al. (1994) 'Augmented Reality: A Class of Displays on the Reality-Virtuality Continuum', *Systems Research*, 2351 (Telemanipulator and Telepresence Technologies), pp. 282–292. doi: 10.1.1.83.6861.

Reed, S. E. et al. (2014) 'Shaping Watersheds Exhibit: An Interactive, Augmented Reality Sandbox for Advancing Earth Science Education', *AGU Fall Meeting Abstract*, Washington, DC, Vol. 1, p. 01.

Schubert, G. et al. (2011) 'Bridging the Gap: A (Collaborative) Design Platform for Early Design Stages', *Proceedings of eCAADe 2011*, University of Ljubljana.

8

NORDIC DAYLIGHT IN 360°

Anette Kreutzberg

Introduction

Nordic Daylight

Nordic light is characterized by the conditions created by its latitude—the low sun height, long pale shadows, low-intensity light, and white summer nights—whereas the light of the South is just the opposite, with high sun height, short dark shadows, and high-intensity light. Furthermore, in relation to light intensity, in the Nordic countries it is not always the sun that is the most intense source of light, especially in the winter season when the sun is very low; the sky provides the highest light intensities, contrary to the South, where sunlight is the primary and most intense source of light. When a cloud covers the sun in the North, it does not necessarily cause low light intensity. If the cloud is relatively thin and has scattered sunlight in it, the white light of the cloud can provide greater light intensity than a blue sky and the sun combined, which is not the case in the South. This means that the sky can be an important source of daylight in the Nordic countries (Mathiasen, 2015).

Although it is important to understand local daylight conditions when designing architectural spaces anywhere, representing the quality and ambience of daylight can be a challenging task. Simulation software such as Radiance[1] and the Velux Daylight Visualizer[2] calculate Luminance, Illuminance, and Daylight Factor values in a digital model to meet building regulations, but the visual quality and ambience of daylight is a matter of perception and is difficult to qualify from a simulation. Scale models and 1:1 mock-ups are therefore widely used as a supplement to study and communicate the experience and atmospheric effects of daylight in architectural spaces (Andersen, 2017; Guzowski, 2018).

Virtual Reality and Daylight

VR can help us to understand the spatial phenomena of light in space by presenting the space in full scale. We have a lifelong experience of the distribution of daylight in 1:1 space in relation to our bodies. Studies of the influence of light on the atmosphere of a space (Stokkermans et al., 2017) and the perception of daylight in VR indicate a high level of perceptual accuracy, showing no significant difference between the real and the virtual environment in the evaluations that were examined (Chamilothori et al., 2018).

DOI: 10.4324/9781003183105-10

Methods

In addition to describing light by its physical composition of electromagnetic rays and particles, it can also be described by its direction, intensity, and colour. Unlike rays and particles, which are measurable but not immediately visible, these are perceived through the sense of sight. Moreover, they are not just visible, but are also an important part of our form perception and thus our understanding of the outside world. Traditionally, these three characteristics define the qualities of light (Mathiasen, 2015).

Northern daylight in Copenhagen, with its unique, soft daylight qualities, forms the basis of the daylight investigations. Three different representations of an architectural space, namely a full-scale daylight studio, its digital twin, and a 1:10 physical scale model, were used to experiment with immersive ways of representing and evaluating the quality and ambience of indoor daylight in VR using 360° photographic captures and 360° rendered images and abstractions.

These 360° panoramas can be displayed on screens with embedded navigational interaction when viewed in a dedicated app. The native Theta app (iOS and Android), used for controlling camera settings, provides instant feedback with a live view from a Wi-Fi-connected smartphone or tablet with a gyroscope. As soon as the panorama is captured, multiple views are available: VR view (single lens), VR view (twin lens), and Standard screen.

1:1 Daylight Studio

The daylight studio is part of the Architectural Lighting Lab located on the top floor of a three-storey building in the KADK (Royal Danish Academy of Fine Arts) campus in Copenhagen. The studio dimensions are W 5.5 x L 8.0 x H 2.7 meters, and it has a window façade facing east-southeast 115°. The studio has grey linoleum flooring and white walls and ceiling, and the metal window frames are coated with glossy white paint. Sequential 360° panorama recordings (Figure 8.1) with 5 sec., 10 sec., and 20 sec. intervals were photographed with ThetaS and ThetaV[3] cameras and compiled as 360° time-lapse videos in Premiere Pro.[4]

A series of 360° photographed panoramas with variable skylight window configurations in both sunny and overcast weather was captured at five different points of view (POV) for comparison.

1:10 Scale Model

The interiors of different 1:10, 1:20, 1:50, and 1:100 scale models were test-photographed in the Daylight Laboratory part of the Architectural Lighting Lab. The Daylight Laboratory provides a mirror box–style artificial sky and a moveable artificial sun. The fact that the camera POV acts as the eye height in VR determines the perceived scale of the scene or environment to be 1:1 regardless of the original or real-world scale if the established eye height in VR matches the user's real-world eye height (Leyrer et al., 2011).

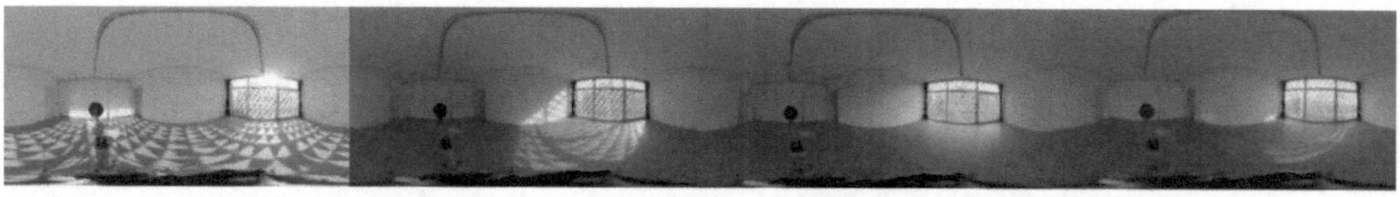

FIGURE 8.1 Extracts from sequential 360° recordings revealing variable sunlight patterns from mounted façade elements, diffuse skylight, and reflections from nearby buildings, all within a diurnal recording

FIGURE 8.2 1:10 scale model photographed with four different skylight window configurations, with overcast sky

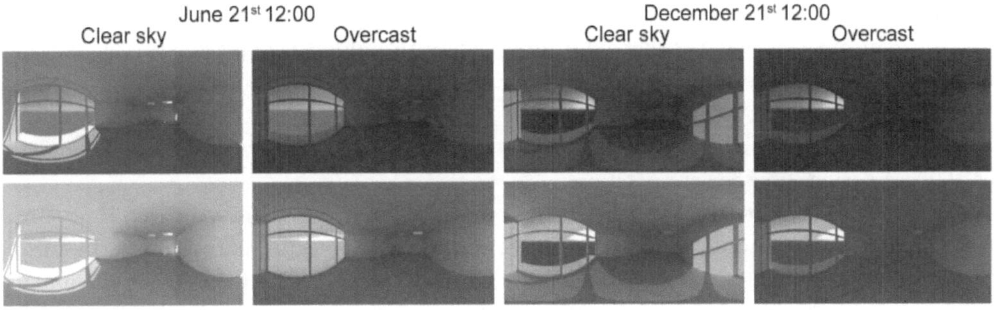

FIGURE 8.3 Top row: RGB render. Bottom row: False Colour Luminance (cd/m^2).

The viewer height is based on an average human eye height of 160 cm. The perception of scale in the architectural scale models viewed in VR is changed by establishing a scaled POV in the 360° panorama corresponding to the chosen eye height (Kreutzberg and Bülow, 2019). A set of support stands for the Theta cameras were designed for upright, rolled, and pitched positions to fit all four model scales.

The 1:10 demonstration model of the daylight studio was photographed in a series of 360° panoramas with variable skylight window configurations in sunny as well as overcast weather for comparison with photographed captures from the 1:1 daylight studio (Figure 8.2).

Digital Model (Digital Twin)

A digital twin model of the daylight studio was built in Rhino, imported to 3ds Max, and rendered with VRay Next. A 360° rendered animation with time and date settings corresponding to the first sequential photographic recordings was made for comparison.

Experiments with separating render passes resulted in alternative abstractions of daylight representation in the form of 360° False Colour Luminance panoramas displayed in VR, as well as unwrapped in 2D. Renderings with a clear and overcast sky were produced in both RGB and False Colour Luminance for comparison (Figure 8.3).

A series of 360° rendered panoramas with variable window configurations and diurnal and yearly sun positions is planned to supplement the 1:1 and 1:10 photographed series mentioned earlier.

Discussion and Conclusion

Time-Lapse

The time-lapse videos compiled from sequential 360° photographed panoramas of the daylight studio were very informative, showing variations in luminous conditions in different weather conditions, thus clarifying the dynamics and complexity of daylight. The very first sequential recording was captured during windy and cloudy weather conditions, resulting in heavy flickering in the compiled time-lapse. It was evident that the daylight condition in the room changed dramatically over time and at high speed. Watching the time-lapse in smartphone VR with the head-mounted display (HMD) was somewhat uncomfortable, due to heavy flickering. However, an alternative viewing on a smartphone without HMD was comfortable and still very informative. The corresponding rendered 360° animation from the digital twin was also informative, although not realistic in terms of shadow detail, demonstrating the path of the sun as stable light with no flickering. Time-lapse videos compiled from sequential 360° photographed panoramas in overcast weather showed little variation in indoor daylight conditions, making time-consuming animation renderings of overcast weather conditions unnecessary.

The single photographic images from the sequential recordings capture the daylight variations, and the unique northern, soft, pale shadows in detail and can provide a valuable reference for 360° renderings used for presentations.

The aim is to compile representative series of 360° photographed and rendered panoramas with variable window configurations in different diurnal and yearly sun positions, for use as teaching resources. Such panoramas are considered a very useful tool for enhancing the understanding of daylight variations and the effects on human perception of daylight in architectural space.

Scale Models

The ability to capture light distribution with photographic precision inside scale models combined with a 360° panoramic VR display enhances and expands the use of illuminated scale models for daylight studies. The 1:10 demonstration model of the daylight studio was very detailed, and had smooth surfaces with similar colours and reflective qualities to the real 1:1 space it represented. The captured images of the 1:10 interior and the reference interior in 1:1 were very similar. Draft models in a variety of scales, materials, and finishes were also test photographed and showed that the daylight distribution and atmosphere of a space illuminated by daylight can be experienced in 1:1 in very early conceptual models, as well as in detailed presentation models.

Rendering

RGB renderings of the digital twin model did not convey the atmosphere of the space or the quality of daylight convincingly. A fair amount of post-production is needed to achieve this. This is a well-established visualization workflow for final presentation renderings, but is not practical for initial design phases depending on fast iterations.

The 360° panoramic False Colour Luminance (cd/m^2) representations were rendered at 24 × 1-hour intervals (00:00, 01:00, 02:00 etc.) on the 21st of every month for a year (Figures 8.4 and 8.5).

When viewed in VR, they provide an alternative abstraction of daylight perception, based on analytical data displayed in a 1:1 3D space.

Unwrapped and displayed in flat 2D, the 360° panoramic False Colour Luminance renderings provide a diagrammatic representation of reflected light data over a full year cycle. The 360° panoramas display all visible surfaces from the POV, as opposed to 180° renderings or perspectives.

Observing the variations of light separately from day to day and season to season, rather than as an annual average, can help to qualify observations and conclusions about a lighting situation.

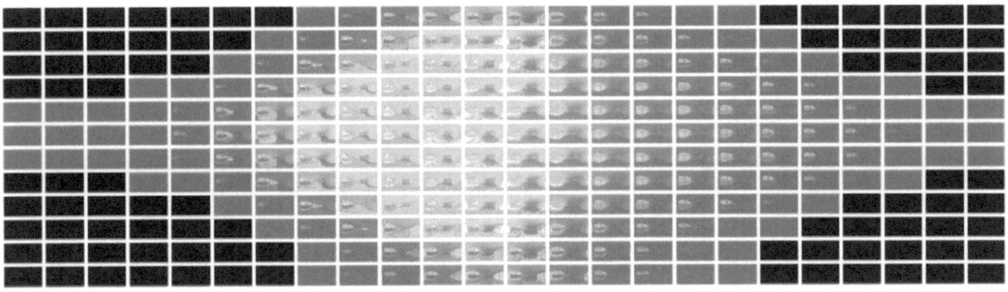

FIGURE 8.4 Copenhagen. False Colour Luminance (cd/m^2). Clear sky. Horizontal 00:00–23:00 Sun Hours. Vertical: January—December.

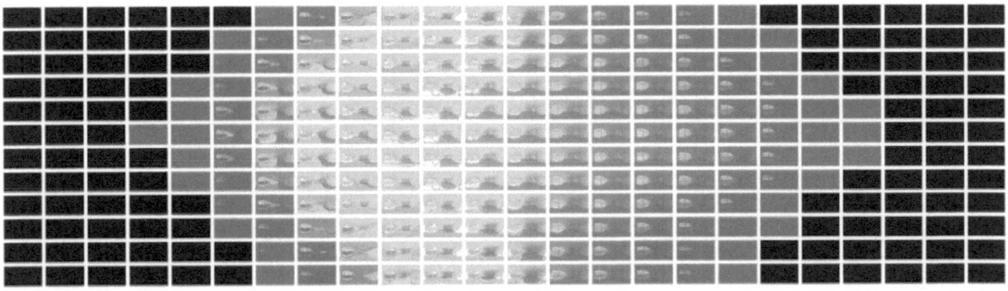

FIGURE 8.5 Lisbon. False Colour Luminance (cd/m^2). Clear sky. Horizontal 00:00–23:00 Sun Hours. Vertical: January–December.

Further analysis of the large quantity of photographed and rendered 360° panoramas already produced may reveal other findings, as may the proposed systematic recordings and renderings of the diurnal and yearly sun path in the daylight studio. In addition, it would be interesting to apply the methods and research approach in further work, in outdoor conditions.

Notes

1. www.radiance-online.org (Accessed: 8 February 2021)
2. www.velux.com/article/2016/daylight-visualizer (Accessed: 8 February 2021)
3. http://theta360.com (Accessed: 8 February 2021)
4. www.adobe.com/PremierePro (Accessed: 8 February 2021)

References

Andersen, M. (2017) 'Understanding the Human Response to Daylight (Interview)', *Daylight & Architecture* (27), pp. 14–31.

Chamilothori, K., Wienold, J., and Andersen, M. (2018) 'Adequacy of Immersive Virtual Reality for the Perception of Daylit Spaces: Comparison of Real and Virtual Environments', *LEUKOS*, Online, pp. 1–24.

Guzowski, M. (2018) *The Art of Architectural Daylighting*. London: Laurence King Publishing Ltd.

Kreutzberg, A. and Bülow, K. (2019) 'Establishing Daylight Studies Inside Architectural Scale Models with 360° Panoramas Viewed in VR', *Virtually Real, eCAADe RIS 2019*. Aalborg, Denmark.

Leyrer, M. et al. (2011) 'The Influence of Eye Height and Avatars on Egocentric Distance Estimates in Immersive Virtual Environments', *Proceedings of the ACM Siggraph Symposium on Applied Perception in Graphics and Visualization*. Toulouse, France, pp. 67–74.

Mathiasen, N. (2015) *Nordisk lys og dets relation til dagslysåbninger I nordisk arkitektur.* Copenhagen, Denmark: KADK. ISBN:978-87-7830-371-4.

Stokkermans, M., Vogels, I., de Kort, Y., and Heynderickx, I. (2017) 'A Comparison of Methodologies to Investigate the Influence of Light on the Atmosphere of a Space', *LEUKOS*, Online, pp. 1–25.

9

CYBER-PHYSICAL EXPERIENCES

Architecture as Interface

Turan Akman and Ming Tang

Introduction

Architecture exists in two domains simultaneously: "the reality of its tectonic and material construction, and the abstracted, idealized and spiritual dimensions of its artistic imagery" (Pallasmaa, 2011, p. 64). The first domain is physical and serves architecture's functionalities; hence it is objective. The latter domain is the one architects have relied on to mediate emotions and enhance the way users experience and perceive architecture and space. However, because of the physical nature of architecture, some historians have claimed that "of all the arts, architecture offered the most restricted scale of emotions" (Zevi and Barry, 1993, p. 192). Throughout history, architects have tried many methods to achieve dynamic experiences in their designs, such as the addition of bays to make space feel more three-dimensional in Byzantine architecture, the movement of the eyes upward in Gothic architecture, undulating surfaces in the Baroque period, and the geometrical patterns in Islamic architecture. Moreover, projects such as Fun Palace by Cedric Price have experimented with different mechanical methods to make the space more dynamic and allow the users to become the protagonists in the overall architectural and spatial experiences (Glynn, 2015; Mathews, 2005).

The Fun Palace project shows that as technology, materials, and construction techniques evolve, architects use what is available at the time, combined with what they have learned from the past, and deploy it to their advantage to break away from the static nature of architecture and enhance the way users experience and perceive their designs. However, any meaningful relationship between modern technology and architecture has been limited because of technology's dependence on a virtual medium. Augmented reality (AR), on the other hand, uses the physical environment as its medium to project digital elements onto the real world, meaning that it is dependent on a physical environment and therefore on architecture (Figure 9.1) (Papagiannis, 2017).

Since the digital elements are projected into the physical world with the correct materiality, lighting, and shadows, this makes it almost impossible to distinguish between digital additions and the physical reality. As a result, new possibilities are appearing for architects. Although AR technology is becoming an emerging tool for architects, the common elements they have relied on, such as materiality, light, and shade, should not be disregarded. AR should be carefully implemented, be compatible with the rest of the architectural and spatial experiences, and enhance their qualities, but how do we test AR additions without having to build the physical

DOI: 10.4324/9781003183105-11

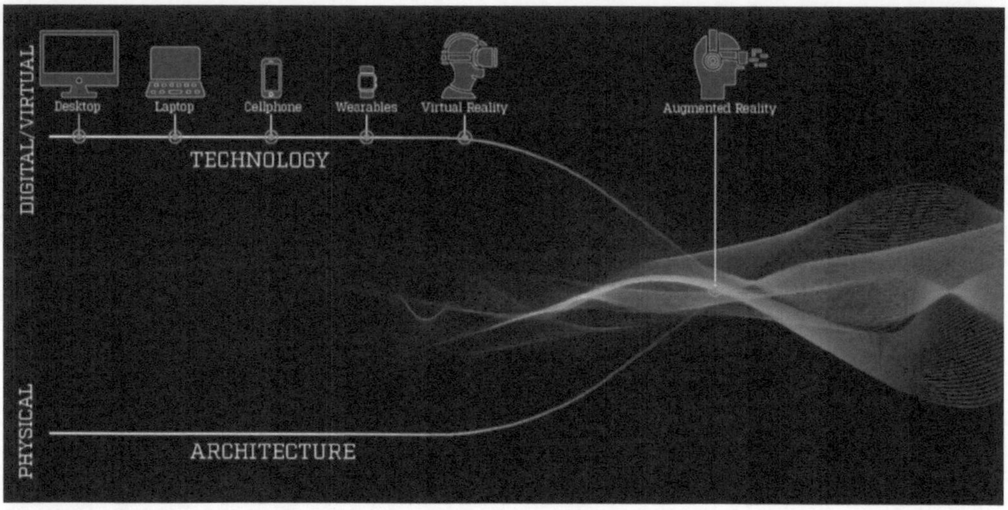

FIGURE 9.1 Technology and architecture

space early in the design process? This is where virtual reality (VR) comes into play. VR has become a powerful representation tool throughout the design process for testing AR effects in a simulated immersive environment. The physical architecture, along with the proposed interactive augmentations, can be tested through VR for user feedback from the early concept design stage onwards. As Tang described the benefit of applying VR to simulate AR experience, "This pipeline enabled students to design, exam, and modify their design while interacting with it. It became a fast cycle of refining and evaluation" (Tang, 2018, p. 87).

Although this chapter does not go into the details of the museum design, it is essential to understand the design, the underlying narrative, and how users were tested on, and evaluated with, VR during the final evaluation process. The proposed AR museum is called the "Museum of Displacement" and was proposed and designed as part of a Master of Architecture thesis in an academic context. The name of the museum is based on the general idea of the displacement of people, which could have many causes, including war, the need for food, natural disasters, or simply the search for a better life. Even though the reasons might be different, they usually all follow similar steps: *Home*, *Passage*, *Arrival*, and *Beyond Arrival*. *Home* would be where a person lives happily but for certain reasons has to move away to a new location. *Passage* would be the experiences during the moving process, usually the main struggles of displacement. *Arrival* would be the experiences of arriving in a new place and would include the experience of being lonely and not knowing anyone. Finally, *Beyond Arrival* would be the positive situation in which the displaced person has adapted to a new location/life and lives happily. The museum is divided into four major sections for users to experience these major stages (Figure 9.2). When combined with conventional architectural elements, AR enhances the qualities of these elements and reinforces the user's experiences and the way in which they perceive architecture, whilst also creating a more immersive storytelling experience. Moreover, the interactive experiences in these sections can be customized according to the local context or target audience.

Methods

In order to create powerful and compelling experiences, a refined version of a cyclical model of action research was used. Whilst it was still in the design process, several test groups walked

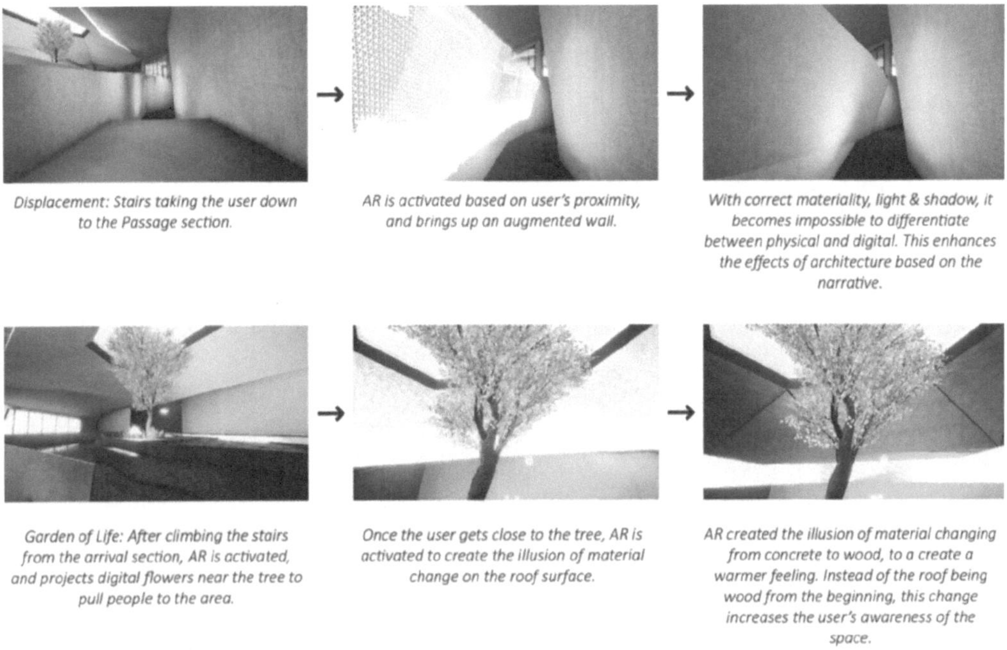

FIGURE 9.2 Experiences in the Museum of Displacement

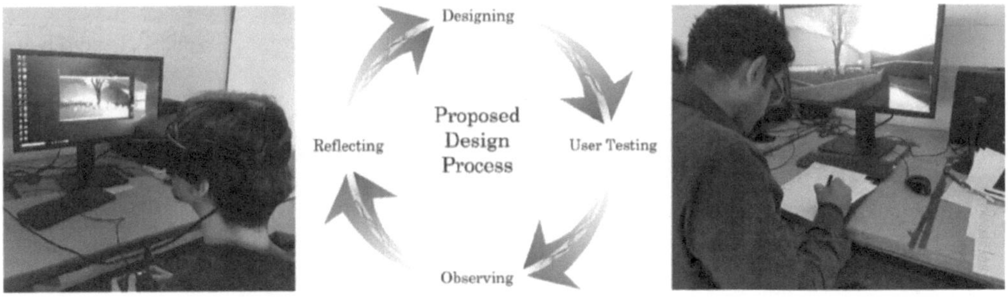

FIGURE 9.3 User testing phase at the University of Cincinnati (Mark Landis on the left, Ganesh Raman on the right)

Source: Photography and diagram by Turan Akman

through the museum via a VR headset. Their reactions were observed, followed by a short questionnaire at the end (Figure 9.3). With the help of this evaluation, the deficiencies in the design were identified and new iterations were created until the designer was happy with the outcome. For example, if a space in the museum was designed for a more emotional experience, the designer would observe the reaction of the user during testing, and if the experience did not reach the desired level, the design would be modified accordingly to enhance the overall experience. The VR process eliminates the need for the building to be fully constructed before testing the proposed interactive digital additions. Moreover, a similar analysis was used to prove the impacts of AR. The reactions of the users were captured to study the whole spatial experience. During this test, the first run provided only conventional architectural elements, with no AR additions, just the representation of a physical building in a simulated VR environment. The second run

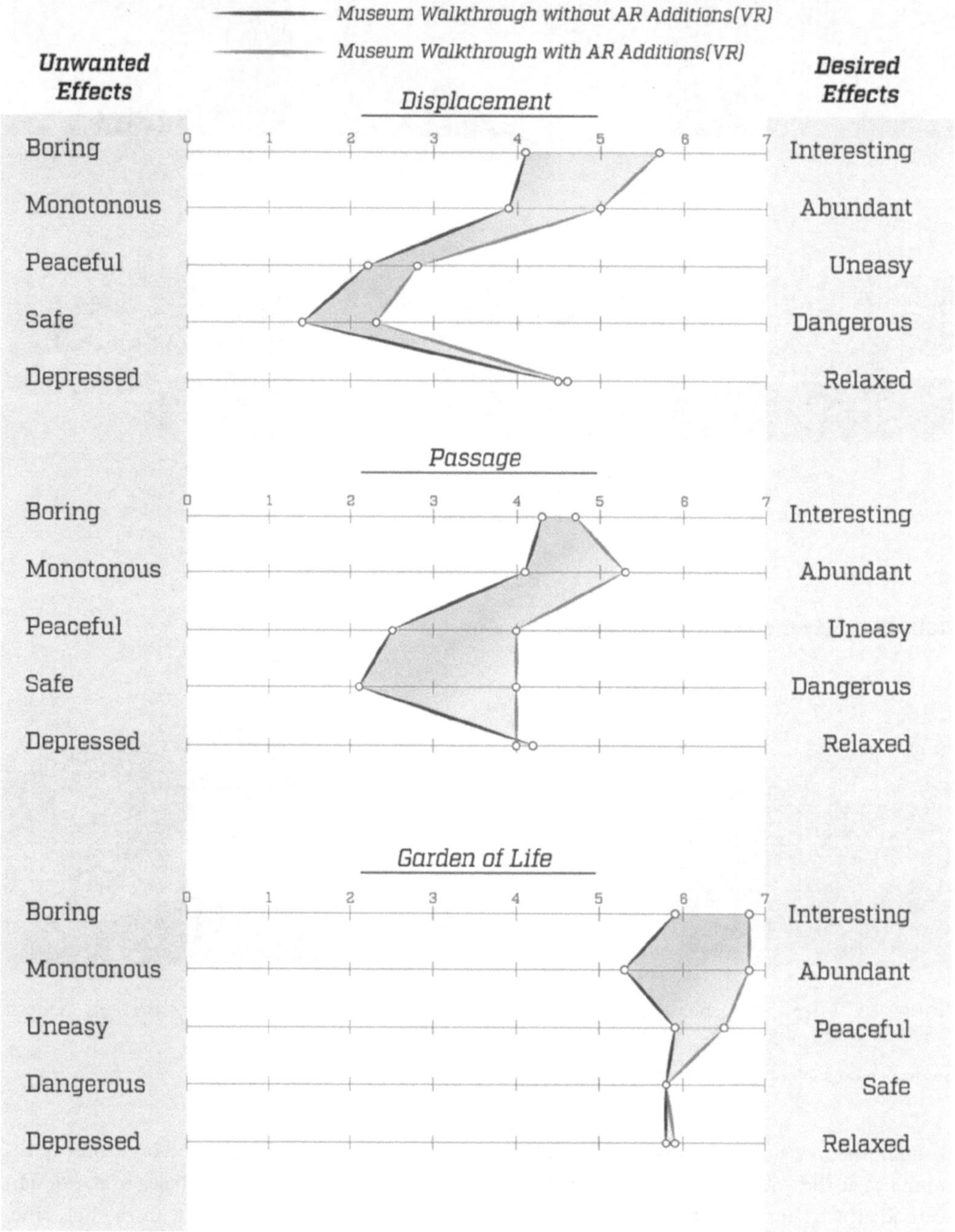

FIGURE 9.4 Test results

provided the same elements, combined with a representation of interactive AR. When the reactions of the users are compared, the capacity of AR to enhance in architecture can be proven.

In order to begin the first set of tests and obtain accurate results, a type of testing that would enable spatial experiences to be measured quantitatively was developed. The semantic differential (SD) method was chosen. This method studies the psychological responses of people in space by giving them a seven-level scale with opposite words at each end and asking them to rate their experiences. Although the method has the scope to test many characteristics, only five different characteristics were chosen and used, based on the desired effects of AR and the museum narrative: interestingness, richness, peace, safety, and depression. Each characteristic was measured by providing two extreme ends of the spectrum. For instance, interestingness was measured on a scale of one to seven, with a score of one indicating "boring" and a score of seven "interesting". Moreover, throughout the test, not every negative word signified an unwanted effect. Some negative words actually represented the desired effect: for example, "peace" was measured in terms of the two extreme words "uneasy" and "peaceful". In some areas of the museum that depicted the struggles of people, a nervous or uneasy experience would be desirable, and therefore the negative word "uneasy" would be the ideal answer from the users.

Findings

The first test was completed by 10 architecture major students. Each student did a walk-through of the museum twice using a VR headset, thus completely immersed in a virtual environment. The first VR experience of the museum offered the conventional architectural elements only, without the digital augmentation, as previously mentioned: the VR scene simply represented the physical part of the proposed museum. The second VR run combined the conventional architectural elements with AR additions to enhance the qualities of these elements and the overall experience of the space. The only variable in these two runs was the addition of AR. At the end of the two walk-through experiences, each person was asked to rate their experience for the first and the second run. The walk-through spaces included the hallway leading the user to the passage section called "displacement", the passage, and the beyond arrival section, which is also called "garden of life". The analysis showed that the physical architecture was not disregarded and still achieves part of the desired effects in the museum. However, the AR additions enhanced the qualities and effects of the architecture (Figure 9.4).

Discussion and Conclusion

Overall, the experiments clearly showed that blending digital elements with the physical world enhanced the qualities of the physical elements and changed the users' perception of space. Using the immersive qualities of VR, the tests were conducted as soon as there was a new iteration of the design. With the quantifiable data collected from the VR representations, the authors concluded that interactive AR experiences can be designed in parallel with the building design, which would enhance the qualities of both and create a meaningful relationship between the physical and digital worlds.

The future phase of this research would involve comparing the data from the VR tests with real-world tests. Instead of walking the user through the whole museum, small scale mock-up spaces could be built, and wearable AR devices introduced to evaluate the user experience in real life.

However, even though VR is an excellent tool to use during the design phase, some users complained of disorientation, and the bulky VR headsets were uncomfortable for some people. Nevertheless, the researchers believe that as technology improves and AR/VR headsets become more ergonomically streamlined, these problems will be reduced.

References

Glynn, R. (2015) *Fun Palace: Cedric Price Interactive Architecture Lab* (blog). Available at: www.interactivearchitecture.org/fun-palace-cedric-price.html (Accessed: 1 June 2019).

Mathews, S. (2005) 'The Fun Palace: Cedric Price's Experiment in Architecture and Technology', *Technoetic Arts: A Journal of Speculative Research*, 3(2), pp. 73–91. http://doi.org/10.1386/tear.3.2.73/1.

Ortega, L. and Bunning, A. K. (2017) *The Total Designer: Authorship in Architecture in the Postdigital Age*. Barcelona, Spain: Actar Publishers.

Pallasmaa, J. (2011) *The Embodied Image: Imagination and Imagery in Architecture*. Hoboken, NJ: John Wiley & Sons Inc.

Papagiannis, H. (2017) *Augmented Human: How Technology Is Shaping the New Reality*. Sebastopol, CA: O'Reilly Media.

Tang, M. (2018) 'Architectural Visualization in the Age of Mixed Reality', *Informa*, 11, pp. 82–87, The University of Puerto Rico.

Zevi, B. and Barry, J. A. (1993) *Architecture as Space: How to Look at Architecture*. New York, NY: Da Capo Press.

PART 3
Context and Ambiguity

This section addresses the topic of **'Context and Ambiguity'** and includes three chapters that present work related to interpreting the digital architectural context, covering virtual reality (VR) representations from point cloud scanning in rehabilitation projects, and the digital recreation and interpretation of endangered or lost heritage.

Joana Gomes et al. present a quasi-real VR experience based on a point cloud model of an existing building, viewed in VR. The authors discuss how interventions involving existing architecture can be enhanced by off-site access to the quasi-real VR experience of the architecture.

Documenting endangered heritage in Palestine is the theme of Ramzi Hassan's contribution. Hassan presents a digital library platform with VR content designed to raise public awareness of cultural heritage sites and provide access to sites that could not otherwise be visited. The platform is based on numerous technologies, including mobile VR technology, augmented reality (AR), and panoramic spherical photogrammetry.

Spyridoula Dedemadi and Spiros I. Papadimitriou reflect on the concept of the virtual monument, presenting a historic site now submerged by the ocean as an explorative VR game. They propose that the VR environment should operate as a design tool as much as a representation tool, enabling relations, connections, and dynamics to be tested. They also outline how virtual wandering constructs subjective narratives which take shape as new, instant, ephemeral monuments.

Follow the QR-code to navigate through the online content of Part 3.

DOI: 10.4324/9781003183105-12

10

A *QUASI-REAL* VIRTUAL REALITY EXPERIENCE

Point Cloud Navigation

Joana Gomes, Sara Eloy, Nuno Pereira da Silva, Ricardo Resende, and Luís Dias

Introduction

Interventions in existing buildings and other built spaces require total control over the construction in question. A design project based on incorrect assumptions has a high probability of resulting in a failed intervention.

This research aims to explore two technologies that are useful in the ideation stage of architecture design, specifically in the case of interventions to existing constructions: 3D laser scanning and immersive virtual reality. Firstly, we made use of a recent surveying technology—3D laser scanning—to carry out a building survey, and secondly, we used immersive virtual reality to visualize the survey results. These technologies were tested within the framework of an academic project in order to discuss how they could assist interventions in built spaces and the extent to which visualization in virtual reality can be an aesthetic instrument for the ideation phase in architecture design.

Nowadays, after reflecting on the various aspects that are gradually becoming obsolete in traditional surveying methods, certain fundamental questions arise: Can point clouds offer architects more than traditional surveying techniques when designing interventions for existing buildings? How can immersive VR visualization of the resulting point cloud help when architects are designing interventions for existing buildings?

New Technologies for the Building Survey

The process of design architecture requires, on the one hand, complete control over the surrounding and existing project space (Pauwels and Di Mascio, 2014) and, on the other hand, the possibility of contemplating what already exists and fictionalizing the future. When involved in interventions to existing buildings, non-rigorous spatial documentation leads to many problems for the architecture project and construction.

New building survey methods have been developed in recent decades which enable information collected from cameras to be instantly translated into three-dimensional information. A built space can now be reconstituted virtually using technologies such as Photogrammetry and 3D Laser Scanning.

These survey tools are used to capture data describing the physical shape of existing buildings and objects. With this we can increase our spatial knowledge, collecting and combining more

DOI: 10.4324/9781003183105-13

data which can be used to create digital models that reproduce the real buildings (Hamani et al., 2014).

In the design and construction stages, the use of 3D laser scanning technology is useful in several tasks, such as obtaining rigorous data to start the design project, off-site visualization of the virtual model in an almost real way, quality control, and inspection. The collected data is stored as a point cloud in which spatial components such as geometry, spatial coordinates, colour, and texture are saved. However, the point cloud is not only a set of geometric and mathematical data, but also a source of data that restores the experience of the building and the various epochs that characterize it. By showing large sets of points in their correct 3D coordinates, a point cloud delivers a very close impression of the scanned surfaces. The point cloud is therefore a 3D model consisting only of points in space, with no topology. Three-dimensional scanning stores all the components, which can be consulted at any time without the need for a new visit to the real place (Shih and Wang, 2004). Moreover, after collection, the data points can be converted into a polygonal 3D digital model by using CAD or BIM software (from this moment on, we will use 'Point Cloud' and '3D model' to refer to the 3D Point Cloud Model and 3D Polygonal Model respectively). Nevertheless,

> the advantages of keeping the scan in point form are what makes it great; the file sizes are much smaller, and the porosity of the point clouds make it possible to see through walls and surfaces, accessing 'hidden' spaces and uncommon views of seemingly familiar surroundings.
>
> *(ArchDaily, 2016)*

The set of points and its floating features are often referred to as beautiful elements in themselves. The density of the points can be altered to create different types of scenes and simplified so that the contours "can sometimes even be more beautiful than the original complexity" (ArchDaily, 2016).

This study uses the point cloud that resulted from a 3D scan carried out as part of the design process and analyses how this can be useful, both in terms of preserving the memory of the built space and facilitating the sharing and discussion of design options among the design team.

Immersive Virtual Reality

Milgram et al. (1994) presented the Reality-Virtuality continuum concept, at the time called Mixed Reality, which has been used and extended up to the present day. In this concept, the Real Environment (RE) and virtual reality (VR) are positioned at opposite ends, while other types of virtual combinations, such as augmented reality (AR) and augmented virtuality (AV), lie between them. Several technological solutions have been used to create alternative realities with different degrees of immersion and feeling of presence, of which 360° video/photos, VR, and AR should be highlighted.

They include a vast repertoire of immersive technologies with the potential to effortlessly transport the user to an augmented or totally new world. Immersive technologies have been considered one of the most disruptive technological developments of our time, due to the new possibilities they offer for communication and interaction between users and devices and among people (Rosedale, 2017). A VR environment is a completely synthetic world that may or may not mimic the real world and in which the participant is immersed. The devices commonly used to present VR to users include head-mounted displays (HMD) and monitors and projections on walls and screens (CAVE, Powerwalls, etc.). VR has brought new opportunities that have totally changed the previous technological solutions and have been immediately accepted by people. In the future, being in a VR space "will be nearly indistinguishable from standing face to face or in a group" (Rosedale, 2017, p. 48).

Some authors are combining point clouds with VR environments in order to obtain an accurate representation and closer-to-reality visualization of real space in the virtual environment. Nagao et al. (2019) use 3D point cloud to automatically generate an appropriate 3D model and replace it with the section to be modified/converted in the VR space. In the field of cultural heritage, Choromański et al. (2019) are exploring the potential of combining high-quality photogrammetric 3D models, virtual reality technologies, and an advanced visualization engine. The aim of the authors is to use this combination of technologies so that the visualization "makes it possible to remotely familiarise museum architecture and history in the closest way to a real visit" (Choromański et al., 2019, p. 266). Using immersive VR to experience digital creation as a point cloud enables people to "re-experience or share an experience of a space with others who may not have had the opportunity to visit the site" (ArchDaily, 2016).

Case Study—Intervention on a 19th-Century Building

Methodology

This work was divided into three phases: (1) preparation and configuration of the equipment and point cloud acquisition; (2) preparation of the point cloud model with specific software (Leica Cyclone[1] and Autodesk Recap);[2] (3) transfer of the point cloud to the Unity[3] game engine to be visualized in VR. The project was partially carried out as an exercise for the final year of the Master in Architecture programme and was aimed at intervention on a three-storey, 250 m^2 building dating from the mid-19th century, situated in the Vila Alta de Alenquer, Portugal.

Development

Cloud Point Acquisition and Preparation

The interior and exterior survey of the building was carried out using the Leica ScanStation P30,[4] resulting in a point cloud of 240 million points (Figures 10.1–10.4). The survey was performed in four hours, with three hours dedicated to scanning the interior area and one hour to surveying the exterior. A total of 34 scans were taken from the ScanStation, most done at the entrance and in the centre of each room. The time taken to prepare the equipment was not calculated but was considerable, as the pavement was often not very stable. For each shot, it took approximately two minutes to collect the detailed 360° view and process it. To prevent blocking relevant spatial information, the collection took place without the presence of people in the rooms. In order to improve the laser range, doors were also removed, and the rooms were partially cleared of non-structural elements (furniture, old equipment, and other objects). Three scans were performed on the ground floor, 11 on the first floor, and 12 on the second floor. The attic was in very poor condition, and only two scans could be performed. Outside, six scans were performed.

After collecting the information using ScanStation, the binary data was transferred to a Windows workstation and converted into the Leica Cyclone software PTX file format, as Autodesk

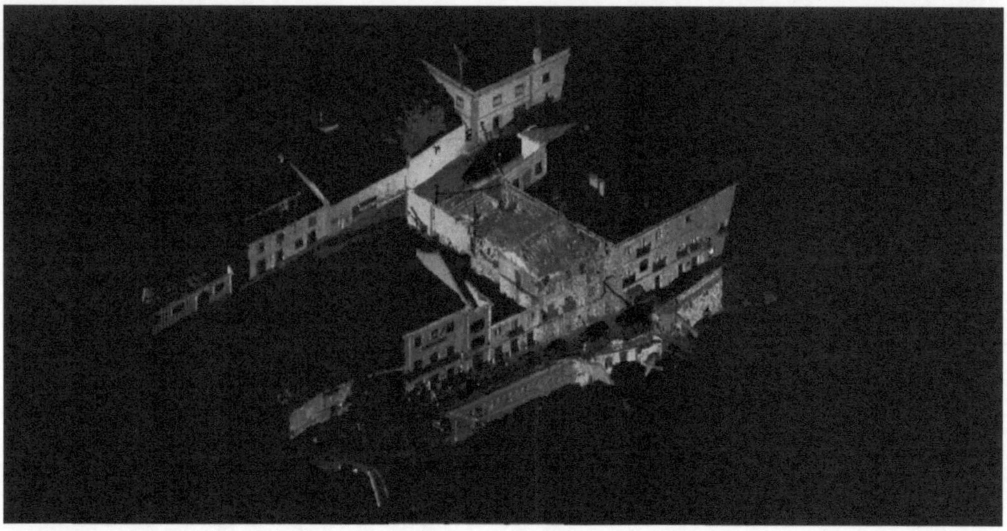

FIGURE 10.1 The entire point cloud in Recap

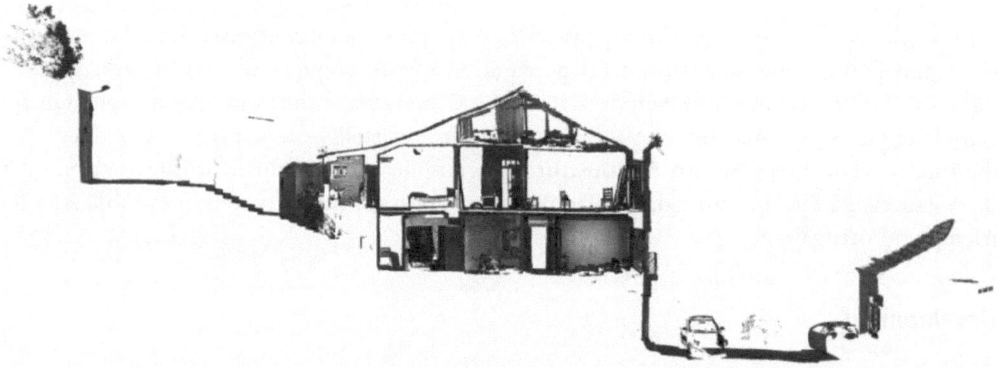

FIGURE 10.2 Longitudinal section through the point cloud in Recap

Recap software does not accept binary files acquired from ScanStation as input. In the unification process, the PTX files corresponding to each scan are imported in Recap and registered. The software first performs an automatic registration but is often not able to detect all the common parts in the scans and at this stage shows the inconsistencies and suggests that these should be merged by the user. Sometimes this process is not accurate, and the user is given the opportunity to impose their own interpretation. Whilst still in Recap software, after unifying the entire file, the user can quickly analyse and identify deformations and anomalies.

Immersive Virtual Reality Visualization

The point cloud was visualized in immersive virtual reality using the Oculus Rift HMD and the Unity game engine. The point was imported to Unity in two steps. First, the point cloud was corrected by importing the main Recap file into CloudCompare,[5] software used to analyse and correct point clouds. The problems that were identified and needed correction were that

FIGURE 10.3 Visualization of the point cloud in Recap software

FIGURE 10.4 Visualization of the point cloud in Recap software

the object scale was too small for Unity and needed to be increased, and the number of points had to be slightly decreased, while maintaining the complexity of the model. In the second stage, two different workflows were developed and tested to obtain the cloud point in Unity.

In one of the workflows, we used CloudCompare to export the point cloud into the PLY file format, which is supported by Unity, and then imported it. Unity software does not support point cloud files, since points are not one of its basic geometries, making it necessary to use the *Point Cloud Viewer and Tools* plugin by mgear.[6] The disadvantage of such a technique is that the final result is not a set of points floating in space, but a mesh with a semi-transparent texture that is produced by the plugin and replaces the cloud point. The algorithm used to generate the mesh from the cloud points is not described, and its parameters cannot be controlled. The VR visualization displays a different environment from a point cloud, visible in Figure 10.5. The texture covering the mesh only mimics a cloud point, and there is a significant loss of detail in the point-to-mesh conversion.

In the second workflow, we developed a C# Unity script that reads the point coordinates from a .txt file and instantiates each point in Unity as a sphere. The script has several parameters: the ratio of spheres per point (decimation factor), the diameter of each sphere, and the far clipping plane of the camera. All these parameters aim to control the computational effort, so that the resulting geometry is manageable for the Unity game engine and Oculus Rift. In this case, only 1 in 40 points was instantiated, the spheres had a diameter of 0.75 cm, and a far clipping distance of 100 m, larger than the model length, was defined. This workflow allowed for individual elements in the VR scene which, at a distance, act like points (Figures 10.6 and 10.7).

For both workflows, only approximately one third (80 million points) of the original geometry was used so that real-time VR rendering could process all the information.

The background in Unity was set to black to emphasize the point cloud floating in space. As the point cloud was captured in grayscale intensity and colour (RGB) information was not included in the points, the colour characteristics could not be imported to Unity. We then opted to design white spheres to generate a high contrast with the dark background.

FIGURE 10.5 Visualization of the point cloud converted to a mesh in Unity software

FIGURE 10.6 Visualization of the point cloud in Unity software with points converted to spheres

FIGURE 10.7 Visualization of the point cloud in Unity software with points converted to spheres

To complete the process, we built the project into an independent application and imported it into Oculus Rift for the immersive virtual reality experiment (Figure 10.8).

We aimed to experience the aesthetic potential of the point cloud and freely navigate through it. Experiencing the point cloud in immersive virtual reality while off-site enabled us to obtain a very clear image of the real scale and connections between spaces. VR also allowed us to contemplate the permeability and dematerialization features present in the building in the VR environment. As it was represented by low-density cloud points (which can be manipulated), it was possible to see through walls, which would be impossible in the real building. With this feature, the building seemed to open up and disperse over random elements connected by

FIGURE 10.8 Visualization in immersive VR with Oculus Rift

Source: Photo by Joana Gouveia Alves

similar coordinates and colours. Immersive virtual reality presents new ways of revealing the world and, in this case, acts as a bridge between the digital point cloud and the experience of the real world.

Discussion

Regarding the research questions raised at the beginning of this paper, it may be said that, unlike a traditional survey, by using the point cloud it was possible to achieve a high level of dimensional accuracy. In fact, the collected data allowed for an extremely accurate visualization of the building, not just in terms of the basic geometry but also the changing geometric characteristics of this heritage building. These are features which traditional surveying techniques do not restore.

The use of 3D laser scanning and the point cloud made it possible to preserve a virtual faithful representation of the existing reality. In the immersive VR visualization used during the design process, the fact that such a model existed enabled us to assess detailed information about the entire building, systematized and organized in a single location that was accessible to all project stakeholders. By using such a visualization technique, it was possible to continually revisit the 'real' building instead of a simplified version of it in the form of a BIM model. The feeling of presence the user experiences when navigating in the point cloud virtual environment 'brings' them back to the real space, with the additional advantage of having only the selected information visible. This also meant that during the design stages the designer could analyse the existing deformations in the building on a case-by-case basis and decide whether or not to maintain certain building elements. In addition, this form of visualization has an impact on the designer due to the constant presence of the authenticity of the building, which they cannot hide away. The fact that this visualization was always accessible during the design stage made the final design more faithful to the existing building and its memory than if the reality had been forgotten. In fact, the point cloud made it possible to take a closer look at the space and understand how the building process had evolved over time. A longer and closer observation using the point cloud enabled us to clearly understand that not all of the building had been constructed in the same period. Very recent interventions had been added in recent decades, and since they had no clear value, the decision was made to keep the original elements and demolish the recent additions.

In addition, the point cloud made it easy to observe the complex construction of the ceilings. To the naked eye this could have gone unnoticed, whereas by using the point cloud it was possible to measure the components accurately and understand how they had been assembled. In fact, dimensions such as the thickness of the panels or direction of the locking plates, which previously would have been considered impossible to deal with, were extracted and analysed in detail. When modelling the building in BIM, every time a doubt was raised regarding dimensions (e.g., the thickness of the window frames), it took just a few minutes to open the point cloud and confirm the data. If the point cloud had not been available, in addition to countless extra trips to the building, these details would have gone unnoticed.

Another extremely valuable aspect of the potential of immersive point cloud visualization for the architectural design process concerns the fact that, after being modelled in BIM software, the new design can be viewed superimposed onto the point cloud of the surrounding areas, thus providing a very realistic view of the future site.

Our aim was to use the maximum number of elements obtained to maintain the authenticity of the building. Nevertheless, for the VR model using Unity we needed to reduce the density of the point cloud so that the model was navigable. We believe that advances in these technologies will allow for a much bigger point cloud in VR. However, at the end of the day, the slow navigation of the model, due to its large size and technological incapacity to render a high frame rate in real time, proved to be a powerful visualization technique, since it enabled us to contemplate the 'forms' at a slower pace, almost as a delirious mind would do. The fact that colour could not be imported to Unity needs further research, since the loss of colour has an impact on the beauty of the point cloud.

Final Remarks

By using the point cloud, building information becomes much more accurate and consistent. It provides accurate bases which, together with other information such as photos, allows for the proper planning of the intervention. The use of immersive VR to visualize point clouds is also very helpful for places with geometric or material complexity, since it provides a high-quality impression of the materiality "without having to render the millions of faces that would be required" (ArchDaily, 2016). In this study, we have focused on the VR visualization of the 3D point cloud model, which is a topic much less frequently studied than the VR visualization of a 3D polygon model. Point clouds have an additional advantage over 3D polygon models, as they require less storage space and computing power.

When applied to existing buildings, the use of 3D laser scans raises some questions. Although the quality of the information extracted is good, it only allows for an analysis of the geometry and structural deformations, whereas invisible information (e.g., internal layers of walls) cannot be collected. From a constructional perspective, this technique still does not provide all the information required and needs to be supplemented with other techniques, such as selective demolition for inspection. However, as an aesthetic medium for architecture ideation, the point cloud provides an incredible source of authentic building elements and allows the designer to feel almost as if they are inside the building. The visualization of a point cloud in immersive VR transports us to a new dimension where not everything from the existing building has a place, only the main essence, levitating in a virtual world.

This chapter discusses how, in addition to their mainstream use, 3D scanning and VR immersive technologies have the potential to open up new creative possibilities in architecture ideation. These possibilities are empowered when design practitioners collaborate with technical specialists such as computer animation engineers. According to Walters and Thirkell (2007, p. 242), the combination of point clouds and VR

> can lead to new creative synergies, resulting in interdisciplinary practice that is innovative both in process and outcomes—whereby art and design practitioners productively engage with specialists in other fields, drawing on their knowledge, skills and techniques in the realization of work made possible through this engagement.

Notes

1. https://leica-geosystems.com/products/laser-scanners/software/leica-cyclone
2. www.autodesk.com/products/recap/
3. https://unity.com/
4. https://leica-geosystems.com/products/laser-scanners/scanners/leica-scanstation-p40-p30
5. www.cloudcompare.org/
6. https://assetstore.unity.com/packages/tools/utilities/point-cloud-viewer-and-tools-16019

References

ArchDaily (2016) *10 Models Which Show the Power of Point Cloud Scans, as Selected by Sketchfab*. Available at: www.archdaily.com/tag/point-cloud (Accessed: 16 June 2019).

Choromański, K. et al. (2019) 'Development of Virtual Reality Application for Cultural Heritage Visualization from Multi-Source 3D Data', *ISPRS Annals of the Photogrammetry, Remote Sensing and Spatial Information Sciences*, pp. 261–267. doi: 10.5194/isprs-archives-XLII-2-W9-261-2019.

Hamani, D., Beautems, D., and Huneau, R. (2014) 'Digital Statement and 3D Modeling for the Restitution of the Architectural Heritage: 3D Virtual Model for Architectural Restoration', *Digital Crafting, 7th International Conference Proceedings of the Arab Society for Computer Aided Architectural Design (ASCAAD 2014)*, Jeddah, Saudi Arabia, pp. 149–160.

Milgram, P. et al. (1994) 'Augmented Reality: A Class of Displays on the Reality-Virtuality Continuum', *Proceedings of Telemanipulator and Telepresence Technologies*, Boston.

Nagao, K. et al. (2019) 'Building-Scale Virtual Reality: Another Way to Extend Real World', *Proceedings: 2nd International Conference on Multimedia Information Processing and Retrieval, MIPR 2019*. IEEE, pp. 205–211. doi: 10.1109/MIPR.2019.00044.

Pauwels, P. and Di Mascio, D. (2014) 'Interpreting Metadata and Ontologies of Virtual Heritage Artefacts', *International Journal of Heritage in the Digital Era*, 3(3), pp. 531–555. doi: 10.1260/2047-4970.3.3.531.

Rosedale, P. (2017) 'Virtual Reality: The Next Disruptor: A New Kind of Worldwide Communication', *IEEE Consumer Electronics Magazine*. IEEE, 6(1), pp. 48–50. doi: 10.1109/MCE.2016.2614416.

Shih, N.-J. and Wang, P.-H. (2004) 'Using Point Cloud to Inspect the Construction Quality of Wall Finish', *Proceedings of the 22nd eCAADe Conference*, Copenhagen, Denmark, pp. 573–578.

Walters, P. and Thirkell, P. (2007) 'New Technologies for 3D Realization in Art and Design Practice', *Artifact*, 1(4), pp. 232–245. doi: 10.1080/17493460801980016.

11

VR AS A TOOL FOR PRESERVING ARCHITECTURAL HERITAGE IN CONFLICT ZONES

The Case of Palestine

Ramzi Hassan

Introduction

According to Hassan (2002), heritage sites are sensitive spatial fabrics that exist in constant and inevitable physical flux, and it is necessary to document their current situation in order to show the impact of these changes. Conventional methods of documenting cultural heritage sites and landscapes, such as photographs, physical models, text materials, and drawings, create an incomplete image of the settings of cultural heritage sites. This makes it necessary to introduce new methods and techniques for documentation. The latest developments in virtual reality (VR) and Information Communication Technologies (ICT) are providing new possibilities for documentation, preservation, and management, making it easier for managers, educators, researchers, and the general public to observe and understand the complications of historical sites interactively and dynamically and provide a comprehensive historical experience of them. This chapter outlines the efforts and research activities being undertaken at NMBU to help document and preserve heritage sites and historically important landscapes in Palestine. More specifically, it focuses on efforts to introduce a digital library based on VR technology that immortalizes historical spots in three-dimensional, VR-ready models, creating a publicly accessible, interoperable digital library of historically important landscapes and architectural heritage sites. The digital library will act as a medium for preservation, documentation, interpretation, and intervention, assisting in research, education, and tourism and raising public awareness of the significant value of cultural heritage sites and historically important landscapes.

Approach and Relevance

The strength of preservation is its mission to empower future generations with the benefits of cultural heritage in full. Much of the information on historical sites is either hidden in archives and libraries, or not linked or synchronized to form a clear and full narrative. Digital technologies present tools and methodologies that can improve the understanding of cultural heritage and landscapes over time. By collecting existing documentation and linking it digitally to particular locations in a virtual environment, we can present a biography of the historical site, from which we can then begin to understand its development over time. This allows us to create a sense of time and appreciation of the past which would be difficult to grasp without the use of

DOI: 10.4324/9781003183105-14

FIGURE 11.1 Digital reconstruction project of Hisham Palace in Jericho

digital visualization. Digital documentation helps bring together and manage the large amounts of information that are distributed over many national archives and unpublished reports. The concept implies cross-disciplinary collaboration with, among others, archaeologists, historians, and archivists involved in efforts aimed at communicating information on cultural heritage based on theoretical frameworks from the digital humanities, cultural theory, history of the built environment, and archaeology. The approach suggests that digital representations provide a method of incorporating heterogeneous, diverse information to present the contexts in which descriptions, texts, photographs, letters, videos, and oral history can be better understood, interpreted, combined, and distributed.

The Digital Library

The concept for introducing a digital platform is a continuation of the research work that has been taking place in cooperation with the NMBU and institutions in Palestine. The project objective is to develop an interactive digital platform for heritage sites and historically important landscapes in Palestine. The concept focuses on 'edutainment', an upcoming field that combines education with entertainment features, thus enhancing the learning environment to make it more engaging and enjoyable. The technological platform is based on commercially affordable technologies and open-source tools such as mobile-based VR technology, augmented reality, panoramic spherical photogrammetry, 360° video capture, spatial databases, Geographic Information Systems (GIS), 3D modelling, 3D mapping, Google Street View, and Google Maps. It was built on the basis of the following (Figure 11.1):

Documentation

Digital documentation plays a vital role in preserving the memory of the heritage. This is a highly relevant aspect, given the problems of physical preservation in Palestine. There are several reasons for this, ranging from the simple effects of time and weather to more serious causes such as the occupation, accessibility, earthquakes, neglect, abandonment, and vandalism. When cultural heritage sites are spread in large amounts across a territory such as Palestine, where access is limited, certain tools are needed to collect and manage the data in order to present it to the community (Figure 11.2).

FIGURE 11.2 Selected projects from the 3D documentation which aims to produce a 3D digital library for historical sites

Storytelling

Technology is changing the ways in which we tell stories, allowing for greater interactivity, participation, and emotional engagement. Therefore, the project introduces innovative technologies for the presentation of complex cultural heritage sites with immersive 3D computer graphics which are based on new concepts, partly adapted from other computer graphics areas to the specific needs for heritage presentations. The focus is to develop new concepts for the integration of historical, architectural, and cultural data related to a cultural heritage site into an immersive VR environment suitable for presentation of the digital content.

Education

VR provides opportunities for interaction with subjects through games or challenges. In addition, various types of information can be added in the VR environment, offering access to a variety of useful information. Due to its entertainment qualities, VR also encourages users to remain engaged while in the virtual environment. The new generation is highly dependent on computers, smartphones, video games, and TV screens. This situation introduces a new pattern of learning. Therefore, it is very important to incorporate these new visual technologies in order to develop on-site educational experiences and enhance public awareness of cultural heritage sites (Figure 11.3).

Community Involvement

Local communities are usually very interested in their heritage and motivated to engage with it. In Palestine, however, this involvement has not been established, due to a lack of knowledge and skills, financial restrictions on heritage projects, or a lack of local capacities. It is therefore clear that community involvement does not happen spontaneously. Community involvement can empower people to take responsibility for the historical environment and provide socio-economic opportunities as well. Therefore, there is a need to incorporate new

FIGURE 11.3 A child experiencing VR demonstrations of a heritage site in a workshop in Jenin, Palestine

tools, technology, and research which can serve to enhance the perceived value of heritage sites for members of the local community. Digital technologies can improve conservation documentation and preservation techniques, enhance interpretation through interactive media, enrich archives with sensory experiences, and augment histories with crowdsourced data. This approach offers the potential to widen public engagement, engaging personal interests in areas such as the protection of local monuments and rational local decision-making in efforts to preserve heritage sites.

Accessibility

In many cases, it might be not possible to make an actual visit to a site. The limitations on visits may be associated with different reasons: the remote location of a site, the fact that it is too expensive, too inhospitable, or too dangerous, or simply the fact that it does not exist anymore. In the case of Palestine, the political situation plays a major role in this. The segregation that has been implemented prevents locals from visiting and experiencing many historical sites and landscapes that are important in national history. One example is the restrictions on visiting historical and holy sites such as the Dome of the Rock and the Al-Aqsa Mosque in Jerusalem. Another example is the restriction on movement between Gaza and the West Bank. In addition, many people from the Arabic and Islamic world are unable to make visits to Palestine. VR technologies could convey an experience of landscapes and sites that are physically and visually inaccessible. VR is, of course, not intended to replace actual site visits. However, it could provide an alternative visual platform for experiencing inaccessible sites and facilitate people's ability to learn and explore remotely.

Tourism

The monuments of the past not only have powerful spiritual potential but also promote the development of the tourist infrastructure, which potentially ensures additional revenue for a country's economy. VR has great potential for marketing destinations and could enhance the promotion and selling of tourism in Palestine. The visuals and experiences that VR offers through its virtual tours makes it an optimum tool for providing rich data for potential tourists seeking destination information. Using VR, a tourist could make better-informed decisions and have more realistic expectations, which may lead to a more satisfactory vacation (Cheong, 1995; Hobson and Williams, 1995). The latest developments represented by the affordability of mobile-based VR technology are providing the momentum for more possibilities for the use of VR for tourism.

Empathy

There is increasing evidence that VR can be effective in evoking empathy (Jeremy Bailenson, 2016). The power of immersive storytelling can create huge positive social changes. This makes VR an important tool for charities. Agencies including Amnesty International and the Clinton Foundation have started using VR to promote their objectives, raise awareness, and encourage donations. The sense of really being there is why some say it is "the ultimate empathy machine" (Chris Milk, 2015). While it is not possible to bring people to the land to witness the struggle and suffering of Palestinians due to the occupation, VR instead has the capacity to bring the land to people from all over the world. This was the case with a recent eight-minute VR documentary film produced by Vrse (Arora and Palitz, 2016) in conjunction with the United Nations. *My Mother's Wing* gives a first-person view of a Palestinian family in Gaza, after the loss of two sons in the war of 2014. According to Gabo Arora (2016), "by leveraging breakthrough technologies, such as VR, we can create solidarity with those who are normally excluded and overlooked, amplifying their voices and explaining their situations".

Discussion

Nowadays, information and communication technologies allow for far more dynamic, interactive, and participative communication. Social networks, as well as apps for smartphones and tablets, offer almost unlimited opportunities for the exchange, dissemination, and circulation of information, enabling everyone to share their views on cultural heritage with a global community. The introduction of a digital library based on VR technology enables heritage sites and landscapes, often inaccessible to the public or even no longer existing, to be recreated and experienced again. It has led to major improvements in the fields of education, tourism, and planning, and thus provides new tools for interpretation and preservation. It has become possible to recreate digital portals by linking information and comparing data on a historical site, which allows for an inclusive understanding of cultural heritage in its topographical and cultural contexts. It also permits multiple researchers, stakeholders, and the public to contribute to the cultural heritage knowledge base. The use of VR to present ancient life in Palestine is an important step towards raising awareness of the cultural heritage, by making it more understandable to the public. The digital library platform will raise public awareness of cultural heritage sites and make them conscious of the richness of the environment in which they are living. Consequently, it will help to protect, preserve, and monitor endangered sites.

References

Arora, A. (2016) *Life and Death in Gaza Captured in 'Watershed' VR Film*. Available at: www.wired.co.uk/article/vrse-vr-gaza-movie-my-mothers-wing (Accessed: 1 June 2019).

Arora, G. and Palitz, A. (2016) *My Mother's Wings*. Available at: http://with.in/watch/my-mothers-wing/ (Accessed: 1 June 2019).

Bailenson, J. (2016) 'Can VR Help Create Empathy around Climate Change?', *TED Talk*. Available at: www.youtube.com/watch?v=zJCD3R3LlSs (Accessed: 1 June 2019).

Cheong, R. (1995) 'The Virtual Threat to Travel and Tourism', *Tourism Management*, 16(6), pp. 417–422.
Hassan, R. (2002) *Computer Visualization in Planning*. Norway: University of Life Sciences (UMB).
Hobson, J. S. P. and Williams, A. P. (1995) 'Virtual Reality: A New Horizon for the Tourism Industry', *Journal of Vacation Marketing*, 1(2), pp. 125–136.
Milk, C. (2015) 'What Happens When We Step Inside the Screen?', *Ted Talk*. Available at: www.npr.org/2015/09/11/439199892/what-happens-when-we-step-inside-the-screen (Accessed: 1 June 2019).

12

EPHEMERAL MONUMENTS

Spyridoula Dedemadi and Spiros I. Papadimitriou

Setting: Interactive Artefact

This research focuses on the archaeological site of Pavlopetri (in Laconia, Peloponnese, south Greece) (Harding, 1969) (Figure 12.1). In Pavlopetri lies a submerged settlement from the Bronze Age, with elements that fascinate and inspire (urban) fantasies. It is an urban landscape, with a structure and substructure (strata) beneath the extreme state of the ruins (abandonment, degeneration, etc.).

At sea level, the visitor can see the ruins of the foundations of the former settlement and interpret them as a slightly deformed map. The sea dominates, protects, and constantly reveals new parts of the settlement buried at the bottom of the sea. To experience the archaeological monument, the visitor needs to be fully submerged: the double meaning of immersion is used here in a ludic sense, literally, in Pavlopetri, and figuratively in the game. In order to generate the digital environment, the existing context was mapped, using photographs, sketches, diagrams, and drawings.

Through a combination of bibliographic research (concerning the archaeological site and similar settlements from the same chronological period) and the new mapping, a collection of models, drawings, diagrams, and photographs was created (Figure 12.2). The material refers to architecture, structure, materiality, and function, as well as the current state of the monument.

The documentation collected data on:

- the architecture of life (houses)
- the architecture of death (intramural cist tombs, carved tombs)
- the art of storage and everyday life (fragments of ceramics)

These elements coexist and share a common materiality with the natural environment.

Game Flow

The user puts on the VR gear and enters the virtual environment. The opening scene is in a kidney-shaped, carved tomb (evoking the beginning in a womb) on the shore of Pavlopetri. The user walks out of the womb and follows the trail of the tombs on the shore. The shore starts

DOI: 10.4324/9781003183105-15

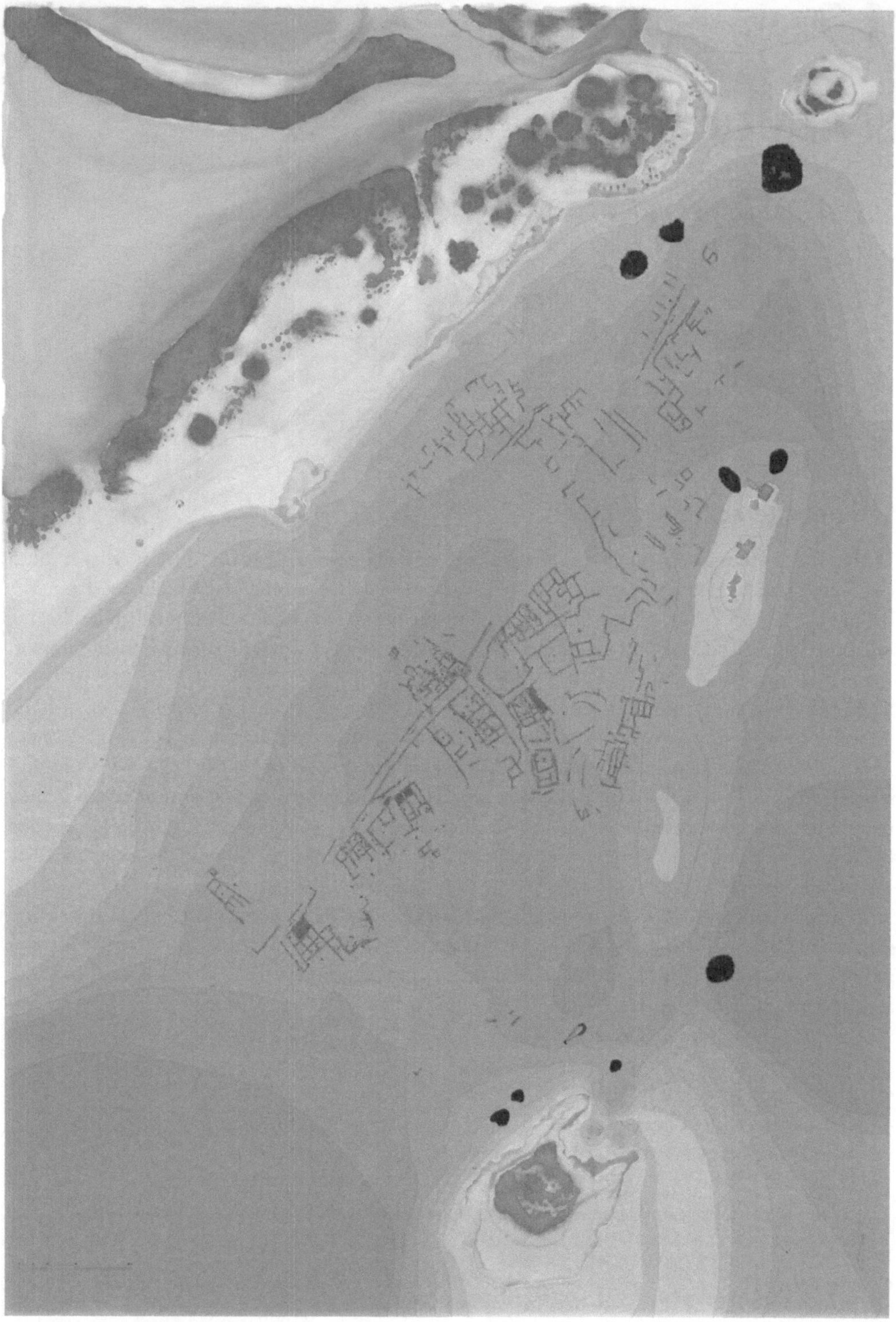

FIGURE 12.1 Map of Pavlopetri

FIGURE 12.2 Catalogue of intramural cists

FIGURE 12.3 The shore reshapes into an archetypical system of platforms.

to transform and reshape into an archetypical system of platforms that fades into the sea (Figure 12.3), tempting the user to dive in. The submerged monument is a single stage, where the user is able to wander/swim in any direction and experience the representation of the settlement and the environment. Fields and objects throughout the site serve as attractors and trigger points: when the user decides to approach any of them, they are activated. Wandering through the ruins of the settlement, foundations, regenerated walls, enhanced graveyards, misplaced and out of scale objects, instant centres and connections are created. The game ends when the user arrives at the island of Pavlopetri. From the top of it, only the sea and the shore are visible.

Memory From Cultural 'Waste'

The experience of virtual wandering in the underwater monument that is constructed constitutes a new historical artefact, which is charged with information and interpretations. On one level, the digitally constructed model maps, digitalizes, archives, and preserves the archaeological monument as a historical artefact (documentation of the digital heritage) and also encourages interaction between the user and the monument, providing a direct interface. Simultaneously, through the multiple personalized narratives of the users, the monument functions as a narrative, an augmented monument that can reconstruct ephemeral, new memories, superimposed onto the historical artefact.

The best way to protect heritage is to augment it. Traditional archaeological research methods catalogue and exhibit the remains of the past as inert matter: a fragment of a wall, for example, is a ruin. However, if it is seen as reactivated information, it can once again become a living and active urban element. The same wall, converted into an urban document, can produce information about the history of the city and the flows and dynamics that once formed what now remains. On this section of wall, on the ruin, on the 'waste' of our culture (Figure 12.4),

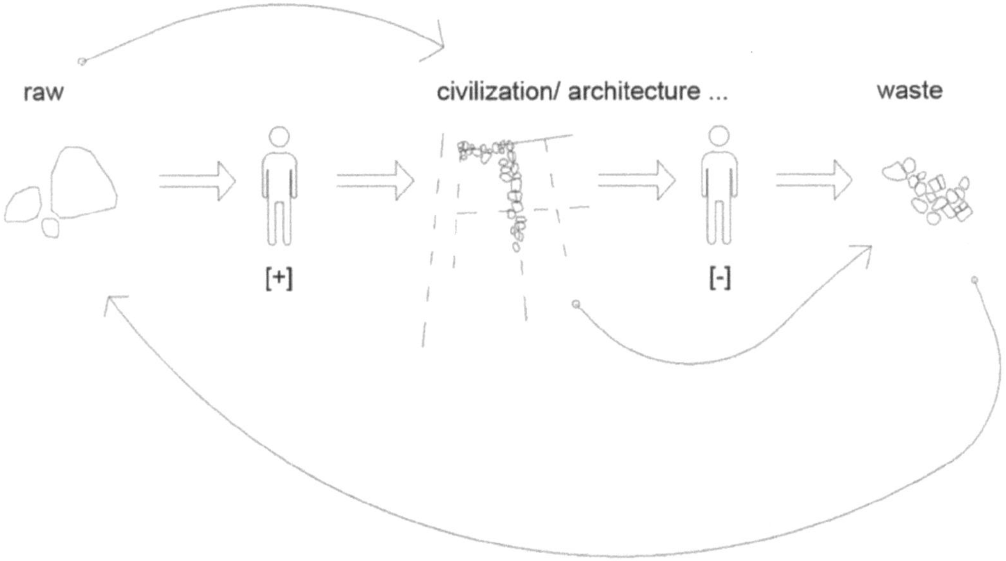

FIGURE 12.4 Archaeology studies the 'waste' of human civilization.

we can, according to V. Flusser, project the memory of the place and the human traces (Flusser, 1999). Theoretically, this is the objective purpose: amidst discontinuities and hypothetical images, the science of archaeology detects the causes, ramifications, and ideas of who we were and who we are through space, time, and life.

Immersion, Narration, Interaction

The project develops through multiple researches and reflections on the technological tools and assets of design and representation that we own/have access to (as architects, artists, and designers). The model/virtual reality environment offers a multi-sensory approach/experience and understanding of space (immersion) and enables a set of rules and protocols to be invented which, as a result, create the experience of the user. In the virtual space, environments, relations, connections, and dynamics can be tested. It is also an evasion of a linear answer to a solid architectural problem as a cause-effect system. The VR environment operates as a designing tool as much as a representation tool, a medium for research and narration.

Narrative plays a key role nowadays. The story that is transmitted predates the transcription of the message, and the project takes place within this narrative. Modern communication is becoming more and more metaphorical. The metaphor replaces the linear cause-effect sequence with multidimensional reasoning and the discontinuity of rhetorical devices. The linear sequence is replaced with a system of leaps and metaphors that can be personalized.

Interaction follows the narrative. According to A. Saggio, interaction is one of the catalysts for the emergence of the new paradigm of information technology (Saggio, 2013). It is the catalytic element of this phase of architectural research, due to the fact that it encapsulates the modern communication system based on the possibility of producing metaphors, the ability to navigate, and the construction of hypertext systems. It positions the subject (user) as the centre of design (alterability, transformability, personalization) instead of the ultimate object (sequence, standardization, copying). Interaction suggests the idea of constant 'spatial transformation', which changes the initially specified limits of time and space.

The Imagined: Protocols for Utopias

In representing reality, we are simultaneously transforming it. In the digital space, matter is information: we are constantly operating information landscapes. We map reality, select specific information from the 'objective reality', and feed it with a reference system and a constructed system of rules in order to link it together and recreate meaning. As a result, we construct subjective models of reality. These subjective realities are more functional: every decision leads to a branching and a decision tree that is constantly evolving.

The archaeological landscape is triggered, and densities, information dilutions, time intensities, obsessions in space are created, and *events* (spatial transformations) take place. Each event, each 'action on the field', is a representation of the imagined and, at the same time, an observation/reflection on the 'real' (Figure 12.5).

The narrative and the representation of the imagined draw on the principles and protocols of three significant utopias from the 1960s. They imply the juxtaposition of the real and the imagined, as presented in the iconic platform of Continuous Monument by Superstudio (1969), the theorem of fields, instant centres, and flows proposed in Takis Zenetos' Electronic Urbanism,

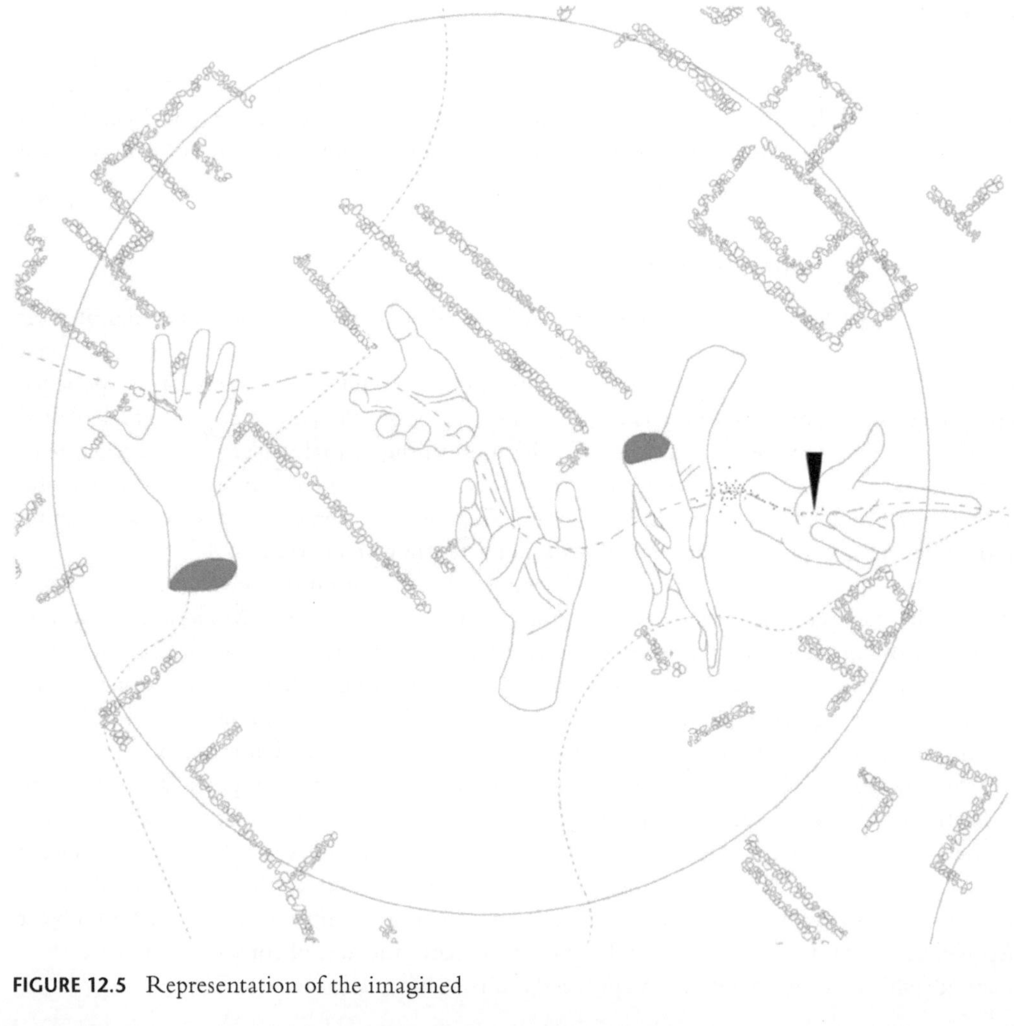

FIGURE 12.5 Representation of the imagined

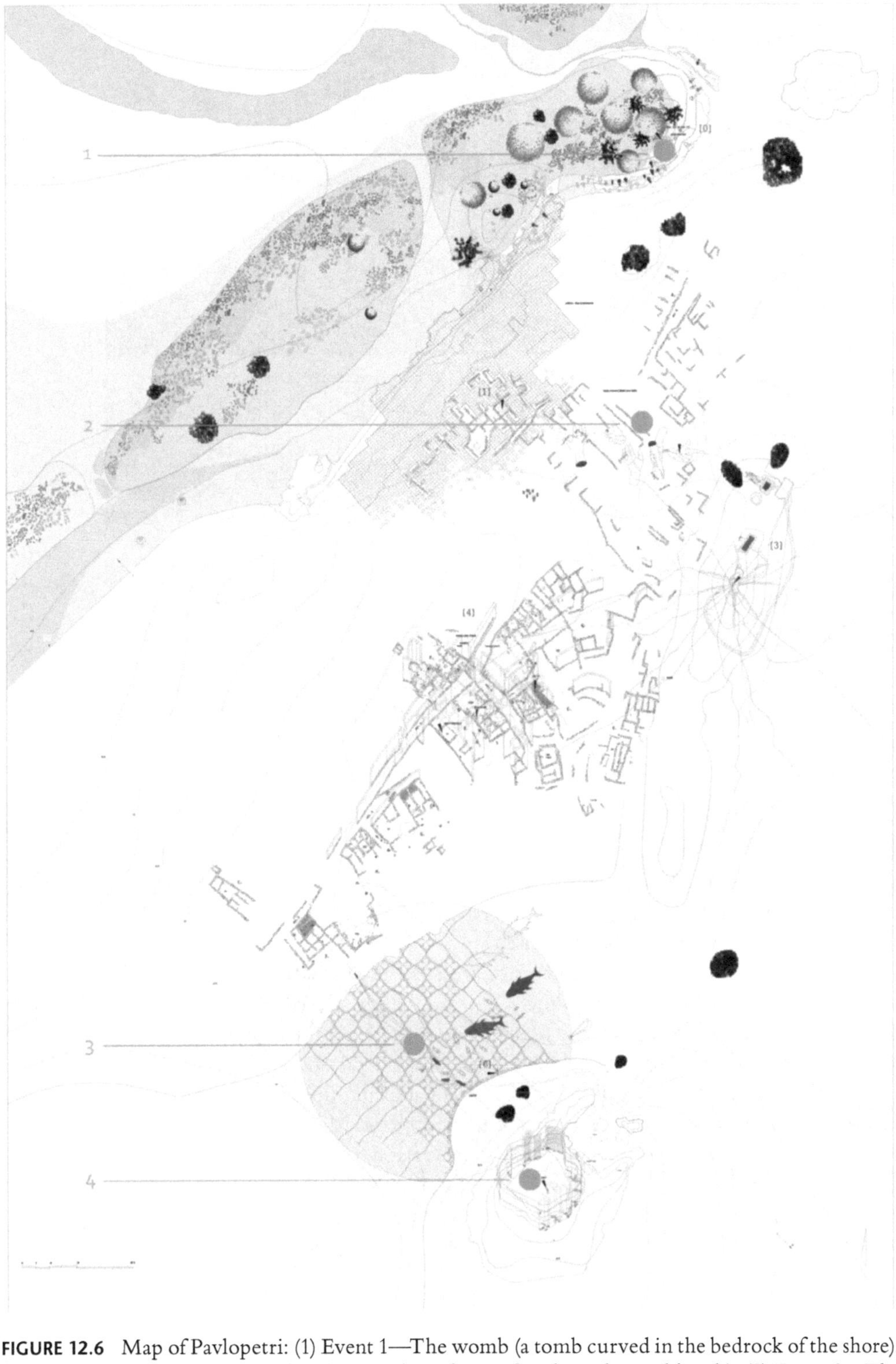

FIGURE 12.6 Map of Pavlopetri: (1) Event 1—The womb (a tomb curved in the bedrock of the shore); (2) Event 2—The hands (a garden of out-of-scale sculptured hands); (3) Event 3—The bridge (a field of instant centers, flows and knots); (4) Event 4—The island (the end).

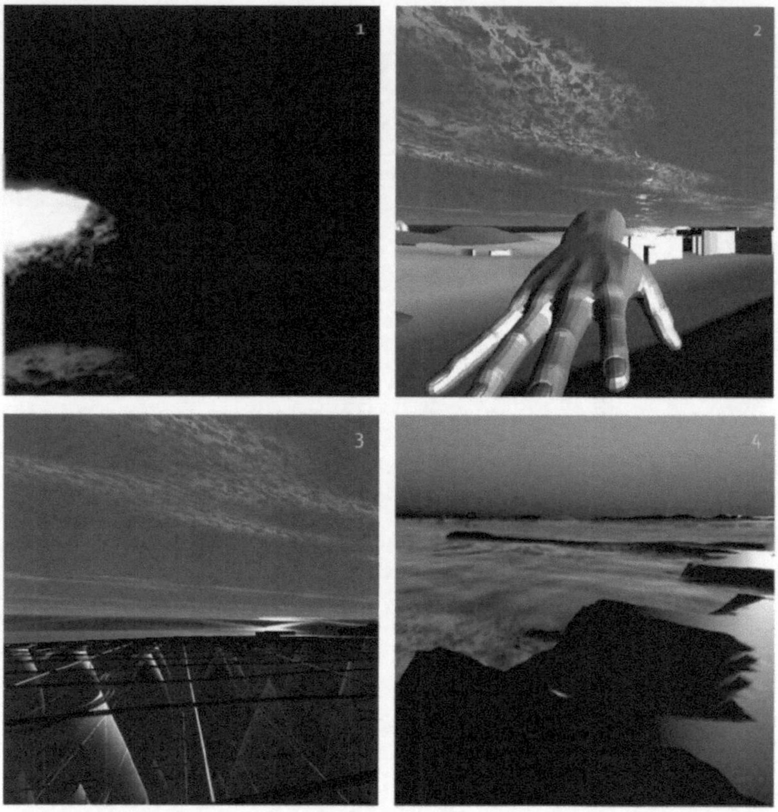

FIGURE 12.7 Screenshots—events regarding the events mapped in Figure 12.6

and the concept of perpetual extension and continuous progress in the almost mathematical work of Ecumenopolis by Konstantinos Doxiadis. Being parasites (as presented in M. Serres' Le parasite, 2009), utopias act as triggers/catalysts for the virtual monument, functioning as means of exaggeration, activation, and stimulation of the existent field for the purpose of quest/pursuit and production of experience in the game flow.

These utopias trigger certain elements or areas of the archaeological site—the carved tombs on the shore, the threshold between the shore and the sea, the cists (burial graves) underwater, the main body of the settlement, the island of Pavlopetri. The user (digital flaneur) determines the route and interacts with all, some, or none of the environments/elements of the site. The interaction between the user and the environment activates the (charged) fields and objects and transforms fragments of the landscape and the monument. Mapping the events and transformations enables the user's subjective narratives to be created, thus generating new subjective digital models. The resulting models are based on assumptions, individual capture, and experience of the (digital) environment and events that have been unfolding, as much as the fluid/subjective distribution of the information (Figures 12.6 and 12.7).

Ephemeral Monument

In the end, a new place takes shape, a hybrid of the real and the imagined. A new 'monument' is generated—a virtual monument, an ephemeral one, that carries the memory of the old one and it is open to interpretation and negotiation.

Each newly constructed user narrative is a scenario extending through multiple and possible or less possible branches and hybrid options. These multiple narratives lead to multiple subjective systems that produce multiple ephemeral digital monuments. When combined, they create an open archive which documents, stores, and reconstructs the memory of the historical heritage. The open archive inclines towards representation of the 'real' monument. Through multiple subjective interpretations of history, we come closer to the objective 'truth'. The more lines and interfaces there are, the more definite the shape is: multiple subjective views of the imagined tend towards the objective view of the real.

References

Flusser, V. (1999) *The Shape of Things: A Philosophy of Design*. London, UK: Reaktion Books.

Harding, A. et al. (1969) 'Pavlopetri, an Underwater Bronze Age Town in Laconia', *The Annual of the British School at Athens*, 64, pp. 113–142. Athens, Greece: British School at Athens.

Saggio, A. (2013) *The IT Revolution in Architecture, Thoughts on a Paradigm Shift*. New York: Lulu.com.

Serres, M. (2009) *Le parasite*. Translated by Heliadis. Athens, Greece: Smili Publications.

Superstudio (1969) 'Design d' invenzione e design d'evasione: Superstudio', *Domus*, 475.

PART 4
Materiality and Movement

This section of the book addresses the topic of **Materiality and Movement**, including three chapters in which the authors overlap between physical and digital worlds, the materiality of architectural artefacts and their ability to move across media, contemplating the emerging potential for expressing ideas in architecture. The synergies between construction and virtual and augmented reality (AR) enhance the creative capacities of architects, introducing immersive technologies not only as a representation tools, but as media that can assist design decisions and facilitate complex fabrication processes.

In this context, James Forren et al. investigate the use of off-loom weaving and AR in the construction of architectural building components and assemblies. The authors aim to develop architectural spaces through an emerging process of collaborative exchange, as they develop a method using AR headworn displays to support off-loom weaving, utilizing gesture and interacting with materials.

As processes of digital design and fabrication have become integral to the design process, architects can seamlessly transfer information across media. Within these lines, Ioanna Symeonidou explores the blending of realities from digital to physical and back to digital. Symeonidou employs computational design tools and constructs digitally fabricated prototypes that inform the design process on issues of materiality. The prototypes inform the design process by considering the material feedback and form. At the same time, revisiting a project with the use of immersive VR and AR technologies results in a blending of realities throughout the design process and the incorporation of design decisions based on the experiences and feedback from both physical and virtual spaces.

The use of AR technologies to facilitate design decisions in architecture may be developed further by virtually replicating the actual construction process. Sara Eloy and Nuno Pereira da Silva implement AR to simulate the flight of drones assembling bricks to construct a wave-like wall. The authors employ an AR optical see-through device to explore the aesthetics of AR and to analyse the potential of this for architecture. The robotic dance performed by the drones and experienced through AR provides a new experience of space and time which enhances creative freedom without the boundaries of (real) reality.

DOI: 10.4324/9781003183105-16

Follow the QR-code to navigate through the online content of Part 4.

13

ACTION OVER FORM

Combining Off-Loom Weaving and Augmented Reality in a Non-Specification Model of Design

James Forren, Makenzie Ramadan, and Sebastien Sarrazin

Introduction

This chapter presents a three-part investigation using large-scale off-loom weaving techniques in conjunction with augmented reality (AR) technologies. It postulates that virtual technologies can change designing and building by facilitating a fluid exchange between people, tools, and materials. By using a flexible building material and augmented reality media, the study explores building methods which work in harmony with intrinsic material properties and physical movement in collaborative building contexts. It is guided by Tim Ingold's principle of 'morphogenesis', which describes the emergence of form through the coordination of designers, materials, and context (Ingold, 2013).

The work is part of a larger research programme conducted with a cultural anthropologist, with the aim of understanding the effect of new materials and technologies on design. The research programme includes studying how new materials and technologies impact designers' thoughts, actions, and behaviours by interpreting tacit, non-verbal communications and behaviour. This chapter addresses the technical aspects of the collaborative research. The first study it presents, *Lap, Twist, Knot*, is a preliminary exploration of off-loom weaving using cement composites (Forren and Nicholas, 2018). The second study, *Augmented Weaving*, explores the participation of non-experts in design and construction by coordinating AR technologies with off-loom weaving techniques. The third study, *Augmented Weave: Urban Net*, is ongoing research which explores full-scale construction, coordinating AR technologies and off-loom weaving with cementitious composites.

Literature Review

Tim Ingold's non-specification model of design and building—developing designs in collaboration with tools, people, and near environments without adhering to strict predetermined drawings and specifications (Ingold, 2013, 2011, 1999)—provides the basic organizing principles for the research. These principles include knowing by doing, working with intrinsic material properties, and attention to embodied practices. They provide a lens through which to interpret technical research in the fields of materials science, computational design, and building. The research draws on the following technical literature: material science studies on cementitious composite technologies (Annesley, 2019; Babaeidarabad et al., 2014; Mercedes et al., 2018);

DOI: 10.4324/9781003183105-17

computational design and building methods for large-scale braiding (Lüling and Richter, 2016; Sabin, 2013; Zwierzycki et al., 2017); and construction methods using AR applications (Jahn et al., 2018). In addition, the research references examples of building construction as performance and collaborative building methods (Nicholas et al., 2014; Halprin, 1969).

Methods

The work of Ingold guides the research aim of developing ways of building which evolve through material engagement, interpersonal exchange, and representations that direct action rather than prescribe form. The first investigation, *Lap, Twist, Knot* (Figure 13.1), uses building methods drawn from movement choreography. The research team developed coordinated movement to construct a large-scale building component from a cement composite. This was initially developed through scale models and captured in scores: diagrams and text directing the sequential positioning of each fibre strand. The final building component—a nine-foot-tall column—emerged from a rehearsed performance of the cementitious fibre under the influence of gravity and manipulated by four design participants.

Augmented Weaving (Figure 13.2) introduced augmented reality technologies and non-expert participation to the choreographic practice. The investigation used Fologram, a graphical algorithm editor application which coordinates parametric computer modelling with AR head-worn displays (HWDs) and mobile devices. The research team adapted the previous method

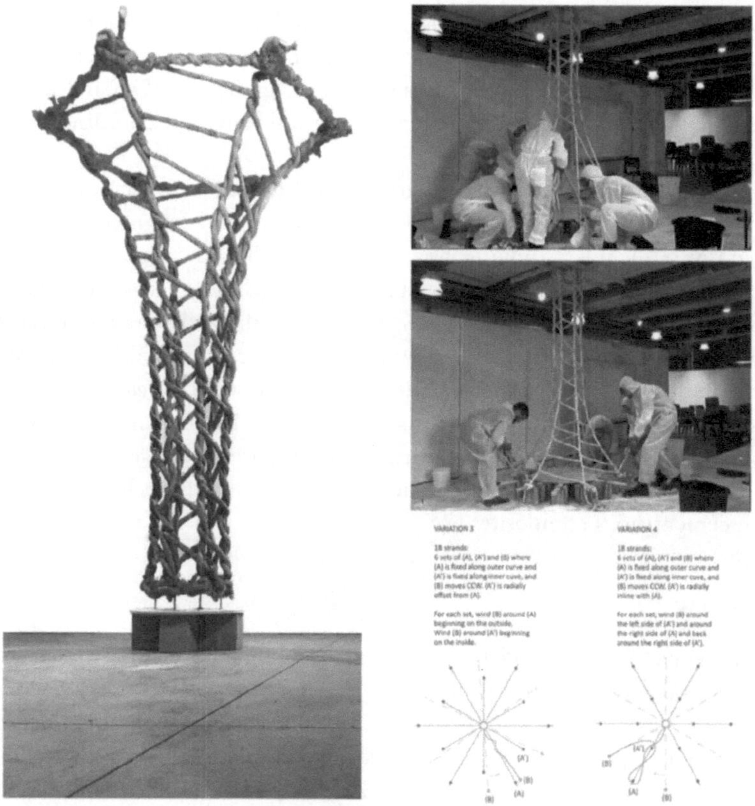

FIGURE 13.1 *Lap, Twist, Knot.* Full-scale investigation of woven cementitious composite using choreographic movement and graphic and written scores.

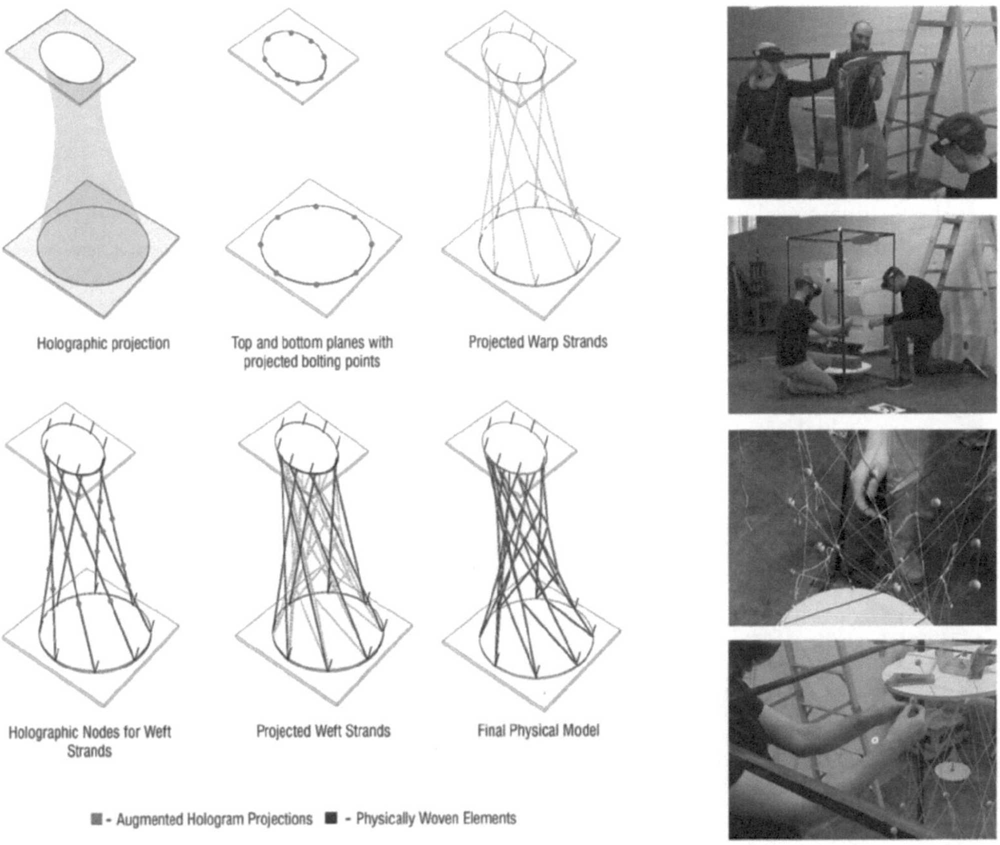

FIGURE 13.2 *Augmented Weaving.* Expert and non-expert encounter in off-loom weaving using augmented reality and interactive, dynamic weaving armature.

of choreographed weaving to a new method using a parametric computational model coordinated with an adjustable physical armature via Fologram. Two research participants, one trained designer and one non-designer, conducted this investigation. The parametric computer model was linked via ArUco tag markers to a flat plate in the armature which could be manipulated by hand. One participant moved the plate and trained the HWD camera on an ArUco marker. The HWD communicated this new plate position to the parametric computer model, updating the virtual position of the plate in the computer model. The updated virtual plate position generated a new form in the computer model. The computer model, in turn, updated the AR HWD projection. A choreographer wearing a second HWD could then see the updated virtual form in physical space, make design evaluations, and request new positions for the plate. Once the final form was determined, the computer model provided virtually projected positions for 'knots' as anchor points and 'twists' as nodal crossings to direct construction of the physical weave. The projected positions for knots and twists were an elaboration on the graphical scores from *Lap, Twist, Knot*. Due to the simple construction detailing of laps, twists, and knots, designers and non-designers in *Augmented Weaving* wearing AR HWDs were then able to collaboratively execute the final form.

The third investigation, *Augmented Weave: Urban Net*, draws on this three-dimensional scoring to explore the potential of the technology for full-scale building with a cementitious composite. The study overlays physics engine modelling simulation to predictively evaluate the effects of gravity and guide the positioning of the cementitious strands (Figure 13.3). Components were constructed in an inverted configuration, then turned upright so that the resulting structures work in compression, belying the thinness of their construction.

The target geometries were derived from a building assembly, generated as a three-dimensional minimal-bending diagram through a computational simulation of gravitational forces (Figure 13.4). This three-dimensional diagram was rationalized into discrete architectural components which were prefabricated in a wooden three-dimensional frame (Figure 13.3). Mounting plates were positioned in the frame according to holographic projections. Drill hole angles and locations for the plates were also guided by holograms. Once the plates were mounted, holograms guided warp strand placement and the location of weft strand hitch-knots along the warp strands. By

FIGURE 13.3 *Augmented Weave: Urban Net.* Holographic projections locating drill holes and mounting plates, directing shape-relaxed forms in a cementitious composite, and providing structural simulation data.

FIGURE 13.4 *Augmented Weave: Urban Net.* Overall target geometry and in-progress assembly of woven cementitious composite building components.

use of interactive buttons, the holographic guide for each strand was individually isolated to direct the strand's placement and identify it by length.

To further advance the computational potential of the process, the investigation also developed a method of characterizing the cementitious composite textile by calculating structural performance values for entry into the structural simulation software Karamba3D. The goal of this characterization was to visualize the structural performance of the building components and initiate real-time structural feedback in the AR interface. The material characterization was achieved by filming a three-point bending test from which the values for ultimate strength, shear modulus, and Young's modulus were calculated. This method of material characterization was verified against a slender steel bar. Although the method treated the composite as a homogenous material, it was an accessible approximation of material properties.

Findings

In line with Ingold's model, the findings and discussion are organized into three categories: people, tools, and materials.

People

In *Augmented Weaving*, the technology facilitated non-expert participation. Non-designer participants were able to direct designers in the shaping of a component and also join them in making it. Clear instructions and a simplified range of options contributed to this success, which included a robust parametric computer definition.

The co-location of new tools and materials also led to new roles in the design and building practice. As the technologies were explored, expertise was developed around certain tasks, and new tasks were developed. During periods of construction, different participants assumed particular roles: mixer, weaver, director. The director would point to positions for the strands and the weaver would continually check in to ensure proper location, while the mixer provided the material. This also highlighted the role of gestures in coordinated positioning and in guiding elements into place.

Tools

The use of sequential visual guides—breaking tasks into visually descriptive steps—proved to be an effective method for building complex forms three-dimensionally. The guides projected in three-dimensional space enabled fabrication and assembly to be accomplished without a single traditional construction drawing. The interactivity of the holographic interface allowed people to manipulate these visual guides and access explicit building information model data, such as strand lengths. This facilitated a straightforward yet precise mode of working with the material that would not have been possible otherwise without considerable effort and elaborate documentation.

Materials

Using this shape-relaxed construction method, the researchers made building components which could support 150 pounds from a material which, tested in isolated bending, only held 10 pounds of weight. The physics engine modeller viewed through the AR interface combined well with the shape-relaxed method of malleable composite construction. Preliminary visualizations with Karamba3D facilitated conversations with engineering professionals. These visualizations have yet to be worked interactively into the design process.

Discussion and Conclusion

The research has added a collaborative building method to off-loom weaving which can be incorporated with large-scale textile construction processes. The investigation has added to research in cementitious composites normally used in building repair by demonstrating an expanded application for building stand-alone structures. Moreover, it has contributed to research in construction using augmented reality by presenting methods for working with woven composite materials and gravitational forces. Finally, with regard to social science research in technology, it offers observations on how AR HWDs might structure interactions between *people* (across disciplines and levels of expertise), *tools*, and *materials*. These outcomes are discussed in more detail next.

People

The current *Augmented Weave: Urban Net* research will culminate in a full-scale construction. This full-scale construction will test user reactions to the structure and use AR HWDs to provide additional content about the structure, which may include visualizing structural data, alternate configurations, instructional demonstrations, and information about the building process. Further development of the public component of the research will involve work with choreography professionals to score and rehearse movements in the process of building with AR HWDs.

In addition, a two-week workshop with student participants will engage novice designers in the design and building methods piloted here. The workshop includes asking participants about their reactions to and experiences with this design and construction method.

Tools

In addition to projecting graphic notation, the use of AR HWDs offers the possibility of projecting heads-up displays of instructional videos. Instructional videos have been used in prior investigations as a type of convention, similar to a construction document, to transfer knowledge across participants and disciplines (Forren and Nicholas, 2019).

Materials

The research continues to develop interactive methods, working with AR and the Karamba3D definition for use in form-finding. The goal is to view the structural implications of strand positions in real time and adjust them interactively. One objective is to develop a building model with which participants can create a physical form and then manipulate it in response to holographic information about the structural performance of the physical form. In order to accomplish this, the physical form will need to be fed into the virtual environment through a scanning protocol, photogrammetry, or a tracking system. Preliminary tests were carried out on a version of tracking in *Augmented Weaving* by placing ArUco markers at the nodal points of the assembly.

These developments facilitated by AR technologies—expert and non-expert exchange, building through gesture, and interacting with materials—contribute to an ecological concept of design that takes a range of influences in architectural visualization and building into consideration. Designing and building with computers in context shifts our understanding of computational design and construction from one that is an insular, expert-driven activity preceding building to one that is collaborative, public, and concurrent with building. This adheres to concepts such as those developed by Ingold, regarding design and building as more than just a rote production of form, but instead the emergent result of exchanges between people, tools, and materials.

Acknowledgements

Primary funding: Social Science and Humanities Research Council (SSHRC)—Canada; the Canadian Precast/Prestressed Concrete Institute (CPCI)

Project Assistants: *Lap, Twist, Knot* (Aziza Asatkhojaeva, Liam Guitard, Ryan Vandervliet); *Augmented Weaving* (Sebastien Sarrazin, Daniel Wesser, Jacinte Armstrong); *Augmented Weave: Urban Net* (Sebastien Sarrazin, Makenzie Ramadan, Aswin Ak, Felipe Guimarães Lima)

References

Annesley, J. (2008) 'Burlap-Crete Explained', *Sustainable Buildings as Art: Explorations in Alternative Architecture & Construction*. Available at: https://annesley.wordpress.com/burlap-crete-explained/ (Accessed: 3 April 2019).

Babaeidarabad, S. et al. (2014) 'Shear Strengthening of Un-Reinforced Concrete Masonry Walls with Fabric-Reinforced-Cementitious-Matrix', *Construction and Building Materials*, 65(29), pp. 243–253.

Forren, J. and Nicholas, C. (2018, October 18–20) 'Lap, Twist, Knot. Intentionality in Digital-Analogue Making Environments', *ACADIA // 2018: Recalibration: On Imprecision and Infidelity: Proceedings of the 38th Annual Conference of the Association for Computer Aided Design in Architecture (ACADIA)*. Mexico City, Mexico, pp. 336–341.

Forren, J. and Nicholas, C. (2019) 'Lap, Twist, Knot: Coupling Mental and Physical Labours in Contemporary Architectural Practice', *Scroope: Cambridge Architectural Journal*, 28(1), pp. 94–107.

Halprin, L. (1969) *The RSVP Cycles: Creative Processes in the Human Environment*. New York: G. Braziller.

Ingold, T. (1999) 'Tools for the Hand, Language for the Face: An Appreciation of Leroi-Gourhan's Gesture and Speech', *Studies in History and Philosophy of Biological & Biomedical Science*, 30(4), pp. 411–453.

Ingold, T. (2011) *Perception of the Environment: Essays on Livelihood, Dwelling and Skill*. Abingdon-on-Thames, New York: Routledge.

Ingold, T. (2013) *Making: Anthropology, Archaeology, Art and Architecture*. Abingdon-on-Thames: Routledge.

Jahn, G., Newnham, C., and Beanland, M. (2018, October 18–20) 'Making in Mixed Reality: Holographic Design, Fabrication, Assembly and Analysis of Woven Steel Structures', *ACADIA // 2018: Recalibration: On Imprecision and Infidelity: Proceedings of the 38th Annual Conference of the Association for Computer Aided Design in Architecture (ACADIA)*, Mexico City, Mexico, pp. 88–97.

Lüling, C. and Richter, I. (2016) 'Architecture Fully Fashioned: Exploration of Foamed Spacer Fabrics for Textile Based Building Skins', *Journal of Facade Design and Engineering*, 5(1), pp. 77–92.

Mercedes, L., Gil, L., and Bernat-Maso, E. (2018) 'Mechanical Performance of Vegetal Fabric Reinforced Cementitious Matrix (FRCM) Composites', *Construction and Building Materials*, 175, pp. 161–173.

Nicholas, P., Stasiuk, D., and Schork, T. (2014, October 23–25) 'The Social Weavers: Negotiating a Continuum of Agency', *ACADIA 14: Design Agency: Proceedings of the 34th Annual Conference of the Association for Computer Aided Design in Architecture (ACADIA)*. Los Angeles, pp. 497–506.

Sabin, J. E. (2013, October 24–26) 'MyThread Pavilion: Generative Fabrication in Knitting Processes', *ACADIA 13: Adaptive Architecture Proceedings of the 33rd Annual Conference of the Association for Computer Aided Design in Architecture (ACADIA)*. Cambridge, pp. 347–354.

Zwierzycki, M. et al. (2017, November 2–4) 'High Resolution Representation and Simulation of Braiding Patterns', *ACADIA 2017: Disciplines & Disruption: Proceedings of the 37th Annual Conference of the Association for Computer Aided Design in Architecture (ACADIA)*. Cambridge, MA, pp. 670–679.

14

BLENDING REALITIES

From Digital to Physical and Back to Digital

Ioanna Symeonidou

Introduction

Architectural research and praxis have substantially changed with the widespread use of digital media, and this has affected all stages of architectural creation, from ideation to construction. Design thinking has radically changed, since ideas no longer originate solely in the designer's mind: a new digital reality exists and is associated with a wide spectrum of technologies that digitally simulate reality, ranging from the digital representation of spaces to computational simulations and immersive experiences of space. The ever-growing interest in digital reality has cross-disciplinary roots and is constantly gaining ground within design research education, preparing the next generation of architects for the challenging yet invigorating role of the "new hybrid practitioner—a kind of architect-engineer of the digital age" (Leach et al., 2004, p. 5).

The studio aimed to highlight hybrid activity, employing analogue and digital media, thus blending realities and inspiring innovative design and documentation methodologies through the crafting of projects that question the boundaries of each medium. This is in line with Mark Burry's observations and suggestion that "before we abandon old tools for new, this is a good moment to put the brakes on. Hybrid activity demonstrates unequivocal benefits to the design process, and slow design has proven to be indispensable for success" (Burry, 2005, p. 31).

On Digital Design and Tectonics

The paradigm shift which computation has brought to architecture not only addresses design thinking and creative processes, but the entire workflow from design to construction and visualization. During the early years of digital design in architecture, projects remained on the computer screen, their lifespan was short, and they were seen as research projects, aimed at visually testing out new ideas and, in very rare cases, constructing some prototypes. In the last two decades, however, the widespread use of digital fabrication technologies in architecture boosted the desire to test things out physically, while digital technologies were seen as an "enabling apparatus that directly integrates conception and production in ways that are unprecedented since the medieval times of master builders" (Kolarevic, 2004, p. 3). Kolarevic further explains that the avant-garde designers of the newly introduced formal complexities were left with no other choice than to closely engage in fabrication and construction. In this respect, the actual

DOI: 10.4324/9781003183105-18

making phase becomes important, not only as a sub-process in the lifecycle of a building, but also as an exploratory medium used to develop new forms, new methods, and new thinking processes. The integration of digital media within architectural tectonics obviously affects several different aspects of the discipline, including the design process, the style, and the entire ecosystem of design knowledge.

It is evident that style and technology affect each other reciprocally. Mario Carpo remarks that "all tools feed back onto the actions of their users, and digital tools are no exception. . . . Manufactured objects can easily reveal their software bloodline to educated observers" (Carpo, 2011, p. 34). At the same time, contemporary aesthetics pushes the technological boundaries towards the utilization of new media, while new technological achievements in architecture, such as the integration of CAD-CAE-CAM workflows, give rise to morphological innovation.

> The use of algorithmic or 'rule-based' design research methods is based within the inherent quality of digital media. This is a new idea of a kind of differentiated 'standardisation' that overturns the traditional paradigm of mechanical repetition that determined so much of early industrialisation.
>
> *(Self and Walker, 2010, p. 28)*

The field of digital tectonics emerged as a collaboration between two domains: the digital culture of sensuous, ephemeral images and a tectonic culture of pragmatic buildings (Leach et al., 2004). Architects and engineers counter-inform the design process towards optimized solutions, generating innovative and unprecedented architectural forms. Wasim Jabi describes this process as the "poetics of digitally conceived, structurally clarified, and directly manufactured architecture" (Jabi, 2004, p. 256).

Digital tectonics reflects on the reciprocities involved in design decisions, building performance, constructability, and sustainable logistics. The technological developments afforded by the digital media allow for the ideation of increasingly complex architectures. Reiser and Umemoto define Novel Tectonics as the systemic ecology

> established in the relationships of exchanges among structure, effects, ornament and program. As compared to twentieth-century expressionism, which foregrounds the formal and emotive characteristics of architecture as the product of purely personal sensibility, we regard expression as the properly impersonal capacity of matter and material systems, in which human will and intentionality play a part but are not the sole determinants.
>
> *(Reiser and Umemoto, 2006, p. 104)*

The design brief was a pavilion that was to be fabricated on a scale of 1:10 in the school lab. The fact that a prototype would actually be constructed was a condition that needed to be taken into consideration. Even in the early design experimentation phase, the students needed to address construction logics and assembly, and develop a strategy for fabrication and a design intuition for structural form. Some student groups worked in parallel on the computer and on draft models, devising strategies for component intersections and material thicknesses and sizes. The great majority of students used parametric tools, such as Rhino and Grasshopper, in order to allow for quick changes and modifications that would occur based on the material properties and structural performance of the mock-ups. Most of the student groups went through several cycles of testing with digital and physical media, counter-informing their designs accordingly.

On Physical Construction and Feedback

Within this novel environment in the design studio, when combined with digital media, hands-on experiments can accelerate the emergence of innovative design ideas; by being in actual contact with materials, the designer develops an intuitive notion of material behaviour over time and the resultant geometry of form-finding processes (Figure 14.1). Similar experiences are recorded by designers who utilize algorithms that simulate material properties, such as elasticity, stiffness, and bending. The Kangaroo physics engine within Grasshopper is a tool that can be used to simulate physical forces, such as stretching and bending material, in the form of digital form-finding. As Rossi remarks, "either from a technical point of view or from a compositional one, in the use of every material there must be an anticipation of the construction of a place and its transformation" (Rossi, 1981, p. 1). Within the studio, students encountered both anticipation and unpredictability with regard to material behaviour. There were some examples in which Kangaroo simulations offered similar results to the physical model, whereas in others the material resistance proved stronger and more difficult to handle, as was the case with a project that used an ad hoc strategy for steam bending (Figure 14.2).

In the domain of digital tectonics, models and prototypes are both design and presentation tools. They are media for presenting an idea, but also experiments in material performance or assembly sequence. They investigate tangible and qualitative characteristics that cannot be evaluated on the computer screen. Whereas digital models prove effective in handling numbers,

FIGURE 14.1 Gridshell pavilion for surfers in Hawaii, by students Nikoleta Diamantou, Ioannis Drakakis, Stratis Lamproulis, and Evangelia Fessa, as part of the Architectural Composition course taught by Professor Ioanna Symeonidou.

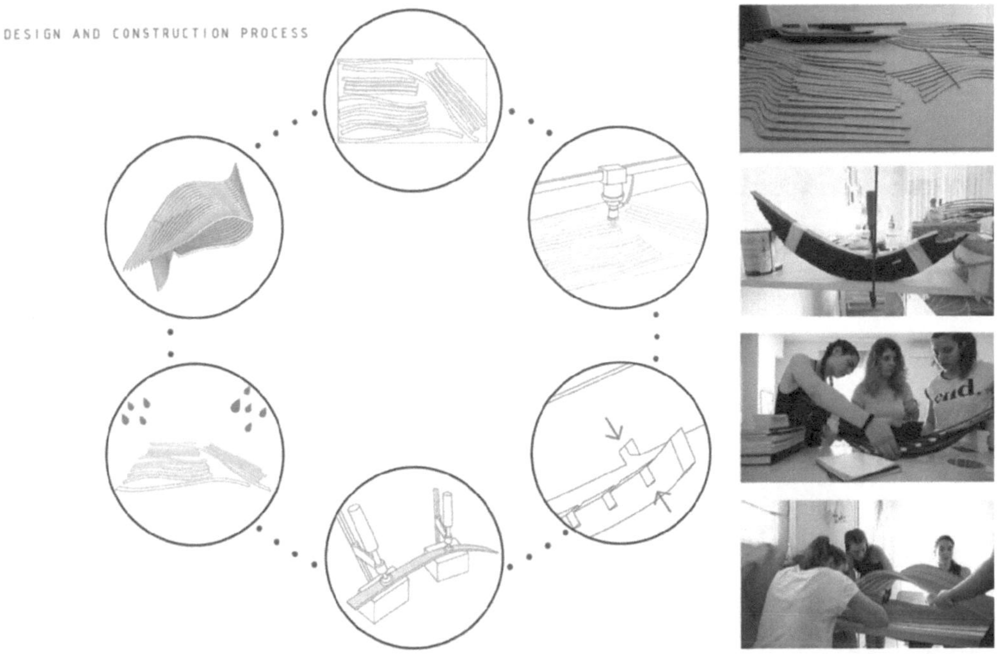

FIGURE 14.2 Construction process and fabrication mock-ups of Drone Pavilion with steam bending plywood on 1:10 scale, by students Mariza Argyrou, Andriani-Melina Kalama, Danai Papoutsi, and Danai Tzoni, during the Architectural Composition course taught by Professor Ioanna Symeonidou

forces, physical simulations, and other quantitative data, built prototypes offer a means of evaluating qualitative data. Materiality and tactility can only be experienced by constructing an artefact.

The design and digital fabrication of scaled prototypes provided very fertile ground for teaching construction, innovation, and inventiveness. The great majority of the structures were modular, and the nodes that connected the components therefore played a decisive role. The immediacy of gaining feedback from fabricated prototypes by assembling and testing both components and nodes proved to be a great asset during the entire process. Reflecting the principles of problem-based learning, students were able to assess the structural performance of the artefact locally and globally and thus pinpoint optimized node solutions, both with regard to functionality and material resistance, as well as considering construction logics and assembly sequence.

On Digital Documentation and Immersion

The last stage of the studio had several aims: on one hand, to document the design process and construction, but also to present the design ideas, digitally place them on the site, and navigate through them with the use of 3D animations (Figure 14.3). At the end of the semester, the students were asked to submit a short film documenting the entire physical and digital process, blending realities and media. The students were given no concrete instructions regarding the technical requirements for the video. The only guideline was that the movie should be both informative as well as immersive; hence they were required to blend the real with the artificial. The viewer had to be able to walk through the pavilion, stand underneath it, and observe the people walking by and the movement of the sun (Figure 14.4). It was very important to ensure

FIGURE 14.3 Still frames from the animation video of Yokai Pavilion, by students Georgia Politi, Georgia Sagatopoulou, Olga Stai, and Sisi Tentzeri, presented for the Architectural Composition course taught by Professor Ioanna Symeonidou

FIGURE 14.4 Images from the digital representations of the Pavilion in Tokyo, designed by students Elisavet Kiretsi, Dimitris Mitsimponas, Zoi Papadopoulou, and Anna Fatourou, for the Architectural Composition course taught by Professor Ioanna Symeonidou

that the building could be understood in context, blending physical and digital images to interpret the scale and its relation to the surroundings.

The students used the models to create experiences in VR which enabled the user to walk through the model, and in AR to experience the project in context when visiting the actual site. For the virtual environment applications, the 3D models of the pavilions were exported in fbx format and imported into Twin Motion in Unreal Engine (Epic Games). Using the VIVE interface, the students could then walk through their models, change the materials and textures, adjust weather conditions and sunlight in order to experience their designs at different times of day, view them from different angles, and understand the relation of the human body to the structure. The AR implementation was created on mobile phones utilizing the Fologram plugin for Rhinoceros 3D. The 3D models were loaded onto the mobile devices, and the scale and orientation were adjusted by placing the marker on the site. In many cases, the AR experience helped the students to understand their projects better in their real context, and some of the on-site adjustments were adopted and informed their designs in terms of location, orientation, and scale. Considering the educational benefits of the VR/AR implementations, it was noted that students would go back to their initial designs and modify them on the basis of the feedback they obtained from these immersive experiences. When compared to previous studios that did

FIGURE 14.5 From the construction process of the 1:10 scale model of the Pavilion in Tokyo designed by students Elisavet Kiretsi, Dimitris Mitsimponas, Zoi Papadopoulou, and Anna Fatourou, during the Architectural Composition course taught by Professor Ioanna Symeonidou

not involve VR/AR applications, it was noted that the students were more aware of the surrounding context, scale, and envisioned experience within the spaces they designed.

In the short films, students combined animations of the design process in Rhino-Grasshopper, and animated explanations of the assembly logic and footage of themselves constructing the models (Figure 14.5). Most of the videos ended with a walk through the project exemplifying different space occupancy and utilization scenarios, focusing on different aspects of their projects, and illustrating a narrative of blending realities.

Conclusions

The studio employed a hybrid design approach that was greater than its parts. Through the active involvement of the students, it was reconfirmed that the digital and the physical should not be seen as competing design media, but instead as complementary design tools that can be blended in several different ways. It had involved several cycles of iterations from one medium to another, initially offering design feedback but eventually contributing to the development of design intuition and sensibility. This is a nonlinear thinking process based on the qualitative characteristics of each medium, the sequence of design decisions, and the moments of failure or success in terms of design intent, all of which contributed to the development of the blended realities of these projects.

Considering the current state of the art of digital media and the apparent limitations, we need to foster innovative thinking. Innovation should not be halted by the media; instead, new ideas should force the media to evolve. Mark Foster Gage claims our generation is the first to be defined by "creative powers and freedoms never before experienced", and, as a supporter of open-ended experimentation, he suggests that new ideas "should be free to accelerate unencumbered in wild and unexpected new directions" (Gage, 2011, p. 1).

Based on the educational experiments presented in this paper, this blended approach in design teaching seems to encourage the exploration of "unexpected new directions". The factors that contribute to innovative design thinking and creativity still remain unexplored, although activating new connections across design processes by blending tools and methodologies appears to maximize learning and inventiveness.

References

Burry, M. (2005) 'Homo Faber', *Architectural Design*, 75(4), pp. 30–37.

Carpo, M. (2011) *The Alphabet and the Algorithm*. Cambridge: The MIT Press.

Gage, M. F. (2011) 'Project Mayhem', *Fulcrum*.

Jabi, W. (2004, November 8–14) 'Digital Tectonics: The Intersection of the Physical and the Virtual', *Fabrication: Examining the Digital Practice of Architecture, Proceedings of the 23rd Annual Conference of the Association for Computer Aided Design in Architecture and the 2004 Conference of the AIA Technology in Architectural Practice Knowledge Community*, Cambridge, Ontario), pp. 256–269.

Kolarevic, B. (2004) *Architecture in the Digital Age: Design and Manufacturing*. London: Taylor & Francis.

Leach, N., Turnbull, D., and Williams, C. (eds.) (2004) *Digital Tectonics*, 1st edition. Chichester and Hoboken: Academy Press.

Reiser, J. and Umemoto, N. (2006) *Atlas of Novel Tectonics*. New York: Princeton Architectural Press.

Rossi, A. (1981) *A Scientific Autobiography*. Cambridge: The MIT Press.

Self, M. and Walker, C. (2010) *Making Pavilions*. London: Architectural Association Publications.

15

THE ROBOTIC DANCE

A Fictional Narrative of a Construction Built by Drones

Sara Eloy and Nuno Pereira da Silva

Introduction

There were two levels of goals for the research presented here. The first involves defining the situations in which robotic construction used for the assembly of parts can be advantageous to architecture and assessing the performance of a robotic building process using a simulation methodology based on augmented reality (AR). The second refers to the title—"The Robotic Dance"—and focuses on the aesthetic potential of AR to simulate the performance of drones while flying and the consequences of this for architecture design, rather than the technical function of drones. This idea draws on the concept that computers can generate human-level creative products such as art, poems, and music (Rodger, 2014; Elgammal et al., 2017). It is not our goal to computer-generate the flight of a drone, but to explore the potential of AR as an aesthetic medium that enables designers to expand their creative process. In order to do so, we designed an AR experience in which visitors to an architecture exhibition could witness a wave-like wall structure being constructed by drones. Using an AR optical see-through device (the HoloLens smart glasses), users can see virtual objects (the wave-like wall) superimposed onto the real world (an exhibition gallery).

This chapter presents a study that forms part of a research project which explores the possibilities afforded by robotic technologies used for assembly purposes, namely robotic arms, drones, and hybrid solutions, in architecture ideation and the building construction sector. The adoption of robotic technology in several industries, such as those in the naval and automotive sectors, has changed production methods and, consequently, the final products. Nevertheless, it has still not been adopted by the building construction industry. In architecture, robotics has arrived through the manufacturing industry with the advent of digital fabrication, and offers a broad spectrum of activities, ranging from pre-design to fabrication, assembly, and on-site construction (Daas and Wit, 2018). In the architecture industry, robotic arms are used mainly to digitally fabricate by subtracting, although there are some examples worldwide of their use in the assembly of construction elements, which is the topic of this research. In fact, the use of drones to assist in the assembly of construction components has advanced very little and is limited to a few experiments carried out by universities in which researchers explore how this technology can be used to build real buildings. In addition to analysing the potential of robotic construction in architecture, we aim to analyse how fictional narratives of construction in AR can be an advantage in this field.

DOI: 10.4324/9781003183105-19

The research questions that are the focus of our work are the following: what AR can explore during the ideation stage of the architecture design; whether the animation of an ongoing construction adds new insights to architectural ideation; whether the possibilities provided by simulation can change the way we design.

This chapter presents a discourse framed by confronting the rationality and efficiency of construction assembly performed by drones and the aesthetics and poetics associated with an animated simulation using virtual technologies applied to the architectural design process.

Robotic Construction

Robotic construction mainly focuses on robotic arms, used to digitally fabricate architectural components by subtracting or adding matter but rarely used in the assembly of construction elements. The use of drones in the assembly of architectural components, which is still in the early stages of development, has advanced to a lesser extent in comparison to robotic arms, which have also proved possible for the same purpose. In fact, this disruptive technological development is confined to a few experiments carried out by some universities, exploring how it can be used in building sites.

At ETH Zurich, the work by the Gramazio Koehler Architects team concluded that these technologies can be used in simple and repetitive tasks, such as quickly placing bricks with a minimal error margin in simple geometries (Bonwetsch et al., 2006). At the University of Stuttgart, experiments carried out by a team headed by Achim Menges and Jan Knippers opened up new perspectives, using carbon fibre modules with integrated sensors and communication technology between devices (Wood et al., 2018).

Experiments undertaken at ETH Zurich, Stuttgart University, and Hong Kong University, such as *The Aerial Construction* (Mirjan et al., 2016) and *Cyber Physical Macro Material* (Wood et al., 2018) using drones, *The Informed Wall* (Bonwetsch et al., 2006), *The Brick Labyrinth* (Piskorec et al., 2018) and *Ceramic Constellation* (Lange et al., 2017) using robotic arms, and *On the Bri[n]ck* (Rocker, 2009) and *ICD/ITKE Research Pavilion 2016/7* (Menges and Knippers, 2017) using hybrid robotic situations, are good examples of the use of such technologies.

The ROB|ARCH and FABRICATE conferences, which have run since 2012 and 2011 respectively, discuss the integration of digital design with digital manufacturing processes and its impact on design and fabrication.

Simulation by Augmented Reality

In the reality-virtuality continuum concept presented by Milgram et al. (1994), the real environment and virtual reality stand at opposite ends of the spectrum, while other types of virtual combinations lie in the middle and a large group of mixed reality (MR) displays also play a role. AR and virtual reality (VR) allow for the creation of alternative and artificial realities that effortlessly transport the user to an augmented or totally new world.

Eriksson (2016) observes that the current times are marked by the "spreading of the virtual into our everyday surroundings, breaking out from the already obsolete box-with-a-window computers at our desks. The possibility of projecting virtual objects, as well as intelligent virtual agents in mid-air, seems inviting and useful" (Eriksson, 2016, p. 260). Regarding the most extreme possibilities for projecting a true mid-air volumetric display with high visual fidelity, Eriksson states that if this is not possible, we will have to resolve the "question of how to feed these illusions into our eyes or the brain" (Eriksson, 2016, p. 260).

When these artificial realities are discussed, three aspects are usually foregrounded. The first is related to how much users "actually know about objects and the world in which they are displayed", which Milgram et al. (1994, p. 287) called the Extent of World Knowledge. The second is Reproduction Fidelity or level of realism, which is the "relative quality with which the synthesizing display is able to reproduce the actual or intended images of the objects being displayed" (p. 289) and depends on both image quality and the feeling of presence. Finally, Milgram et al. (1994, p. 290) refer to the "extent to which the observer is intended to feel 'present' within the displayed scene" and calls this the Extent of Presence Metaphor. These three concepts shape the way we experience the virtual world and have differing roles and levels of importance in different contexts.

The Robotic Dance

As previously stated, in order to respond to our research questions, an AR experience was designed to simulate the construction of a wave-like wall structure performed by drones.

Virtual Environment

The virtual environment was designed so that a wave-like wall structure was being built virtually in the middle of the exhibition gallery while visitors walked through the space. The VR graphics were not designed to look photorealistic, since the goal was not the representation of detailed materiality or light. The head-mounted display (HMD) matched the positions and orientations of the real space of the exhibition gallery. The aim was to give visitors the impression that the wall could be, or was being, built in the room. Hence, accurate and precise low-latency tracking, together with good calibration and viewpoint matching, were essential. The visualization of the drones building a wall was not interactive, and the users could only walk around the virtual built site, but not interact with the construction. Both visual and audio stimuli were provided for visitors.

Methods

The experience was created by using a combination of digital tools. The methodology chosen for this AR experience comprised three steps: (1) definition of the construction process and site conditions, (2) 3D modelling and animation and transfer to AR, (3) analysis of the simulation. The following software was used: Rhinoceros 3D and Grasshopper (for the 3D model of the wall), 4D Cinema (for the animation), and Unity (for the visualization in AR) (Figure 15.1). With Rhino and Grasshopper, different alternatives were designed for the wall. The wall (parametric design), the two landing platforms (where the drones take off and grab a brick), and the bricks themselves were modelled in Rhino. When the desired wall solution was found in Rhino, the model was imported in 4D Cinema, where the drone flight animation was developed. The visualization in VR was accomplished by importing the model to Unity, where physics was added to the bricks, table, and drone elements.

The Robotic Dance experience was presented to visitors via a Microsoft Hololens AR HMD, with the aim of achieving the harmony described by Heim (1998, p. 14) as the wish not to replicate the primary world in cyberspace by substituting it, but by paying attention to "both tendencies within—to the realist and the idealist in us". During the AR experience, when wearing this see-through device, the visitor sees the real world as well as the virtual objects overlaid on it.

Findings and Discussion

The Robotic Dance experience led to a discussion on both the use of mixed realities for simulation and drones for assembly proposes, and the exploration of the aesthetic medium in

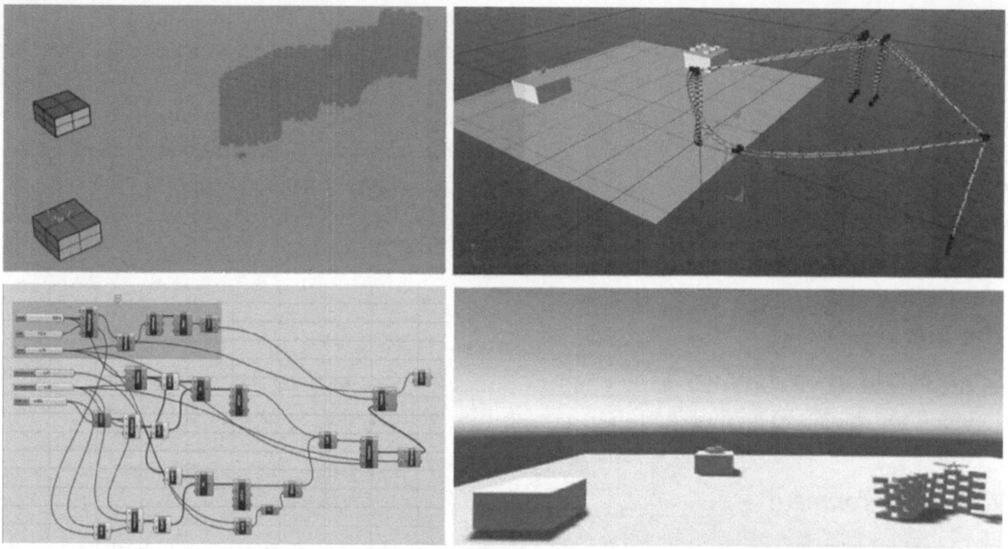

FIGURE 15.1 3D model of the wall, the two landing platforms and the drone in Rhino and grasshopper script for the wall design: (right top) 3D model in 4D cinema where all the animation was developed; the visible path represents the drone trajectory (take off, flight, landing); (right bottom) 3D model in Unity.

architectural ideation. On one hand, the technological solution of using drones for assembly purposes represents, in this discussion, the rationality, efficiency, and immediate results that technology brings to architecture. On the other hand, the AR used in the fictional narrative of the drone construction enables us to explore the non-rational, the aesthetics, and the contemplation of the architectural ideation. While the first set of features is broadly discussed in the field of robotic architecture, the scientific and architecture community has paid much less attention to the second.

Using the Milgram et al. (1994) concepts of Extent of World Knowledge, Reproduction Fidelity or level of realism, and Extent of Presence Metaphor, it is possible to analyse the extent to which these concepts could be applied to the present experience and the impact they would have on the use of virtuality as an aesthetic medium in architectural ideation.

Given its technological nature, AR does not need a completely modelled world, since it uses the real world and adds virtual objects to it. In this sense, AR provides the closest authentic reality possible in the Milgram reality-virtuality continuum. The Extent of World Knowledge (EWK) is therefore realized to a great extent, and the virtual objects are the elements by which representation is questioned, in terms of 'authenticity'. The next questions regarding EWK are 'where' and 'what' the objects are. In order to approach this, we aimed to design an experience that overlaid a construction of a wall in the exact physical space intended for the real construction. 'What' in this case is a brick with a clear size, a not-defined material. This knowledge, given to the observer, is therefore the only relevant knowledge for the purposes of the AR simulation.

The sense of realness is not provided by a photorealistic representation of the built wall, using basic graphic design, but by the position of the virtual wall and the surrounding real elements that enables the wall to grow continuously, without touching any real element. The audio stimuli which accompany the visitor throughout via HoloLens, referencing the flight of a drone, enhances the sensation of realness.

FIGURE 15.2 The view from HoloLens, showing the real world (the exhibition gallery) and the virtual wall

HoloLens has a small field of vision which does not permit the user to see all the virtual objects that should be in the scene, particularly above and below the transparent screen. Although at first the virtual objects look as if they actually exist in real space, the user is unable to feel totally present when parts of the virtual objects are cut out of the field of vision. Yet, despite this drawback, AR still breaks down the distinctions between virtual objects, real space, and the self. As announced by Eriksson (2016), in the future, virtual and real worlds will mainly be blended, and the current division between virtual and physical will gradually disappear.

In this experience, users cannot interact with the drone construction in any other way than by visualizing it from several angles and hearing the drones flying (Figures 15.2–15.5). The possibility of interacting with the construction, for example by starting a new construction scenario or changing the position of the landing platforms, is part of our future work.

Final Remarks

AR opens up new and disruptive means of visualization and interaction within architecture design, based on virtual worlds in which virtual objects and worlds are present everywhere. As Eriksson (2016, p. 256) states, "The virtual is not a separate universe and going there does not mean leaving the physical behind". In 1998, Heim anticipated how virtuality would create a field for discussion:

> The journey to virtuality launches us onto an open field. Whichever way we choose to travel makes a big difference. The route of virtual realism is not an easy one. Nor can it be traveled once and for all. It is a continual balancing act, one that has already begun and that requires ongoing attention.
>
> *(Heim, 1998, p. 15)*

FIGURE 15.3 The second author using the HoloLens to see the Robotic Dance

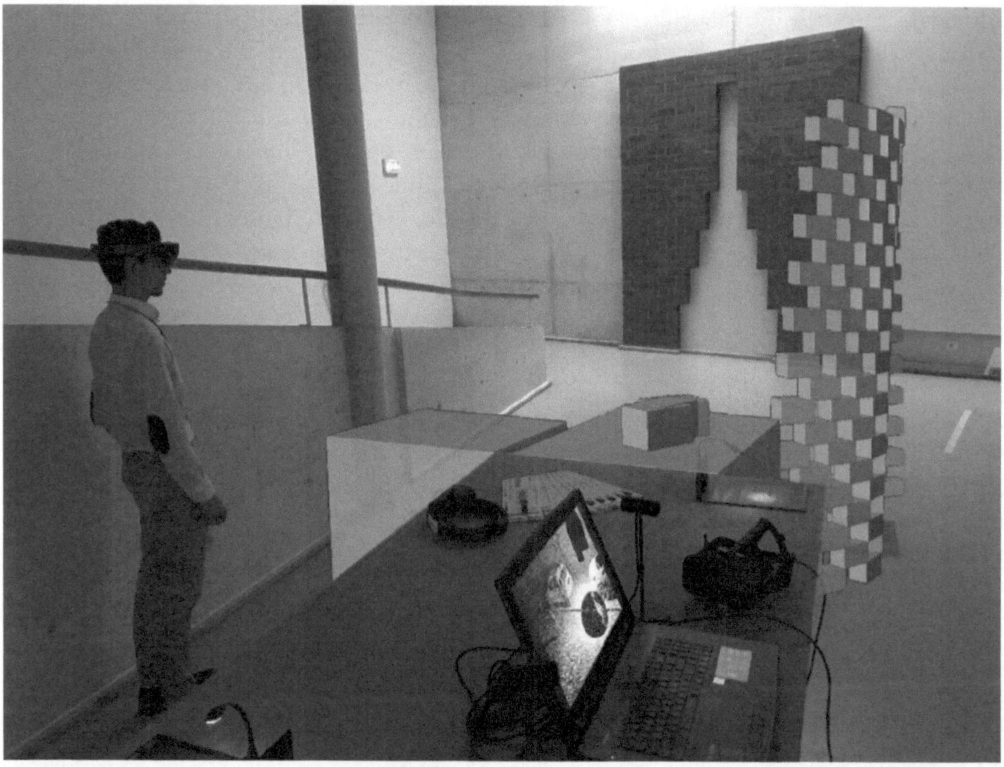

FIGURE 15.4 The second author using the HoloLens to see the Robotic Dance

FIGURE 15.5 Visitors using the HoloLens during the exhibition
Source: Photo by Mariana Veríssimo

Moreover, what other narratives of space does AR technology empower in architecture?

Firstly, it has the potential to effortlessly transport the user to an augmented or totally new world in a way that no other existing solution has been able to achieve.

Secondly, a new combination of space and time should be considered. The tireless flight of the drone transports us to a city that is always awake, where the production chain never stops. There is neither a beginning nor an end; the drones are continuously building a wall that starts up repeatedly. Simultaneously, we can pause, go back, or even stop the construction, thus transgressing the conventional boundaries of space and time.

Thirdly, it offers new possibilities for communication and interaction between humans and the devices, and among humans. In such a virtual space, more than one person can be immersed in a real-scale simulation of a building, thus providing the full interaction which immersive technologies enable. This interaction not only allows for visual and audio stimulus, but also the possibility of exploring the virtual object in a *quasi*-physical way by walking up to it and around it.

In addition to the concepts of EWK and realness, AR also enables several design possibilities to be explored during the architecture ideation stages, thus enhancing creative freedom without the boundaries of (real) reality.

Finally, the experience involving drones also explored their specific feature of limited visibility. In the built scenario, the drones perform a dance similar to the one described by Brady (2017) when he refers to the act of "visualizing the other". Drone visuality is

> undermined by limited bandwidth, . . . 'latency', . . . 'blinking' (when a drone needs to move and another one cannot replace it immediately), resource constraints and the 'soda straw' effect (the drone camera's inability to visualize more than a small proportion of the total field).

This dance, although not relevant in a real construction scenario, is an add-on in this simulation since time enables us to contemplate it.

References

Bachelard, G. (1964) *The Poetics of Space*. Boston: Beacon Press Books.

Bonwetsch, T. et al. (2006) 'The Informed Wall Applying Additive Digital Fabrication Techniques on Architecture', *Synthetic Landscapes: Proceedings of the 25th Annual Conference of the Association for Computer-Aided Design in Architecture*, Louisville, pp. 489–495.

Brady, A. (2017) 'Drone Poetics', *New Formations: A Journal of Culture/Theory/Politics*, 89–90, pp. 116–136.

Colletti, M. (2013) *Digital Poetics: An Open Theory of Design-Research in Architecture*. Farnham: Ashgate Publishing Limited.

Daas, M. and Wit, A. J. (eds.) (2018) *Towards a Robotic Architecture*. Novato: ORO Editions.

Elgammal, A. et al. (2017) 'CAN: Creative Adversarial Networks, Generating "Art" by Learning about Styles and Deviating from Style Norms', *International Conference on Computational Creativity (ICCC)*. Atlanta, GA, US, pp. 1–22.

Eriksson, T. (2016) *A Poetics of Virtuality*. Gothenburg: Chalmers University of Technology.

Heim, B. M. (1998) 'Virtual Realism', pp. 1–15. Available at: www.mheim.com/.

Lange, C. J., Holohan, D., and Kehne, H. (2017) *Ceramic Constellation Pavilion*. Available at: http://rocker-lange.com/blog/?p=1785 (Accessed: 1 June 2019).

Menges, A. and Knippers, J. (2017) *ICD/ITKE Research Pavilion 2016–17*. Available at: https://icd.uni-stuttgart.de/?p=18905 (Accessed: 1 June 2019).

Milgram, P. et al. (1994) 'Augmented Reality: A Class of Displays on the Reality-Virtuality Continuum', *Systems Research*, 2351 (Telemanipulator and Telepresence Technologies), pp. 282–292. doi: 10.1.1.83.6861.

Mirjan, A. et al. (2016) 'Building a Bridge with Flying Robots', in Reinhardt, D., Saunders, R., and Burry, J. (eds.) *Robotic Fabrication in Architecture, Art and Design 2016*. Cham: Springer International.

Piskorec, L. et al. (2018) 'The Brick Labyrinth', in Willmann, J. et al. (eds.) *Robotic Fabrication in Architecture, Art and Design*. Cham: Springer International, pp. 490–500.

Rocker, I. M. (2009) *Studio: Ingeborg M. Rocker, on the Bri(n)ck: Architecture of the Envelope*. Available at: www.studioplex.org/node/390 (Accessed: 1 June 2019).

Rodger, C. (2014, June) 'Reading the Drones: Working towards a Critical Tradition of Interactive Poetry Generation', *Formules 18: Littérature et Numérique*, pp. 237–255.

Wood, D. et al. (2018) 'Cyber Physical Macro Material as a UAV [re]Configurable Architectural System', in Willmann, J. et al. (eds.) *Robotic Fabrication in Architecture, Art and Design 2018: ROBARCH 2018*. Cham: Springer International.

PART 5

Body and Social

The **'Body and Social'** section includes three chapters in which authors discuss and present work related to the bodily experience in virtual reality (VR) and the use of mixed realities within communities to engage citizens with architectural solutions.

Together with the trend of moving to digital that has emerged over the past decades, virtual experiences have recently gained momentum due to the COVID-19 pandemic travel restrictions. In this context, the need for online solutions for collaborative working, communications, shopping, and entertainment has been boosted.

From this frame of reference, Markéta Gebrian et al. present and discuss an experimental solution developed in a social VR platform, NEOS VR, where visitors can be present in an immersive and interactive space experience.

Carla Leitão also focuses on the central role of the user, discussing new forms of creating space that do not use physical limits but rely on augmented concepts of 'alive' materials and spaces. Her contribution presents critical thinking on 'alive' spaces in which digitally networked materials, spaces and bodies establish new realities that train the users in new intuitions.

Engaging people in participatory design processes has been a longstanding aim in architecture, although it is also difficult task to accomplish. Misunderstandings in interpreting drawings produced by architects is one of the reasons for such difficulties. The work presented by Ana Moural and Ramzi Hassan focuses on the social dimension of bringing architecture to a wider public and explores ways of doing so by using VR.

Follow the QR-code to navigate through the online content of Part 5.

DOI: 10.4324/9781003183105-20

16

DESIGNING THE BODILY METAVERSE OF LISBON

Markéta Gebrian, Miloš Florián, and Sara Eloy

The Inspiration: Lisbon, the Earthquake, the *Elevador*, and the Art of Vieira da Silva

Bodily Metaverse, the experimental project presented here, was developed during a stay in Lisbon at the Information Sciences and Technologies and Architecture Research Center (ISTAR).

In Lisbon, a city with seven hills which have a huge impact on its landscape, old yellow trams and elevators help people travel more easily up and downhill in the city centre. The *Elevador de Santa Justa*, built in 1902, is one of the most emblematic elevators, transporting passengers from the downtown *Rossio* area of the city to the *Largo do Carmo* uphill in the city centre, where several *miradouros* (viewpoints) offer beautiful views over the Lisbon hilltops.

The surrounding area is rich in history. In November 1755, there was a huge earthquake in Lisbon, followed by fires everywhere in the city, culminating in a tsunami. This combination of catastrophes destroyed most of the city of Lisbon. Immediately afterwards, King José I appointed the Marquis of Pombal to organize the reconstruction of the city. Pombal's plan started with "the development of four options that included rebuilding the city as it was, reconstructing the city with minimal improvements to the street pattern, undertaking a total rebuilding effort or starting fresh on a new site" (Mullin, 1992, p. 1).

> The different proposals included a regular grid of rectangular city blocks, including a certain standardization as well in architecture. This design principle created an urban tissue with completely different proportions when compared with the previous medieval urban structure still presents in the resilient section of the city, in the Alfama and Castelo hill. The hygiene concerns, an important issue of the time, forced a regular structure that granted better ventilation, sun light and easier access.
>
> *(Sanchez, 2017, p. 3)*

The city centre, or *Baixa*, was planned in identical rectangular blocks with straight streets leading to the River Tagus (*rio Tejo*). Both the new structures and those that remain from the time before the earthquake are visible in the city. The hills were not damaged by the tsunami and still have very old, winding streets: the neighbourhood of Alfama is a typical example of this layout.

For this project, it was decided to focus on the 1755 new urban plan for the area surrounding the *Elevador de Santa Justa*, due to its innovative features. This new urban plan was built much earlier than the famous *Eixample* urban plan, or *Plan Cerdá*, in Barcelona, for example, produced

DOI: 10.4324/9781003183105-21

by Ildefons Cerdá in 1860. In addition to the urban planning references and the *Elevador*, Lisbon artists such as Maria Helena Vieira da Silva[1] were also an inspiration for this work. Vieira da Silva's (1908–1992) paintings of cities are full of rectangular elements and irregular, blurred poetic grids reflecting the existing structure of the cities of Lisbon and Paris. They are abstract reframings of cities in which the artist plays with colours and sizes, in the same way that we aimed to explore them in social VR environments. The 3D digital metaverses proposed in this project are inspired by the existing architecture of the *Elevador de Santa de Justa*, the *Chiado-Rossio* area in Lisbon, and the work of the Portuguese artist Vieira da Silva.

Digital Metaverses and the Role of Social VR

Several actions usually undertaken in the physical world are now moving to the virtual world online. In the future, certain current online activities such as networking, working, educating, socializing, and shopping may take place in 3D virtual shared worlds via social VR platforms, which provide a more immersive experience. The first author's research on social VR started in 2015, and the city of Barcelona in 2018 was the subject of the first case study in which architecture was interpreted in an artistic VR environment. In the case of Barcelona, concrete construction elements such as walls, floors, ceilings, and roofs were explored as if none of the real-world conditions existed.

In the case of Lisbon, the research focused on architectural elements such as the *Elevador* and the city blocks, and on testing levels, floating VR *miradouros*, and using the colours and shapes of the traditional Lisbon decorative tiles (Figure 16.1). The strategies used to move users were

FIGURE 16.1 (Top) Photos of the *Elevador de Santa Justa*; (bottom) photos taken from the *Elevador de Santa Justa* looking down at the *Baixa* district of the city centre

walking, flying, and teleporting in space to the different VR *miradouro* levels to engage them in an immersive experience in which the existence of their own avatar (hands and head may be visible) enhances the feeling of presence. The *Elevador* was used as a landmark, with a tall vertical element giving form to this concept, which can teleport avatars in VR to upper spaces with floating *miradouros*. The concept of different levels of *miradouros* and moving scenarios where avatars can float in the virtual space of NEOS VR was inspired by Vieira da Silva's paintings. The concept of the Bodily Metaverse of Lisbon is that avatars emerge on the ground in the middle of the city blocks and can move around slowly at ground level until they find the VR elevator. When they encounter the elevator, they can be speedily teleported to the upper floating levels of the VR *miradouros*, where a panoramic view can be accessed. These levels float slowly in virtual space, and their textures change slowly and continuously when avatars step onto them, offering an artistic view of the warm tones of the city of Lisbon.

The Introduction of Online Social VR Platforms and NEOS VR

In a lecture given at the Betlémká Chapel in Prague in November 2017, Beatriz Colomina raised the question of what would happen to existing cities when people no longer paid attention to them. Colomina's question triggered two questions related to the current project: What will happen in virtual space if people start inhabiting it? How can virtual space be designed to trigger emotions in people?

Vincent Guallart argues that the physical laws of the real world are not necessarily applicable to the virtual world. He also states that

> this virtual world could be a clone of a real world, or generate infinite possible spaces, like a world with infinite times and therefore infinite possible, parallel histories.
>
> Quasi-real spaces.
> An acoustic space: a music room.
> A fractal trajectory.
> A mountain of infinite dimensions.
> A cloudy dawn: a city.
> Settings for virtual meetings and real use.
>
> Spaces and computer programs accessible from an intermediate space that can lead to a virtual world full of real content.
>
> *(Guallart, 2003, p. 167)*

In 1999, the film *The Matrix* envisaged a virtual environment that was unrecognizable from the real city. In 2003, the Second Life game offered VR environments to be explored by user avatars that could navigate around the architecture and landscapes. Real architects also played Second Life and built models of their own in which physical rules were not applied. Commenting on Second Life, Rose states that "it is a world in its infancy, unavoidably complex, useful, unpredictable and legitimate, with countless advantages over the real one" (Rose, 2007).

Today, several social VR platforms are available: the best known are Facebook Spaces,[2] Sansar,[3] AltSpace VR,[4] and HighFidelity.[5] NEOS VR,[6] available free online on Steam VR, was the social platform selected for this project. Data is saved in the NEOS cloud, and 1 GB of free space is available for importing 3D models into NEOS VR. Currently, NEOS VR is mainly used as a platform for avatars to meet online, create their own worlds and import 3D models, then move around the metaverse and share and show the 3D space to other avatars in VR. It is also possible to enter and test VR worlds that have been created by other NEOS VR users. For architects, NEOS VR may be used in two main ways. Firstly, it can be a means of visualizing their 3D models, either imported from other 3D modelling software or modelled directly in NEOS VR. It is also possible to create interactive environments that resemble games by using LOGIX, an advanced visual programming language. Our prediction is that the second use will be developed by architects in the near future, when virtual worlds are used to manage some of the activities and tasks that people currently perform in the physical world. Recently, the presence of society on the web has increased significantly due to the COVID-19 crisis and subsequent lockdown measures. Suddenly, everyone needed to adapt to the new ways of interacting online with each other. Due to work commitments, studies, or simply because people wanted to keep in touch with friends and family, society quickly went online. Given these developments, it is reasonable to predict that social VR platforms will replace 2D screens and even physical contact in some situations in the future. In this case, online virtual environments will need to be designed, and architects will be the first in line for the job.

Virtual Worlds in Cyber Art

In 1995, Michael Naimark presented the project "Be Now Here" (1995), an installation which enabled visitors using 3D glasses to visit cultural heritage sites such as Jerusalem, Dubrovnik, Timbuktu, Angkor, and Cambodia by navigating through photos from real sites.

In 2001, the Blast Theory group,[7] in collaboration with the Mixed Reality Lab at the University of Nottingham, created "Can You See Me Now". Blast Theory creates interactive art to explore social and political questions, positioning members of the audience at the centre of their work. In "Can You See Me Now", real people play, using mobile devices with satellite tracking, and have a corresponding avatar in the virtual domain. "The boundary between the urban space and the virtual worlds blurs. Though the users do not see each other, they occupy the same space" (unknown author, in Ars Electronica 2018 event).

Both examples are relevant to the concept presented in this project: in using VR environments to experience distance places, the Naimark project is a precursor, while the Blast Theory project is a game related to the experience of a real city. Although it is very common these days to navigate through real cities with the help of virtual maps such as Google Maps, this was not the case in 2001. Nowadays we use our smartphones and Internet to navigate with Google Maps, and the computer calculates our journey through the city. In VR, guided navigation does not play the same role: distances are not significant since we can fly above the city and be teleported speedily to our destination.

The Design Process for the *Elevador de Santa Justa* Experience

The design process that was followed for this work was divided into several stages to organize the elements and movements in VR 3D space. The goal was to design moving floors, or *miradouros*, and static environments, such as the ground. The NEOS VR program was used to create virtual worlds within which several new textures were developed by means of digital collage to represent the visual identity of Lisbon.

The two main steps in the design process for the Bodily Metaverse of Lisbon were:

- Design in Rhinoceros 3D: the *Elevador*, ground, hill, and floating levels were modelled in Rhino using an exploratory design strategy (Figures 16.5–16.7).
- Design in NEOS VR: firstly, the 3D model from Rhinoceros was exported to NEOS VR, and new elements were added. Secondly, the 3D model was tested with the free immersive head-mounted display HTC Vive in immersive navigation. Both the movement features of

teleportation and the changing scenarios of the *miradouros* will be further developed by using LOGIX visual programming in a cross-disciplinary collaboration with programmers.

The entire 3D model of Lisbon occupies a rectangular base measuring approximately 342 m by 263 m. The 3D model of the *Elevador* is 63 m long, 14 m wide, and 80 m high, larger than the existing one to emphasize its presence. The sizes are derived from the real sizes used in the Marquis of Pombal masterplan and the Lisbon city blocks in the *Baixa-Chiado* area.

The symbolism of the *miradouros* and the *Elevador* was the main concept in this project. The design process started with the *Elevador* as the main element in the composition, deliberately stressed to emphasize its presence. The *Elevador* was intended to be a landmark in the composition, and therefore a high vertical sculpted shape was chosen to capture the attention of the VR users (Figures 16.2 and 16.3). The long horizontal extension leading from VR elevator is inspired by the existing passageway that connects the *Elevador* to *Largo do Carmo*. Instead of a passageway that connects one place to another in the real world, obeying physical laws, the VR elevator in the VR platform allows the visitor to explore the passageway and discover an open area at the end overlooking the exuberant urban complex. This interpretation is more artistic than architectural, since it is not based on the physical rules that apply to architecture.

There are three possibilities for movement in the Bodily Metaverse of Lisbon. The first is walking, which means a slow form of flying performed on the ground. The second option is flying, which the avatar can use when it is in the *miradouros*. The third is teleporting, which happens when the user is close to the VR elevator, which will rapidly teleport them either to the upper level and the VR *miradouros* or down to the ground. It is only possible to be transported up to the *miradouros* or down to the ground via the VR elevator. The concept for the VR *miradouros* is that of a more peaceful presence in the composition, gliding slowly through space and changing texture when an avatar approaches the VR level.

After the 3D model in Rhinoceros was defined, it was exported in FBX format from Rhinoceros to NEOS VR. The position and rotation of the model was then set up in the new virtual

FIGURE 16.2 Flying above and around the VR elevator (view from the NEOS VR experience)

FIGURE 16.3 VR elevator and floating level above, view from an avatar flying over a lower *miradouro* (view from the NEOS VR experience)

FIGURE 16.4 Floating in space close to a *miradouro* with a view of the river (view from the NEOS VR experience)

world in NEOS VR. Using digital collage, new textures inspired by references to Lisbon were defined and used in NEOS VR. In the VR environment, the model is structured as floating levels, floors, the elevator, and the hill (Figure 16.3). The river is also present in the background as a memory of the view from the *Elevador Santa da Justa miradouro* over the *Tejo* (Figure 16.4).

Final Remarks

The Bodily Metaverse of Lisbon did not aim to reproduce the literal city of Lisbon, but to offer an interpretation based on experiencing the city through a new medium.

The approach to social VR illustrated in this chapter is based on designing space for people to inhabit not the physical space of architecture, but virtual spaces which obey different rules. In general, architects use the virtual world to represent past or future projects they want to build in the real world, and their designs therefore obey the rules of the physical world: for example, elements need to be constructible using physical materials, gravity exists and is applied to these elements, and users are human beings that walk. In the VR world, all these rules can be forgotten, presenting a whole new set of possibilities for architects. In VR, our body—i.e., the body of our avatar—has options for movement that are different from the ones available to humans in the real world, and designers can take advantage of this.

Moving around Lisbon city centre essentially involves walking up and downhill and using elevators and trams. In the Bodily Metaverse of Lisbon, these movements take place via the VR elevator, and the movement up and down creates a virtual state for the user. The elevator functions as an arrow, pointing to floating levels that represent different viewpoints—the *miradouros*. These *miradouros* have an important presence in the NEOS VR world as they introduce changing worlds. In fact, the key concept in this project is that if an avatar approaches a floating level, its texture changes and displays some other digital collage of traditional Lisbon tiles.

This project aimed to question the boundary between digital art and architectural space in virtual reality. The chosen case study and process allowed for the creation of an artistic and architectural VR environment that is aesthetically pleasing and represents a new architectural output designed for real users to inhabit. Designing artistic and architectural spaces related to existing sites, cities, culture, history, and patterns can be accomplished in VR in a very innovative way.

This project is the first step in designing a Bodily Metaverse of Lisbon. The use of this type of social VR enables the designer to invent and discuss a new type of architectural world. Users of NEOS social VR need to be registered and can find friends there or be invited by friends to join and explore their VR worlds. Architects can now establish themselves as designers of

FIGURE 16.5 Lisbon city blocks and the R elevator (view from Rhinoceros)

FIGURE 16.6 VR elevator and a *miradouro* (view from Rhinoceros)

FIGURE 16.7 VR elevator and floating levels (view from Rhinoceros)

virtual worlds that can be used and visited in a virtual and collaborative way by a large number of people. Recently, during the COVID-19 crisis, many of our activities moved online to web pages and video conference calls. It is easy to envisage the use of VR headsets for collaborative online activities in virtual online worlds and social VR platforms in the future. Architects are the best candidates to design these 3D virtual worlds.

Notes

1. On the work of Maria Helena Vieira da Silva, see http://fasvs.pt/en/coleccao/vieira
2. www.facebook.com/spaces
3. www.sansar.com/

4. https://altvr.com/RecRoom
5. https://highfidelity.com/
6. https://neosvr.com/
7. www.blasttheory.co.uk/

References

Guallart, V. (2003) 'Digital', in Gausa, M., Muller, W., and Guallart, V. (eds.) *The Metapolis Dictionary of Advanced Architecture: City, Technology and Society in the Information Age*. Barcelona: Actar.

Mullin, J. R. (1992) 'The Reconstruction of Lisbon Following the Earthquake of 1755: A Study in Despotic Planning', *The Journal of the International History of City Planning Association*, 45.

Naimark, M. (1995) *Be Now Here*. Available at: www.naimark.net/projects/benowhere.html (Accessed: 14 June 2020).

Rose, S. (2007) 'Buy! Buy! Buy!', *The Guardian*. Available at: www.theguardian.com/technology/2007/jul/09/news.architecture (Accessed: 14 June 2020).

Sanchez, J. M. P. (2017) 'Evolution of Lisbon's Port-City Relation: From the Earthquake of 1755 to the Port Plan of 1887', *PORTUS Plus the Journal*, 7, pp. 2–16.

17

INCEPTIVE REALITY

Carla Leitão

Introduction/INQUIRY

This chapter aims to present preliminary findings from research that looks at potential reciprocal concepts between architectural design, immersion, and virtual environment design. The inquiries have a deeper interest in understanding future frameworks and typologies for architectural design products that integrate 'alive' materials (Sterling, 2005)—smart materials that connect physical materials and spaces to digital materials and processes.

The findings emerged from experimental design studios, seminars, and independent projects developed at the Rensselaer Polytechnic Institute School of Architecture from 2014 to 2020, exploring VR, AR, MR, and XR constructs/environments in an immersive collaborative room, as well as in VR.

Among other sources, the relevant background context of inquiry is present in works which explore the intersection between design approaches and concepts of the virtual and of experience, such as Peter Sloterdijk's view of architecture as the art of creating 'immersion' by forging a simultaneity of at least two points of view from and into the same space (Sloterdijk, 2006), and Mark Wigley's pre-history of virtual architecture, particularly his 'inside viewpoint' on the architectural design 'mind/drive', which can be read as a navigation structure, program, or effect by a user (Wigley, 2007). In addition, in Marcos Novak's definition of Liquid Architectures, through philosophical underpinnings, 'becoming' is linked with 'the digital': "I use the term liquid to mean animistic, animated, metamorphic, as well as crossing categorical boundaries, applying the cognitively supercharged operations of poetical thinking" (Novak, 1991, p. 250).

Locus of Experience: Projection Room (CRAIVE Lab) Versus Solo Perceiver (VR)

Studio projects in two locations enabled the user's body to be tested under two conditions: a collaborative immersive space where the body is free to roam within a physical space and interact physically with others, and the virtual space of isolated perception, or the VR headset/screen.

The Collaborative Room experience took place in the CRAIVE Lab (Collaborative-Research Augmented Immersive Virtual Environment Laboratory) facility—a 360°, 39'x32' visual and audio (132-speaker) projection room located in the RPI Tech Park (Director, Dr. Jonas Braasch).

DOI: 10.4324/9781003183105-22

Experiences created for the CRAIVE Lab have to contend with the in-between space—the distance/space between a screen that contains users. In exclusively virtual environments, it is easier to transport the body into the experience, where it feels and projects itself through its fictional protocols (engaging more easily with its 'simulation').

Design Directions: Control Viewpoint or Dream State

In our Architecture Design courses (the one-year undergraduate thesis studios, one-semester vertical/option design studios and elective seminars), this research approach and the environments provide a platform for reflecting on data translation, site, and program, developing new roles for architecture as a perceptive device, aesthetic mediator, and communicative interface that can activate and act on multifaceted aspects of reality.

The design studio topics focused on a preliminary fictional split between virtual constructions:

Control Viewpoint: virtual space/structure as place for immersion and navigation of physical realities as augmented by their virtual data characters. The Oblivion and Control Room Studios designed 'cockpits' to access uninhabitable landscapes (toxicity, security). The Protoroom and Impermanence Studios highlighted reflections on interfaces and transparency, interactivity, and performance, whilst exploring new logics for public and institutional space, infrastructures, and governance (Figures 17.1 and 17.2).

FIGURE 17.1 In "Interposition, Infiltration, Interference" by Kristen Van Gilst, the courtyard of a City Hall is converted into a forum for discussion and voting on several local and district issues via mediating pixel links that stand in for metrics of response and access to video fragments: the courtyard becomes a network of overlapped topical spaces.

Source: Karen Van Gilst in Control Room Studio, 2017

FIGURE 17.2 In "Intimatopia", Jerry Huang creates a landscape that meshes virtual territories in physical maps by allowing users to produce surrounding spatial environments through the use of digital audio production tools.

Source: Jerry Huang in Impermanence Studio, 2019

Following a branch of cultural history predicated on cybernetics and institutional power, as traced by Eden Medina (2011) and Cormac Deane (2015), topics and projects in these differently designed Control Viewpoint studios tested critical inquiries into libraries, control rooms, and urban dashboards and their close links with surveillance systems, as presented by Shannon Mattern (2015) and Evgeny Morozov (2014), in addition to potential restructuring frameworks, as glimpsed in Benjamin Bratton's *The Stack* (2016).

The projects also examined the opportunities afforded by augmented perspectives and representation and their potential for present and near-future challenges visualized in concepts such as Timothy Morton's 'hyperobject' (2011) and Adam Greenfield's frameworks for post-smart city, post-human environments (Greenfield, 2017).

Dream State (Inception): virtual space/structure as a projection for immersion of the body and mind following new rules that reassemble fragments of the real, through new types of coherency. The Inception Vertical Studios explored dream and play landscapes, designing cohesive new landscapes, interactive audiovisual experiences using game design engines and interactive platforms (e.g., Unity, Processing, MaxMSP).

The Dream State or Inception Studios consider that our perception of reality has always had virtual dimensions (examples being thoughts or dreams) and that we may be expanding this aspect of experience through digital materials whose impacts are becoming increasingly evident.

The Inception Studios acknowledge the demand for representing contradictions as cohabiting dimensions and for exploring impossible, discontinuous, or paradoxical configurations, including personal reconstructions of past memories, and dreams, 'suspension of disbelief' experiences, scientific theories, 3 1/2D & 4D space and non-spatial dimensions, among others. As a process, this design edits design procedures into combined layers and fragments using tools that allow for apparent continuities and fictional cohesions—modes that can be recognized as figures and grasped by the body trained in intuition of the physical.

Lingering questions posed by authors of digital architecture from the '90s and 2000s and new media theorists apply here. Brian Massumi talks about a 'duplicity of form': the dual way in which agents receive the form or image of something. This happens "spontaneously and simultaneously in two orders of reality, one local and learned or intentional, the other non-local and self-organizing" (Gregg and Seigworth, 2010, p. 203). Hence, apprehension occurs in two simultaneous, non-integrated, separate ways: intention and affect, meaning and sense, perception, and experience. Marcos Novak's writings on eversion align with William Gibson's claim that modes of being in cyberspace have for a long time 'colonized the physical' to such an extent that currently they sound archaic. Eversion is "the Obverse of Immersion" (Novak, 2002), what Kathryn Hayles has called the fourth phase in the history of cybernetics "mixed reality . . . environments in which physical and virtual realms merge in fluid and seamless ways (Hayles, 2010, pp. 147–148).

'Gameplay' sequence and narrative structures are intrinsically tied to scale and contiguity, and different forms of experiencing coherency and cohesiveness. However, the studio focus on the primacy of experience for its own sake alters traditional gameplay concepts of reward, instead offering intrinsic conditions for space play that can become other models for 'level' and thus generate representational dilemmas and constructs. This redirection focuses again on the environment itself and its apprehension—and on the whole-to-parts relationship that reveal its (non-fragmented) cohesive potential.

The Reality of Inception

Much of the discourse around immersion and virtual environments focuses on 'framing'—that which is located between the experience and the user. Sloterdijk proposes that "immersion as a method unframes images and vistas, dissolving the boundaries with their environment" (2006, p. 105). Grau claims that the history of immersion art has a media history that dates back to wall paintings in the Roman Villa dei Misteri near Pompeii for their elimination of boundaries between viewer space and painting space (Grau, 2003, pp. 25–27).

For Crary, the panorama of the 19th century instilled a promise that could not be sustained:

> a structure that seems magically to overcome the fragmentation of experience in fact introduces partiality and incompleteness as constitutive elements of visual experience. . . . That a perspectival representation allowed only a partial and delimited opening onto that world was offset by the universality and rationality of the laws by which it was composed.
>
> *(Crary, 2005, pp. 21–22)*

Alex Galloway observes that the interface of the '90s perhaps never left us, arguing that a state of ambiguity is important to the figure at the interface, to enable it to continue to mediate on representation in itself, as well as representing the 'window' (threshold) (Galloway, 2012).

In the design of mixed environments, nearly all users become hyper-users, as the environment senses them in order to activate itself. In the Control Viewpoint Studios (Oblivion, Control Room, Protoroom, Impermanence), the gamification of reality becomes a problematic of user access, a means of making domains, characters, and connections to reality actually closer for users to grasp.

In the Dream State Inception Studios, the hyper-user peels away (Figure 17.3), starts sequences and opens doors (Figure 17.4), inputs sound waves that change the space, and observes them from multiple points of view (Figure 17.5) or activates layers of the space through animated character-objects (Figure 17.6).

FIGURE 17.3 Xscape, by Taelinn LaMontagne and Alanna Deery, deploys a running user gaze that peels away building skins, revealing species, events, and non-linear narratives.

Source: Taelinn LaMontagne and Alanna Deery in Inception Studio, 2020

FIGURE 17.4 Impossible House, by Page Bickham and Ayesha Ayesha, produces the components and reassembling logics of a proto-logical dream sequence, using objects, spaces, elements, and movement as triggers for events, passageways, effects, and material transformations.

Source: Page Bickham and Ayesha Ayesha in Inception Studio, 2020

FIGURE 17.5 Indeterminacy (Ryan Hu/Luke Korzenko) is a space that listens to a user and its sounds, producing an involving detailed matrix of their characteristics. The user location and sound source can be split, creating other domains of spatiality for the subjective experience.

Source: Ryan Hu and Luke Korzenko in Inception Studio, 2020

Mixed environments mimic the relationship between structure and ornament through their performative scaffolds and layers—the entities that receive and display information (layers) and those that connect them with each other and ultimately with the user (scaffolds). The degree to which layers/ornaments can complexify their relationship to scaffolds/structures is still a good measure/criteria for the success of the environment as friction between coherence and fragmentation—'material' tectonic qualities emerging as architectural bodies themselves. Dream spaces constantly change the association figure (structure), converting it into a sign/layer (Figure 17.4), while spatial illusions (layers) add a near-structural feel to reality (Figure 17.6), and mirrors impart new 3D spaces to surfaces (Figure 17.7).

These environments mainly restate problems associated with memory and identity, through sequence and expectation as related to movement and narrative, by positing experience as remembering. Multi-layered realities are still translated/received as sequences (by a user)—assuming the role of a correlating guiding spatial structure that either emphasizes spatial contiguity as a linear time sequence or serves as a scaffold that enables spatial discontinuities to create alternative or parallel time sequences.

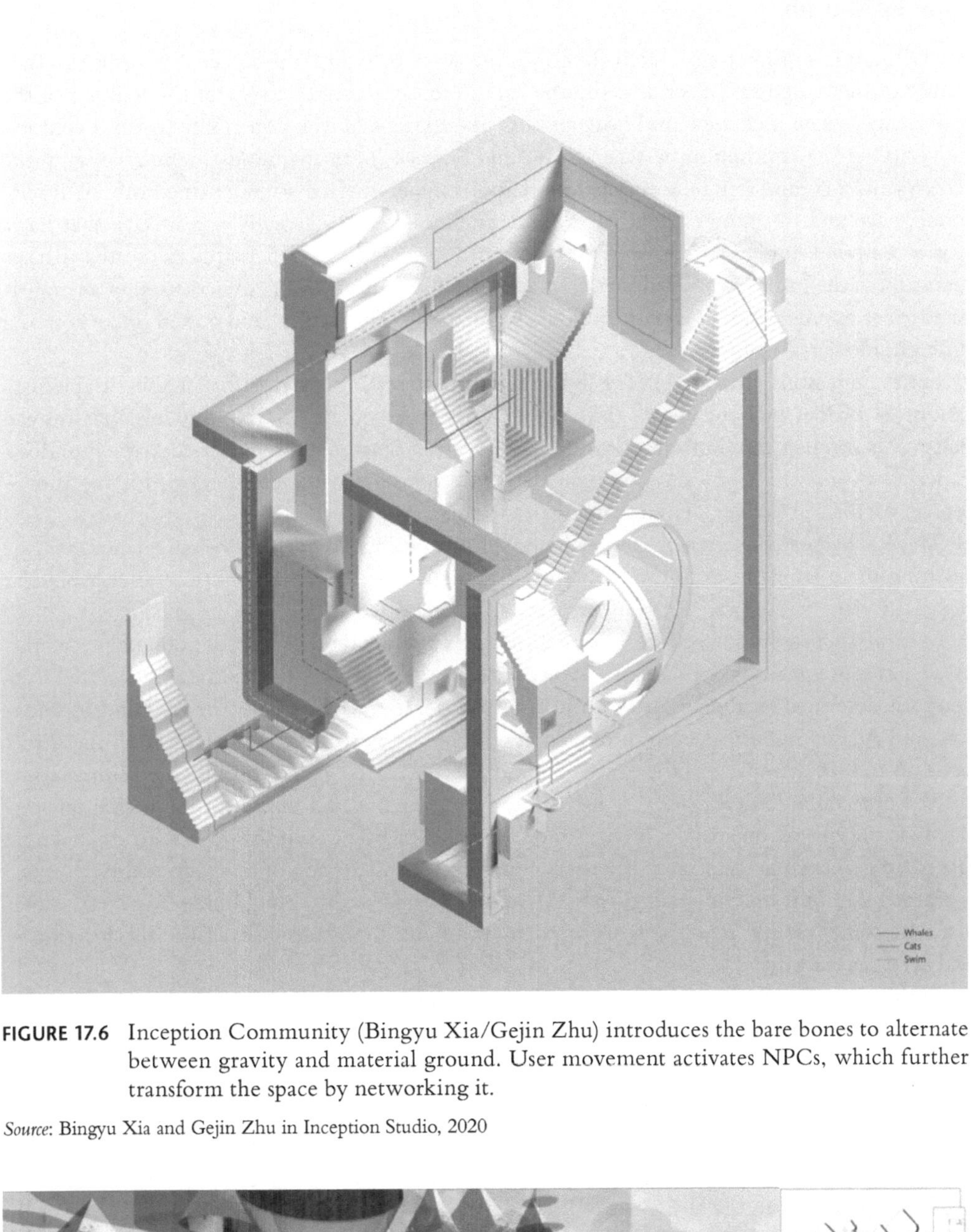

FIGURE 17.6 Inception Community (Bingyu Xia/Gejin Zhu) introduces the bare bones to alternate between gravity and material ground. User movement activates NPCs, which further transform the space by networking it.

Source: Bingyu Xia and Gejin Zhu in Inception Studio, 2020

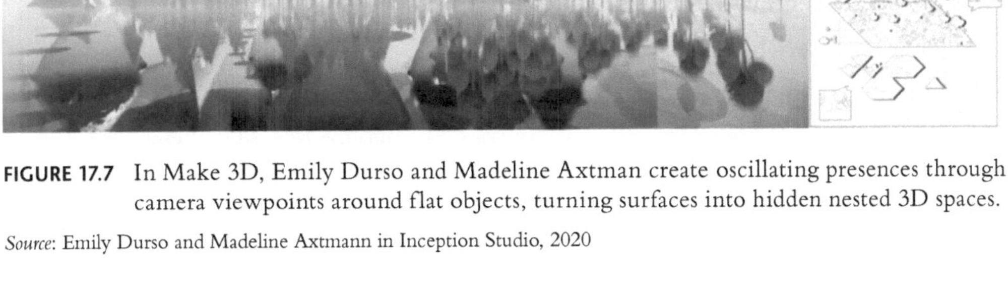

FIGURE 17.7 In Make 3D, Emily Durso and Madeline Axtman create oscillating presences through camera viewpoints around flat objects, turning surfaces into hidden nested 3D spaces.

Source: Emily Durso and Madeline Axtmann in Inception Studio, 2020

Final Reflection

Alicia Imperiale (Imperiale, 2000) describes the ways in which the screen has been the flattening of the structures of sensing and the role of sensing as structuring of the making of the experience, when mediated, and how authors like Marcos Novak contribute to this evolution by verifying the continuum between Space and Surface (both manifolds), acknowledging the screen's all-encompassing new character—that of a hyper-surface—integrating both mediating intelligence and incommensurability: "the computer screen . . . really is a surface that has a spatio-temporal dimension that and allows one to interact with hypersurfaces created mathematically in the space of the computer" (Imperiale, 2000, pp. 70–71). Any creation of any fabricated space or environment is both completely 'virtual' (a fabrication) and mixed (incorporating different mediated realities).

For these reasons, the CRAIVE Lab has been an interesting location for architectural explorations as it does not encourage the user to surrender completely to protocols, but instead delays this through the framing of the space—creating what is known in media as a 'window' experience—in which any environment delays becoming a complete reality—for the user—forever oscillating between environment and room.

This has helped contextualize processes and effects usually dedicated to virtual environments—rescuing them from the allure of 'content's' transient desires—within more indescribable and hopefully richer tectonics. VR-only projects have benefitted from those insights.

Critical discussions on types of behaviour fostered by digital media and its potential networks, as well as representations of landscapes that are both its active background and generated outcome, as described by Benjamin Bratton, Shannon Mattern, Evgeny Morozov, Timothy Morton, and Adam Greenfield, have provided a welcome framework for engaging with the direct political and social impacts of the earlier-mentioned constructs, seeing through their shiny layers.

The new architectural spaces are not created by using physical limits but by relying on augmented concepts of 'opening' which, as the Control Viewpoint Studios show, is all about a new flat space managed by ecologies of sensors and their reconstruction of access to reality.

Immersion in inceptive reality is also all about sensors—conceptual ones—the entities that translate some 'reality' into the fabricated environment: their sensibility, filtering, location—and their networking.

In the Inception Studios, navigation of the incommensurable re-emerges as a quest, as virtual reality now reattaches itself, through mixed reality, to unpacking dimensions of the real. Both models—modelling and mining—rely on managing perception and comprehension. It is an opportune moment to own this perceptive machinery, when comprehension is challenged by new entities that are too vast to be easily read in time and space (Morton, 2011), but must urgently be made present.

Acknowledgements

I am grateful to Jerry Huang and Samuel Chabot for long-term support and access to the CRAIVE Lab, and to Prof. Jonas Braasch for his visionary directorship of the CRAIVE Lab and continuing support for our endeavours in it.

References

Bratton, B. H. (2016) *The Stack: On Software and Sovereignty*. Cambridge, MA: MIT Press.

Crary, J. (2005) 'Géricault, the Panorama, and Sites of Reality in the Early Nineteenth Century', *Grey Room*, 9, pp. 5–25.

Deane, C. (2015) 'The Control Room: A Media Archaeology', *Culture Machine*, 16, Drone Cultures. Available at: https://culturemachine.net/drone-cultures/ (Accessed: 4 February 2021).

Galloway, A. R. (2012) *The Interface Effect*. Cambridge, MA: Polity Press.

Grau, O. (2003) *Virtual Art: From Illusion to Immersion*. Cambridge, MA: MIT Press.

Greenfield, A. (2017) 'Blockchain beyond Bitcoin: A Trellis for Posthuman Institutions', in *Radical Technologies: The Design of Everyday Life*. London: Verso Books.

Gregg, M. and Seigworth, G. J. (eds.) (2010) *The Affect Theory Reader*. Durham, NC: Duke University Press.

Hayles, N. K. (2010) 'Cybernetics', in Mitchell, W. and Hansen, M. (eds.) *Critical Terms for Media Studies*. Chicago: University of Chicago Press, pp. 144–156.

Imperiale, A. (2000) *New Flatness: Surface Tension in Digital Architecture*. Basel: Birkhauser.

Mattern, S. (2015 March) 'Mission Control: A History of the Urban Dashboard', *Places Journal*. Available at: https://placesjournal.org/article/mission-control-a-history-of-the-urban-dashboard/ (Accessed: 22 January 2021).

Medina, E. (2011) *Cybernetic Revolutionaries: Technology and Politics in Allende's Chile*. Cambridge, MA: MIT Press.

Morozov, E. (2014, October 13) 'The Planning Machine: Project Cybersyn and the Birth of the Big Data Nation', *The New Yorker*. Available at: www.newyorker.com/magazine/2014/10/13/planning-machine (Accessed: 22 January 2021).

Morton, T. (2011) 'Zero Landscapes in the Time of Hyperobjects', *Graz Architectural Magazine*, 7, pp. 78–87.

Novak, M. (1991) 'Liquid Architectures in Cyberspace', *Cyberspace: First Steps*, pp. 225–254.

Novak, M. (2002) 'Eversion: Brushing against Avatars, Aliens, and Angels', in Clarke, B. and Henderson, L. D. (eds.) *From Energy to Information: Representation in Science and Technology, Art, and Literature*. Stanford, CA: Stanford University Press

Sloterdijk, P. (2006) 'Architecture as an Art of Immersion', translated by Engels-Schwarzpaul, T., *Interstices*, 12(2011), pp. 106–109.

Sterling, B. (2005) *Shaping Things*. Cambridge, MA: MIT Press.

Wigley, M. (2007) 'The Architectural Brain', in Burke, A. and Tierney, T. (eds.) *Network Practices: New Strategies in Architecture and Design*. New York, NY: Princeton Architectural Press.

18

VIRTUAL REALITY IN LANDSCAPE DESIGN

Findings From Experimental Participatory Set-Ups

Ana Moural and Ramzi Hassan

Background

Why Does Virtual Reality Come With So Many Challenges?

Many aspects could be addressed under this topic, the first being a considerable degree of uncertainty about the unknown. VR can indeed change the way we interact with the real world and with each other (Bailenson, 2018). Additionally, there is some uncertainty about which of the several VR options may be most suitable for a given purpose. The choice of technology should not only take the ultimate goal into consideration (e.g., presenting an ongoing design, allowing stakeholders to run through a suggested design multiple times, or communicating a result), but also the available resources. Producing such an environment can be considered challenging and time-consuming. A regular 3D model of a project scenario is typically used as base to create VR content. Nevertheless, practitioners who are willing to take the first steps must go through a process of learning. However, there are no available protocols to follow, which may lead to inappropriate choices and technical complications. In order to prevent this, expectations should be carefully managed, and easy and accessible solutions should be approached first to facilitate a smooth start.

What Is Currently Available on the Consumer Market?

VR has followed an unstable path towards mass adoption, which has created some degree of uncertainty regarding its value and whether it is worth allocating resources to a process that might not be firmly established yet.

The first commercial head-mounted display—Oculus Rift—became available to general enthusiasts in 2012, followed by the first mobile VR solution—Google Cardboard—launched two years later. Since then, there have been two main VR trends: wired and mobile solutions. Whilst the first requires external hardware, portable devices open up for new possibilities (Gill and Lange, 2015). Mobile solutions include both smartphone-based and stand-alone devices (Anthes et al., 2016; Emidy et al., 2018). Stand-alone devices may provide better performance and graphics, but smartphone solutions are available for anyone who owns one of these mobile computing devices.

DOI: 10.4324/9781003183105-23

From 3D Model to Virtual Reality Content

Even though most 3D modelling software can produce VR content, aspects such as the type of VR that is going to be used, level of realism and interaction should be decided in advance. Following the classification of visual output devices as wired and mobile by Anthes et al. (2016), we suggest two categories of virtual environments that are best suited to each type of device:

- Real-time rendering in wired VR: 3D navigable environments require a continuous rendering process, so the user can browse freely around the model. Multiple exploration possibilities bring additional challenges: optimization of geometries to prevent performance issues; high computer power to handle graphically demanding tasks; high navigation skills.
- 360° panoramas in mobile VR: Panoramic computer-generated renderings allow for visualization of a given environment by limiting the user to pre-selected points established by the designer. This is a very effective way of keeping the user focused on one particular scene. Additionally, pre-rendered images are not graphically demanding, which brings affordable mobile solutions into the range of possibilities.

Designers use various digital applications to produce project drawings and create 3D models, but there is some uncertainty about when to bring the 3D model into VR. The designer should think about the type of information that is going to be communicated and the stage when it should be introduced. Even though it is usually linked to very accurate and realistic environments, it can be used in the preliminary stages, in which case there are also other types of VR which do not require any 3D modelling (e.g., 360° photos or videos captured with 360° cameras).

User Experience as a Limitation in Virtual Reality

Mandal (2013, p. 1) argues that VR "allows to see the surrounding world in other dimension and to experience things that are not accessible in real life". An experience is "a story, emerging from the dialogue of a person with her/his world through action" (Hassenzahl, 2010, p. 8). When it comes to VR, the experience with the interface—user experience (UX) (Moural and Øritsland, 2019)—allows the user to enter a different dimension. Building upon the hierarchy of needs in VR (comfort, interpretability, usefulness, and delight) suggested by Cronin (2015), we present and discuss UX aspects considered as limitations to particular experimental set-ups. In addition, we provide some suggestions on how to minimize each aspect and enhance the overall experience.

User Experience Considerations of Implementing VR in Participatory Set-Ups

The findings on user experience taken from two experimental participatory set-ups (an outdoor mobile VR experience and a participatory workshop) involving an existing design and a hypothetical one developed by master's students in landscape architecture will now be examined. Both set-ups were used as case studies for the present research. However, since neither the design nor the outcome are matters for discussion in this study, the feedback collected during the sessions will not be presented.

The on-site experience took place at the site in order to enable the participants to compare the existing situation with the computer-generated panoramas of the hypothetical design

(Figure 18.1). In the workshop, the group was presented with 360-degree photos of the existing site and the 360-degree computer-generated panoramas previously used in the on-site experience (Figure 18.2). Both set-ups were arranged outside our research-controlled environment, which meant moving the equipment to different locations. Very short initial training sessions were required, as there were very strict time constraints for both events. Hence, smartphone mobile VR appeared to be the most suitable solution. The following are reflections and considerations on implementing VR within participatory set-ups.

Orientation: It should not be assumed that VR has the potential to replace pre-established tools. In fact, our experience suggests that plans should be used as additional orientation tools

FIGURE 18.1 On-site VR experience

FIGURE 18.2 360-degree photo of the site (left) and 360-degree computer generated panorama of the hypothetical design (right)

within the virtual environment. In this case, the site was very familiar to all the participants, which made it easier to navigate in VR. The use of at least one plan seems to give the participants a preliminary overview of the virtual environment.

Visual content: Both experiments were conducted in the autumn-winter period, whereas a summer scenario was displayed in VR. This mismatch led to uncertainty and reduced the level of immersiveness. Additionally, we noticed some discomfort with regard to highly detailed environments, as the users took some time to get used to them.

Providing VR images that are close to the current physical conditions and keeping the balance between level of detail and exposure time seem to be key aspects.

Navigation: As it is a quite recent technology, optimal interaction methods have not yet been determined for mobile VR. Most solutions use specialized control methodologies, which prevent users from establishing consistent interaction patterns among VR applications. The workshop was therefore arranged as a walk-through in which the facilitator took control of the virtual experience and guided the group through the given panoramas. This reduced the training session and facilitated navigation skills. While experiencing the guided tour, some participants were able to combine listening to the facilitator with visualizing the virtual environment, whereas others took the headset off to focus on her talk.

Limiting the level of interaction and providing users with time to adjust to walk-throughs are aspects which should be carefully considered.

Situation awareness: VR is about immersing the user in a simulated environment while they engage in natural interactions with it (Zhou and Deng, 2009), but the physical environment and its constraints should not be disregarded. Innovative tools may require different settings and additional caution. While the participants were isolated in VR, we noticed some degree of stress linked to being physically in an environment without any situational awareness. With the on-site experience, this led to discomfort, as the participants were able to perceive the city surroundings while visualizing a different scene. In the workshop, outsiders walked into the meeting room and passed by the group. While some did not notice, others stopped using VR to check on the situation.

Based on those experiences, it appears to be relevant to consider the physical characteristics and constraints of the set-up, given that the experience is very likely to be affected by this.

Physical set-up: In the workshop, the group sat in a 'round table' arrangement, which led to a conflict between seating and the conditions for exploring the 360° environment. Even though being seated was not stated as a mandatory condition, the participants tended to remain in this position. Surprisingly, some realized that they could explore the environment better if they stood up (Figure 18.3), and those who did so claimed they had a better experience.

By keeping a manageable group size, providing a flexible set-up, and encouraging the group to take advantage of it, certain aspects of the user experience can be explored better.

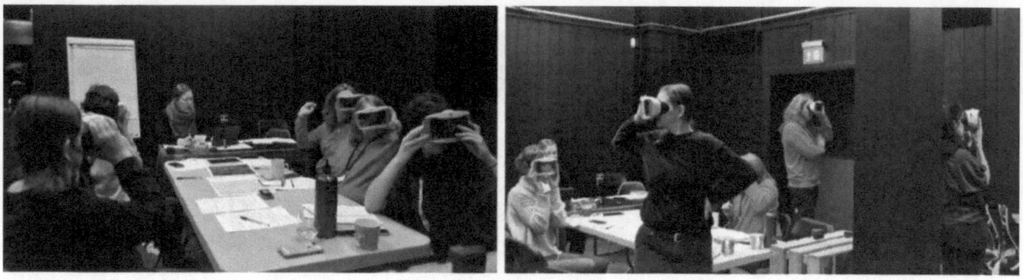

FIGURE 18.3 All the participants remained seated throughout the first part. After a while, some decided to stand up to improve the experience.

Equipment: The headsets had no head straps, as ViewMaster Deluxe VR was designed to be used for short periods. In the workshop, due to long periods of usage, some participants leant over the table, while others just reduced the exposure time. On the other hand, having no head straps was mentioned as a good way to prevent dizziness and tiredness, as the headset can easily be taken off.

The on-site experience ran with no major technical issues, whereas the workshop posed some challenges. As time passed, some devices were affected by performance issues and replaced by new ones. These interruptions seriously affected the flow of discussion.

For medium/long sessions, an adjustable holding system for the VR headset should be provided. Additionally, performance issues are not always easy to predict, and it is recommended that a break should be scheduled in advance to reset all devices or recharge them.

Simulation sickness: Less performative devices and limited experience with VR are likely to lead to discomfort. Dizziness, nausea, eyestrain, and visual fatigue were noticed in both set-ups. In most cases, the symptoms were associated with long periods of exposure, which made people less willing to use it.

The VR system should be chosen according to the requirements for each specific situation and its suitability in each case. Nevertheless, navigation should be limited to short—although multiple—periods of time.

Outlook

The aim of this chapter, which is based on the findings from two different participatory set-ups, is to contribute critically to thinking about the aspects of user experience that may have created barriers to the adoption of VR in landscape architecture. Even though VR has made considerable progress, it must be acknowledged that it has only been on the consumer market for a very short period of time. Hence, it is still seen as a recent technology that is not sufficiently well established for practitioners to be provided with information on how to make the best use of it. However, we also consider that landscape architects should be less apathetic and play an active role in this development by exploring this new tool. The study aims to contribute to a better understanding of how to communicate, design, and implement VR in participatory workshops.

References

Anthes, C. et al. (2016) 'State of the Art of Virtual Reality Technology', *Proceedings of the IEEE Aerospace Conference*. Big Sky, MT, pp. 1–19.

Bailenson, J. (2018) *Experience on Demand: What Virtual Reality Is, How It Works, and What It Can Do*. New York: W. W. Norton & Company.

Cronin, B. (2015) *The Hierarchy of Needs in Virtual Reality Development*. Available at: https://medium.com/@beaucronin/the-hierarchy-of-needs-in-virtual-reality-development-4333a4833acc (Accessed: 22 January 2021).

Emidy, P. T. et al. (2018) *Development of a Mobile Website for the Worcester Art Museum*. Available at: https://digitalcommons.wpi.edu/iqp-all/2200 (Accessed: 22 January 2021).

Gill, L. and Lange, E. (2015) 'Getting Virtual 3D Landscape Out of the Lab', *Computers, Environments and Urban Systems*, 54(2015), pp. 356–362.

Hassenzahl, M. (2010) 'Experience Design: Technology for All the Right Reasons', *Synthesis Lectures on Human-Centered Informatics*, 3(1).

Mandal, S. (2013) 'Brief Introduction of Virtual Reality & Its Challenges', *International Journal of Scientific & Engineering Research*, 4(4), pp. 304–309.

Moural, A. and Øritsland, T. A. (2019) 'User Experience in Mobile Virtual Reality: An On-Site Experience', *Journal of Digital Landscape Architecture*, 4, pp. 152–159.

Zhou, N. N. and Deng, Y. L. (2009) 'Virtual Reality: A State-of-the-Art Survey', *International Journal of Automation and Computing*, 6(4), pp. 319–325.

PART 6
Projects

The final section of this book presents a curated selection of projects by leading architecture offices and academia. The contributions are divided into three parts that reflect their focus—creating, experiencing, and enhancing space. The contributions are diverse and cover a wide range of approaches to using mixed realities during the design process in architecture, with an emphasis on an aesthetic approach.

The three chapters in **'Creating Space'** present work related to the definition, design, and creation of new spaces. Helmut Kinzler et al. from Zaha Hadid Architects present a multi-presence design platform and design space that allows for the creation of a new and neutral ground for co-production. Ruth Ron and Renate Weissenböck explore the design of hybrid spaces, producing augmented living spaces by superimposing virtual spaces onto real living spaces. Alexander Grasser develops work on digital design methods and presents a digital tool for designing new shapes, using augmented reality (AR) to make full-scale installations visible and interactable.

'Experiencing Space' is the most widely researched mixed realities field in architecture. This section presents five contributions from several designers. María López Calleja describes how virtual reality (VR) and AR have been used in MVRDV practice in recent years. The project by Sean Pickersgill also shows how VR visualization can enable a close-to-reality experience of space and therefore facilitate discussion processes within communities. Eva Castro presents solutions developed in the context of academic work that explores VR narratives beyond the constraints of a specific environment, in which analogue atmospheres and digital environments work together. In another contribution, Castro also explores how AR tools are used to (in)tangibly augment physical realities, providing them with fictional contexts. Marcos Novak presents two paired experimental projects that implement multi-user social virtual technologies and discusses their social, conceptual, formal, computational, architectonic, and aesthetic potential.

'Enhancing Space' presents five contributions that describe methods and tools used to enhance the characteristics of a place by superimposing new virtual elements onto it, using both VR and AR techniques.

Kyriaki Goti, from Some People, and Christopher Morse, from SHoP Architects, explore the use of a VR tool that enables people to customize and visualize their personal solution for a

DOI: 10.4324/9781003183105-24

small structure for cities designed to provide a personal space in crowded urban environments. Rudolf Romero, from 01X, proposes a solution for a virtual museum, using VR referencing, both for the works exhibited and the architectural features of the museum.

Julien Rippinger and Arthur Lachard use AR as a reverse window opening onto the observer, where pleasant virtual aesthetical perspectives are overlapped onto the physical space. Pablo Baquero et al. explore how different digital technologies can be combined and reserved during the design process, whilst also investigating the augmentation of the physical world during this process, with the design of a large-scale biomorphic spatial structure. Marcus Farr and Andrea Macruz also use AR to explore materiality and the overlapping relationships between virtual space and virtual stimuli and human sensory experience. The authors study the buildable with not yet buildable elements and how people perceive augmented experiences, rather than those which are purely virtual.

Follow the QR-code to navigate through the online content of Part 6.

6.1

Creating Space

19

ZHVR BIGWORLD

Helmut Kinzler, Risa Tadauchi, and Daria Zolotareva

Introduction

BigWorld is a multi-presence design platform and design space. Initiated by the ZHVR Group, this research and development project has emerged from ZHVR's broadened understanding of the requirements for cybernetic architecture.

Our industry's prior attempts to automate the design process have perpetuated a discontinuity between architectural disciplines. Even with the current, rapid technological development of live-link and real-time collaboration tools, most available software still offers its own specific functionality while remaining incompatible with competitors' products and platforms. This has prevented cross-disciplinary connectivity; even building-information modelling (BIM), despite forming part of our present-day delivery standards for complex architectural projects, is no exception.

The key challenge for the ZHVR Group is to confront the traditional lack of holistic thinking that results from these isolated authoring spheres and their differing design ecosystems (Figure 19.1). BigWorld aims to reintroduce collective connectivity into architectural project development through dynamic assemblies and by establishing manners and rules dependent on a given project's culture, to create a new, neutral ground for co-production.

Brief

BigWorld: The Entire Architectural Ecosystem

BigWorld is a multi-participant platform in which each user can create their own proprietary space for company assets, databases, simulations, and other information. Significantly, this platform introduces access for all parties involved in the appointment, design, management, and execution of the architectural project, while also offering access and functionality for manufacturing, construction, archiving, research, and public engagement. BigWorld thus aims to include all the entities involved in the exploration of architectural space.

Each project emerges inside a dedicated project space, which is created and accessed by collaborators working simultaneously and in parallel, with all datasets co-authored throughout the project's lifetime. These unique databases are accessible to all parties, while the evolving results are held as permanent three-dimensional archives, as revisitable libraries of projects, their assets, and their development histories.

DOI: 10.4324/9781003183105-26

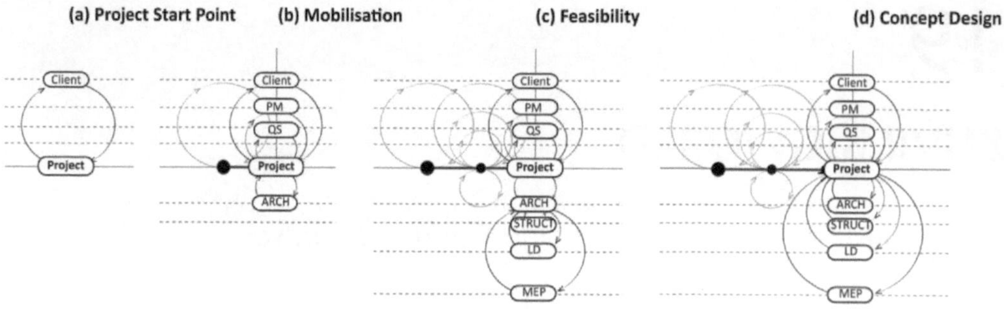

PM (Project Manager)
QS (Quantity Surveyor)
PO (Project Operators)
ARCH (Architects)
STRUCT (Structural Engineers)
LD (Lighting Designers)
MEP (Mechanical, Electrical and Plumbing Engineers)
AC (Acoustic Consultants)
HAAV (Home Automation + AV Consultants)
AC (Acoustic Consultants)
CTR (Contractors)
P+CA(Public + Commercial Access)

FIGURE 19.1 Assemblies of cross-disciplinary project authors within a pilot interior project

Source: Zaha Hadid Architects, Big World (2019)

Functional Distinction

BigWorld maintains the assigned contractual roles and liabilities of all collaborating disciplines within each project space.

Co-authoring cannot be conceptually discussed without also considering the individual data input from each author. The recent computerization of the architectural design process, with software-dependent design solutions that necessitate an adaptation of design workflows, has introduced additional constraints on the accessibility of project data, both during and after the project development. To date, any data associated with an individual author's production is initially rooted in its own software and platforms, with each of these independent data-cluster roots self-contained within the individual author's sphere. Accordingly, there is a need to synchronize the project's data organization to match the real-world contractual set-up and concurrently enable multi-author access.

The permanent global space within BigWorld provides access to the listed local project databases that serve each participant throughout each project, while this access is managed and assigned according to overall contractual agreements. This permanent space exists outside any given architectural project and is a prerequisite for the collaborative concept.

Capturing the Dynamic Process and the Project Timeline

Within BigWorld, each project ecosystem exists in four dimensions. All onboarded participants occupy either a pre-appointment space, an appointment space, or a post-appointment space, as viewed from the traditional architectural project timeline (Figure 19.2). While these periods are variable, and despite the contractual periods being limited, all participants can also maintain their professional presence and services within BigWorld after completing any specific project.

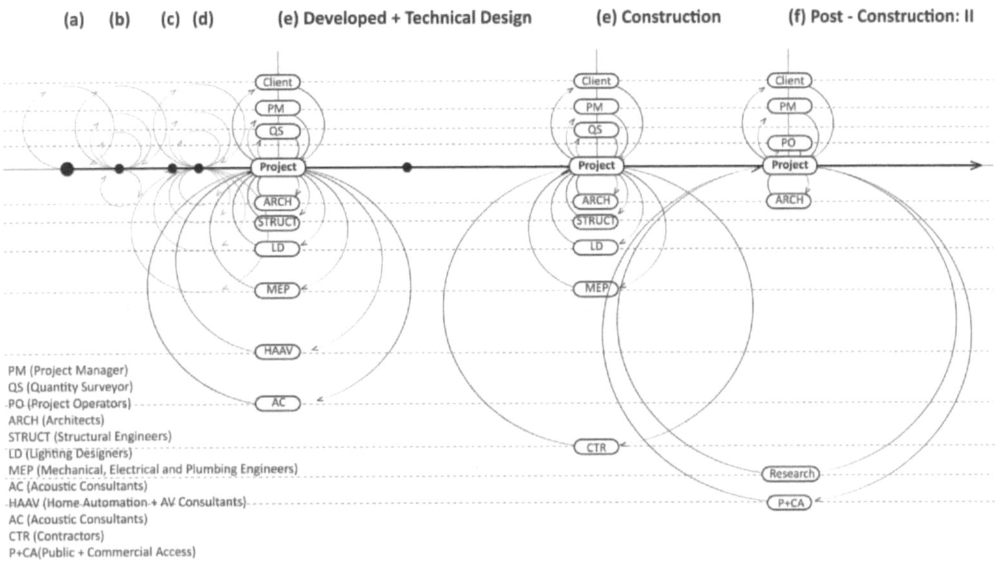

FIGURE 19.2 Project evolution over time, a pilot interior project

Source: Zaha Hadid Architects, Big World (2019)

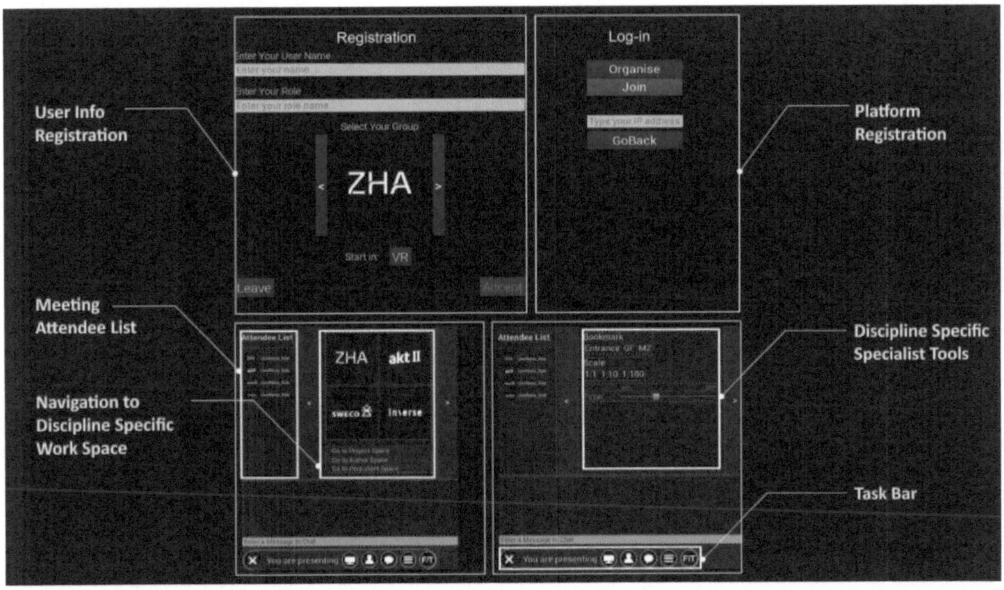

FIGURE 19.3 Sketch for a modular User Interface design for networked VR space

Source: Zaha Hadid Architects, Big World (2019)

Phase 1: Pre-Appointment

The onboarding process for BigWorld defines each participant's commercial roles and licences in accordance with the physical-world architectural industry. Each participant's entry recognizes the participant's profile, portfolio, qualifications, and professional registrations (Figure 19.3).

The requirement for all participants to obtain and maintain a compatible computer network and hardware system to enable any onboarding and subsequent participation is essential to BigWorld.

Phase 2: Appointment

The appointment phase aligns with the duration of the services contract, during which time the participants operate in the dedicated project space. These appointment-phase activities comprise project assembly formation and services delivery.

Within each project-level contractual role, all BigWorld content is integrated with various intellectual property profiles as part of each participant's onboarding and is dynamically controlled via tag systems. These responsive systems draw and call up the assets timestamps to manage privileged access to the infradata, as well as the copyrights, project packaging, and version controls.

Each contractual party is able to author their own assets and databases as required for their discipline and defined by the terms of their contract. The collaborative development process between these parties, which occurs inside the singular design space, allows project-wide evaluation with simultaneous reviewing and commenting by client parties and other participants. These multi-author contributions collectively form emergent libraries which reflect and document the architectural design discourse.

All outcomes are transferred to, and hosted within, BigWorld's permanent space, offering further commercial opportunities for participants.

Phase 3: Post-Appointment

Upon project completion, the project data is accessible for cultural archiving, review, and feedback, and for commercial record-keeping. This data can also be handed to any ensuing service provider, owner, academic body, or commercial partner for purposes such as public relations, academic research, and building management.

As part of BigWorld's holistic nature, its extensive documentation allows all cultural processes and project development narratives to be embedded within the infradata, providing a wide knowledge base for scientific research and a magnitude of embedded narratives for cultural evaluation. This information can be retrieved and experienced virtually using any standard VR hardware interface, and offers an unprecedented, cross-disciplinary perspective.

Outlook

A Co-Authoring Project-Hosting System and a BigWorld Future

BigWorld is envisaged as a platform for the production and integration of generative, computer-aided design methodology alongside contemporary architectural discourse. BigWorld's open ecosystem encompasses all aspects of design and production for all project parties, with visualization being just one of many possible functions. ZHVR is principally interested in the opportunity for collaborative design and production with permanent hosting of all resulting architectural solutions (Figures 19.4–19.8).

The scalability of the BigWorld platform accommodates projects of all sizes and reflects the varying complexity of architectural projects and their on-boarded project networks. Professional user profiles and BigWorld databases can be updated in real time, while the entire BigWorld

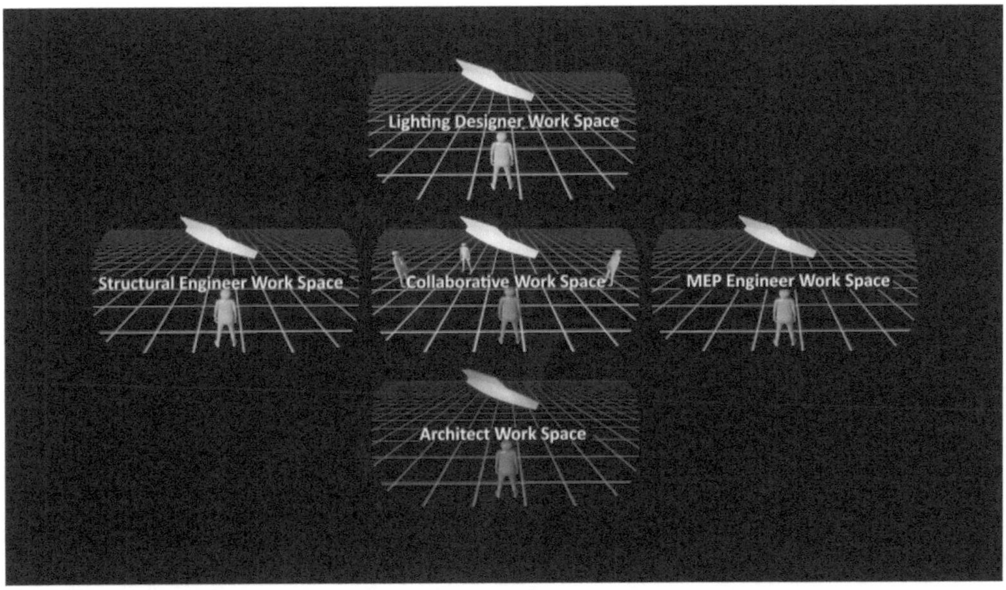

FIGURE 19.4 Networked VR co-authoring space with individual IP protection

Source: Zaha Hadid Architects, Big World (2019)

FIGURE 19.5 Networked VR reviewing space for client presentations

Source: Zaha Hadid Architects, Big World (2019)

network can be surveyed to inform the growth and adaptation of our physical world architectural project management system, potentially with the guidance of artificial intelligence.

ZHVR intends BigWorld to evolve into a self-referencing platform for design and digital construction, expanding the accessible design space through industry networking and multiple

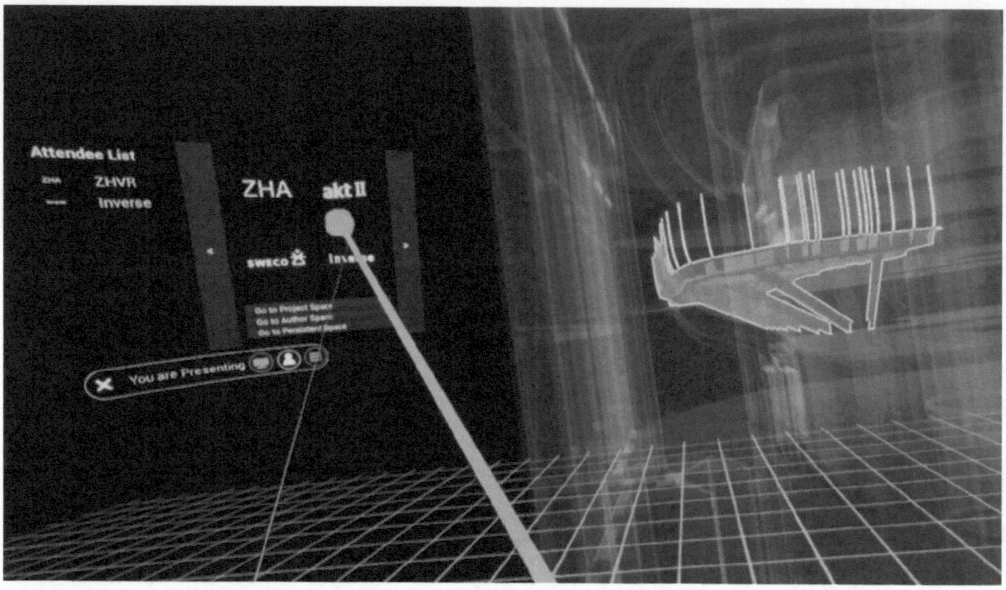

FIGURE 19.6 Networked VR authoring space for the structural engineer

Source: Zaha Hadid Architects, Big World (2019)

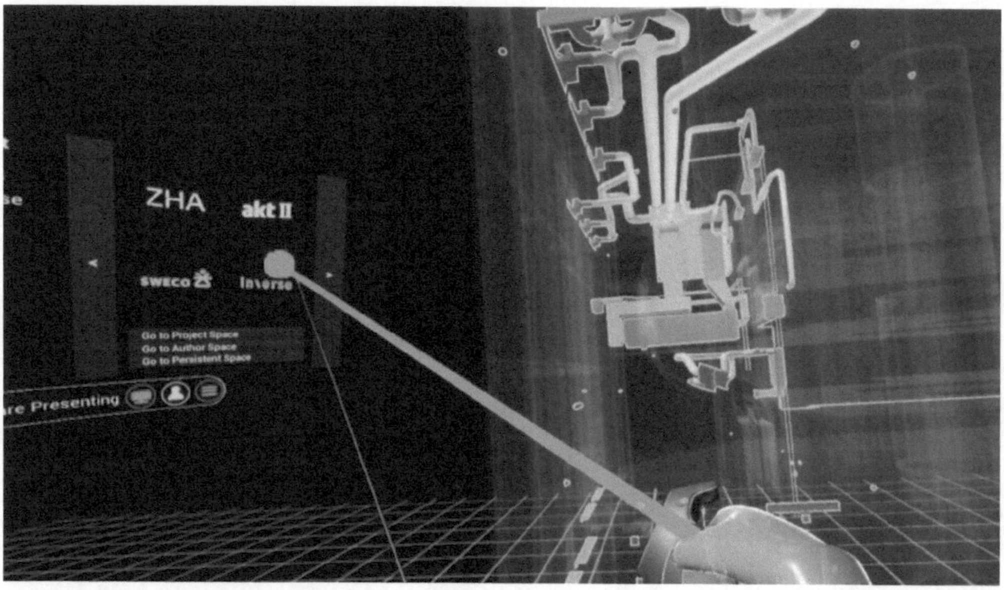

FIGURE 19.7 Networked VR authoring space for the MEP engineer

Source: Zaha Hadid Architects, Big World (2019)

hardware platforms. This permanent global space and its constituent project spaces will together create an active, accessible digital realm for architectural space, supporting the evolution of design. With this infrastructure in place, BigWorld will offer unique, permanent access to the entire architectural production ecosystem.

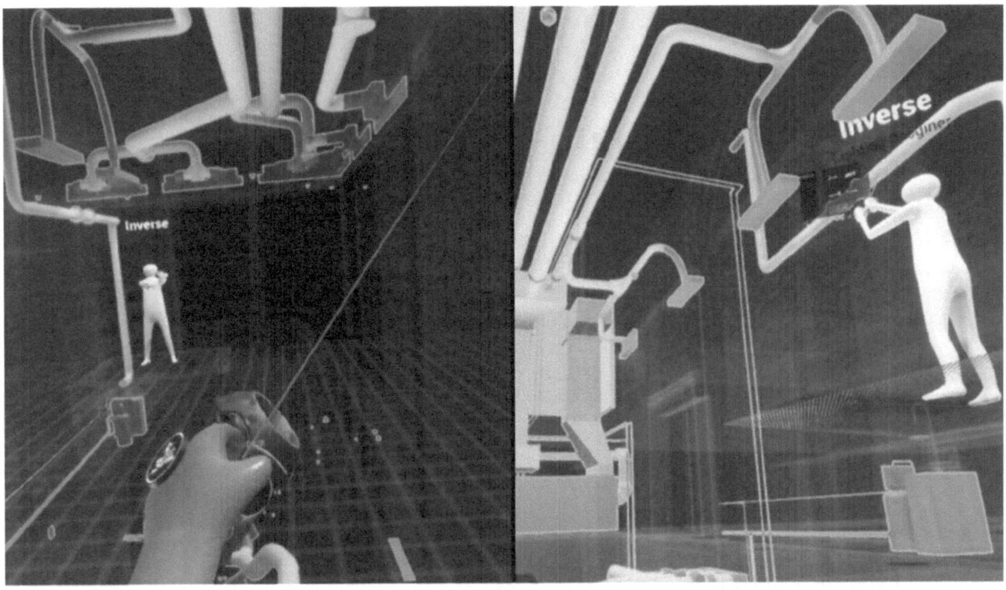

FIGURE 19.8 Networked VR authoring space for the MEP engineer and lighting designer

Source: Zaha Hadid Architects, Big World (2019)

Acknowledgements

ZHVR would like to thank our collaborators: Inverse Lighting Design, AKT II, Pharos Architectural Controls, Sweco, and Luke Fox for copy editing and proofing.

20

THE AESTHETICS OF HYBRID SPACE

Ruth Ron and Renate Weissenböck

Instigated from the fundamental characteristics of virtual reality (VR)—immersion and interaction—this project presents hybrid reality environments that explore the properties of 'spatial continuity'. The "Digital Hybrid" project consists of various virtual spaces with unique aesthetics, fused together by superimposing real living spaces onto digitized fragments of remote homes to produce augmented living spaces (Figure 20.1). The topic of digital continuity is investigated on multiple levels, enabling new modes of interaction and communication by virtually merging remote spaces, producing new forms of aesthetics, transporting spaces from real to virtual and vice versa, and exploring the transition from one space into another.

The project builds on the concept of blending disparate scenes into one consistent space. Using augmented reality (AR) capabilities, we leverage the newly established 'virtual continuity' to design unique hybrid environments, generating physically impossible domestic spaces configured according to social activities. By overlaying selected sections of people's homescapes, we create a range of compositions with differing qualities, scales, and densities.

The "Digital Hybrid" investigates the speculative extension of physical architecture, blending real environments with digital ones. It experiments with visual strategies for creating continuity between disparate spaces gathered from a socially networked group of people from the USA, Europe, the Middle East, and New Zealand. The domestic living areas are combined into a series of heterogeneous virtual environments, each with a specific theme guided by the type of social interaction it accommodates (Figure 20.2). The spaces are fused into a 'smooth' hybrid, gradually transitioning from one to the other. They maintain their unique qualities, while creating a superimposed sense of aesthetics.

In much the same way as artistic techniques, such as early 20-century avant-garde collage and assemblage, were adapted for personal computer software GUI, this project applies 'cut', 'copy', and 'paste' operations to three-dimensional domestic sections. This generates new conditions that 'passively' respond to or 'actively' stimulate social atmospheres, such as intimate conversations between friends or lively cocktail parties (Figure 20.2). The spatial combinations play with traditional perspective, gravity, and physical coordinates by assembling, rotating, and scaling fragments, free from physical restraints (see Figures 20.1–20.4).

Process

The workflow used to generate these spatial configurations started with meticulous photo-capturing of each collaborator's spaces. The sequence of photographs needed to be taken in a specific

DOI: 10.4324/9781003183105-27

FIGURE 20.1 A hybrid space with all five participants' living rooms (New York, Florida, Israel, Austria, New Zealand), consisting of 3D mesh models. Top (from left to right): models of each living space, selected fragments of each person's living space, conglomerated model. Bottom: perspective.

way—gradually moving around the room to capture images with largely overlapping content. Subsequently, the photo sequences were imported into photogrammetry software (Agisoft Metashape). According to the camera positions when the images were taken, the software constructs 3D point clouds, meshes, and texture maps from the image information. The visual qualities of the resulting 3D models were affected by the number of original photos, the amount of overlap of adjacent photos, the resolution, and the light conditions in the room. In addition, the settings of the photogrammetry software defined the precision and density of the point clouds and meshes which were generated. We discovered that each and every step in this complex procedure can create curiously unexpected self-replications, artificial topographies, glitches in surface continuity, and fragmentation of space itself.

In the next step, the models were imported into 3D-modelling software (using Rhinoceros 3D). We split and exploded the scanned rooms and recombined their fragments according to the imagined activity in the hybrid space, depending on the occasion and number of participants. Several hybrid space combinations were therefore created as 3D environments, then loaded into an AR application (Fologram). By connecting the computer to mobile phones equipped with this specific application and utilizing them as AR devices, we were able to spatially experience

FIGURE 20.2 A sequence of hybrid space compositions created according to different social scenarios: top—tea-time; middle—book club; bottom—cocktail party; perspective of 3D mesh models

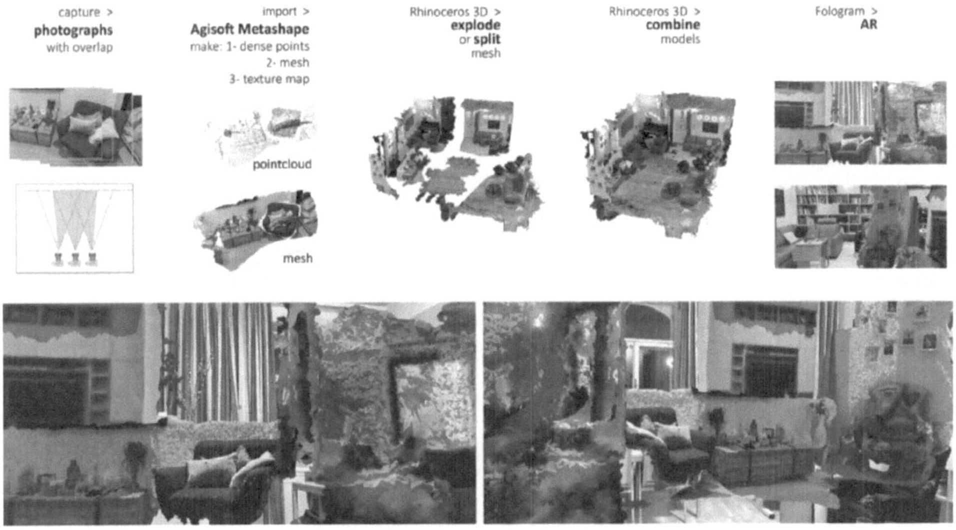

FIGURE 20.3 Top: description of the 3D model construction process (from left to right)—photo-capturing, photogrammetry modelling, 3D editing, 3D hybrid construction, AR implementation back into the domestic space. Bottom: images of an AR hybrid environment using Fologram in Austria.

FIGURE 20.4 Top: experimental studies of transitional modes of hybrid space formations, perspectives of 3D meshes and point cloud models. Bottom: hybrid space variation, consisting of 3D mesh models and point cloud models.

the hybrid constructs in 1:1 scale, as a continuation of our real living spaces into the digital fragments of our friends' homes in distant locations (Figure 20.3).

Conceptually, using rapidly advancing technological developments, we imagine that the spatial conglomerations could be reconfigured according to different needs, such as the activities of the participants, different occasions, or guests moving through the space. As shown in Figure 20.4, these environments could consist of solid surfaces and point clouds cross-dissolving and reassembling.

Reflecting on the project, we envisage that such hybrid spaces can extend and enhance the sensorial experiences of the participants. This has the potential to change the way in which we communicate and interact with each other, using a new kind of social-spatial platform in which our environments are augmented by digital visualization, while allowing us to remain anchored to the real world of our home. In developing this project, we discovered many opportunities that we would like to investigate in the future. By overcoming the geographical separation of traditional architecture, we aim to extend the visual experience of the space with additional acoustic and haptic qualities.

Acknowledgements

The authors wish to thank the collaboration of Dror Goldberg (New York, USA), Rebeka Vital (Ramat Hasharon, Israel), and Michael Weir (Wellington, New Zealand).

21

VOXELCO—PLAYING WITH COLLABORATIVE OBJECTS

Alexander Grasser

VoxelCO explores the potential of playing with collaborative objects in real, augmented, and mixed realities, proposing an architecture of socially augmented fuzzy formations.

"We learn about our reality through exploration, observation and play", Galit Ariel argues, in her book *Augmenting Alice* (Galit, 2017, p. 170). Exploration and observation are quite familiar in our world of efficient architectural design and education, but usually there is not much play. Collaborating and playing with clients, colleagues, students, objects, and discrete units offers a huge potential if we look at it in the way Ian Bogost proposes: "Play is in things, not in you" (Bogost, 2016, p. 91). Playing with collaborative objects in real, augmented, and mixed realities involves deep engagement with them until they reveal their capacities, potentials, and something new. As Bogost puts it: "Fun is the feeling of finding something new in a familiar situation" (Bogost, 2016, p. 6): collaborative objects are trying to find these fun moments in a familiar architecture.

This project proposes the application of the architectural platform VoxelCO, a platform that enables us to interact, engage, and play with collaborative objects. It is developed as a multi-player, cross-platform application running on desktop PCs and mobile devices.

VoxelCO provides a platform for playful engagement in multiple realities in Digital, Augmented, and Real Playgrounds (Figure 21.1). In the Digital Playground, VoxelCO provides a continuous shared environment that allows for real-time collaboration and participation. Online players can instantiate voxels individually or together with other online users, to aggregate shared voxel formations. In this highly dynamic design environment, a metaverse of fuzzy voxel formations emerges. The Augmented Playground, VoxelCO, running on mobile phones, extends this playful engagement to multiple realities by enabling real-time collaboration in augmented reality (Figure 21.2). Augmented reality provides a sense of scale, density, and resolution, as well as a deep engagement with the virtual formations. Furthermore, it encourages social interaction, as multiple users can discuss every design decision with each other, therefore socially augmenting the voxel formations. In the Real Playground, a set of discrete wire-grids and connectors are used as real building blocks (Figures 21.3 and 23.4). VoxelCO's augmented reality overlay provides step-by-step instructions to assemble the voxel formations.

"Design can become massively accessible through the participation of users via websites and video games, where relevant patterns are inevitably scarce and acknowledged as design contributions", Jose Sanchez (2019, p. 27) argues in "Architecture for the Commons". VoxelCO tries

DOI: 10.4324/9781003183105-28

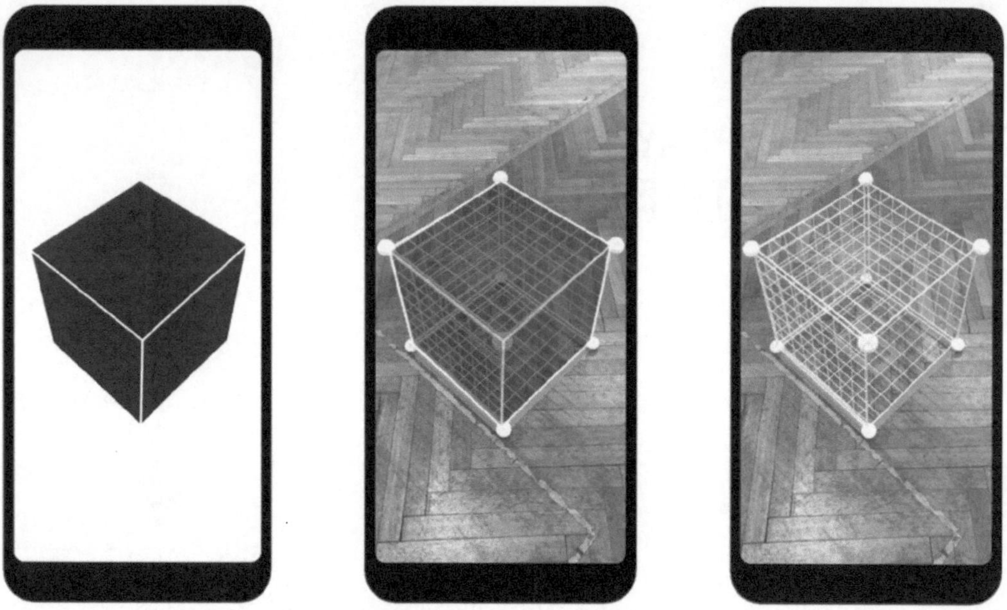

FIGURE 21.1 Digital, Augmented, Real Playgrounds

FIGURE 21.2 Collaborative VoxelCO gameplay at the Augmented Playground

to follow this idea with a simple game logic and a focus on social interaction and part-to-part collaboration. It is an architectural platform that is highly accessible, providing integrated augmented reality to engage deeply with collaborative objects.

Acknowledgements

The author wished to thank the following collaborators: VoxelStage Collaborators: Alexandra Parger (NanaDesign), Anna Brunner (Fifteen Seconds); VoxelStage Tutors: Alexander Grasser, Alexandra Parger, Eszter Katona, Kristijan Ristoski; VoxelStage Students: Nadina Bajric, Emir

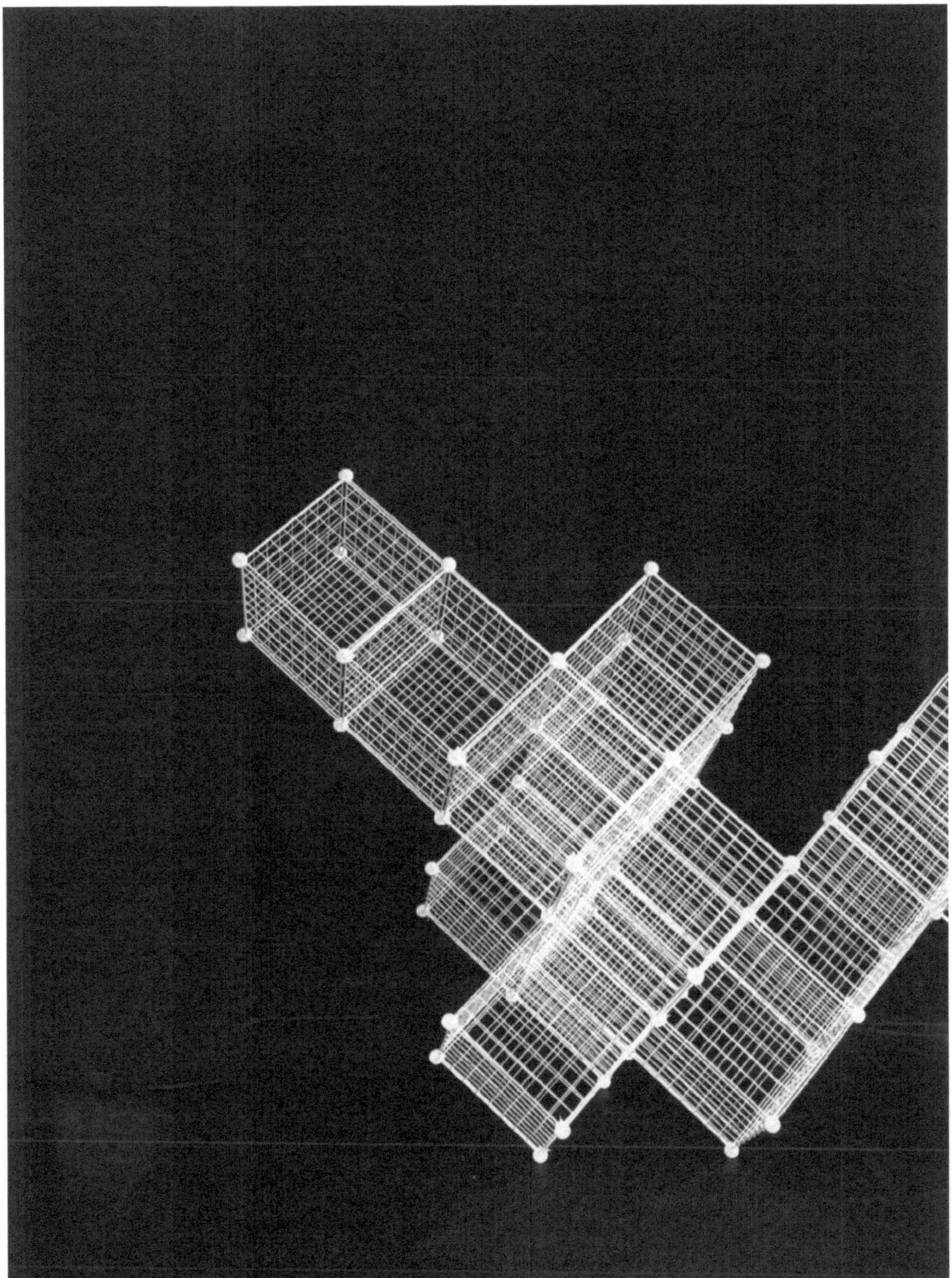

FIGURE 21.3 Socially aggregated voxel formations at the Real Playground

Dostovic, Dijana Imsirovic, Jelena Josic, Larisa Kolasinac, Anela Milkic, Inas Dizarevic, Fabian Jäger, Matea Kelava, Bianka Marjanovic, Sali Ren, Sarah Salkovic, Anela Smajlovoic, Mirna Vujovic, Fabian Rigler, Cornelis Backenköhler; Institute of Architecture and Media, Prof. Urs Hirschberg.

FIGURE 21.4 Case study project: VoxelStage

References

Bogost, I. (2016) *Play Anything: The Pleasure of Limits, the Uses of Boredom, and the Secret of Games*. New York: Basic Books.

Galit, A. (2017) *Augmenting Alice: The Future of Identity, Experience and Reality*. Amsterdam: BIS Publishers.

Sanchez, J. (2019) 'Architecture for the Commons: Participatory Systems in the Age of Platforms', in Retsin, Gilles (ed.) *Architectural Design* (89) 'Discrete: Reappraising the Digital in Architecture'. London: Wiley.

6.2

Experiencing Space

22

MVRDV VIRTUAL SPACE

María López Calleja

As a research-driven architectural practice, our work at MVRDV draws on the cutting edge of architectural knowledge, incorporating research and thinking in urbanism, sustainability, sociology, materials development, and more: our interest transcends architectural style, residing more in architectural design methodology. Our methods allow us to research the questions surrounding our projects in terms of programme, context, and typology.

However, we understand that our approach can be overwhelming for some people. Our designs often push the boundaries of what people assume architecture can do. In order to facilitate open and productive discussions, we believe that architecture needs to speak to people immediately. We aim to create remarkable architecture that needs to be understandable and hence also draw on the cutting edge of architectural representation.

Years ago, MVRDV presented their work with screenshots of 3D software onto which black cut-outs of people had been pasted, in order to give an idea of scale (Figure 22.1 and 22.2). Since then, the technological standard has been raised; computer games and movies are the new common ground. Because of this, people's willingness (or perhaps even ability) to read abstract impressions has declined, both among the general public and our clients.

New technologies now enable us to launch all kinds of visions of the future, from the functional and realistic to the utopian and provocative, and to make them understandable for all audiences. Applications incorporating virtual reality (VR) and augmented reality (AR) technologies, for example, have a wide range of uses, from design and collaborative decision-making to construction—and ultimately the presentation of the project. New VR devices enable us, as designers, to take clients and future users inside conceptual designs, as can be seen in the following four projects.

Markthal

The Markthal is a sustainable combination of food, leisure, living, and parking, a building in which all functions are fully integrated to celebrate and enhance their synergetic possibilities. With its unique arched structure and unusual achievement of turning a private development plan into a public building, the Markthal makes Rotterdam home to a new urban typology, a hybrid of market and housing. It was also one of the first buildings in the world that could be seen through augmented reality.

DOI: 10.4324/9781003183105-30

FIGURE 22.1 Impressions of the Oslo Opera project, MVRDV, 2000

FIGURE 22.2 Impressions of the Oslo Opera project, MVRDV, 2000

FIGURE 22.3 The Markthal in AR

Source: Image from HNI, Het Nieuwe Instituut, 2014

In 2010, the Netherlands Architecture Institute (NAI) developed the world's first augmented reality architecture application, named Sara. Users could view information on existing buildings and browse through 3D models of buildings in development, featuring photos, video, 3D models, scale models, and interesting details about each building design. The first building to appear in 3D via Sara, almost five years before the project was completed in real life, was the Markthal.

Users standing in the Markthal site, which broke new ground when the app was launched, could point their phone at the construction site, and the app would show photos, video, 3D models, and details of the Markthal design (Figure 22.3).

Supervision of Eindhoven City Centre

MVRDV founding partner Winy Maas was selected as one of three supervisors invited to oversee the development of an area of the city. Entrusted with the city centre, MVRDV launched a study of the area to produce guidelines for how Eindhoven could develop under the supervision of Winy Maas.

The research aimed to show how the city could grow with the provision of more housing, mixed-use facilities, and green public spaces, and ultimately how the city could strengthen its position as the centre of Brainport Eindhoven, the leading innovation, technology, and research region in the Netherlands.

In collaboration with the municipality of Eindhoven and Dutch Rose Media, MVRDV presented the project during the 2018 Dutch Design Week with an exhibit named *Future040*.

In a large empty greenhouse on Stadhuisplein, visitors had the opportunity to walk through a 5 m × 6 m 3D model to explore the future centre of Eindhoven using AR-enabled tablets provided in the exhibition (Figures 22.4–22.6).

FIGURE 22.4 The Future040 exhibition space and future centre of Eindhoven in AR, Dutch Design Week 2018

FIGURE 22.5 The Future040 exhibition space and future centre of Eindhoven in AR, Dutch Design Week 2018

Visitors could select certain future city projects, and artists' impressions and access further information about the projects. After visiting the Design Dutch Week stand, they could take home a card (Figure 22.6) and use the Future040 app to explore a small 3D model of the city.

Zaanstad Cultural Cluster

The centre of Zaanstad has been transformed since 2001 to comply with the style of the nearby UNESCO World Heritage site, the Zaanse Schans. The architectural highlights of this transformation include the city hall, in the shape of oversized Zaan houses, and the Inntel hotel, which resembles a large stack of the same green houses.

In 2015, MVRDV won the competition to design the Zaanstad Cultural Cluster. Our proposed design is, of course, also inspired by the history of the Zaan region and the traditional Zaan houses. We began with a compact volume and then turned the typical Zaan house inside out, creating a complex arrangement of internal spaces with a film theatre, library, performance centre, pop music centre, music school, design centre, and local radio station (Figure 22.7).

In order to present the spatial arrangement of the design, we took the opportunity to stage virtual meetings 'inside' the in-progress design, using simplified models in the initial design stages, then moving to more elaborate ones. This enabled us, together with the client and stakeholders, to walk around the site in a virtual tour of the design, exploring potential modifications together.

FIGURE 22.6 Supervision of Eindhoven City Centre, MVRDV, 2017. Image used in the card to download the Future 040 app.

FIGURE 22.7 Zaanstad Cultural Cluster, MVRDV, 2015

Resilient by Design

In 2018, as part of the international HASSELL+ team, MVRDV re-imagined a series of San Francisco Bay Area waterfront communities in the Resilient by Design Bay Area Challenge. This called on entrants to develop plans that responded to urgent environmental and emergency needs, but also to create vibrant, fundamentally public places for everyday use. Bringing Dutch expertise to the team, MVRDV helped to ensure that HASSELL+ understood water: designing for water, living with water, and the immense social potential that waterfront places offer communities when they are connected to them.

The resulting proposal envisioned a network of green spaces, creeks, and revived high streets that would serve as points of collection, connection, and water management from the ridgeline to the shoreline and across the bay via an enhanced ferry network.

For residents, though, the scale of the transformation required throughout an entire region can be difficult to comprehend—not to mention the scale of the global challenges that necessitate such a project. Part of our competition entry therefore included a method for contextualizing the proposal on a more familiar scale.

MVRDV developed a toolbox of ideas to facilitate these urban transformations. In order to engage future users, we proposed an AR approach that could overlay toolbox elements onto physical spaces, melding imagined design solutions with reality and thus bridging the potential disconnect that Bay Area residents might feel between their everyday reality and their resilient potential future (Figure 22.8 and 22.9).

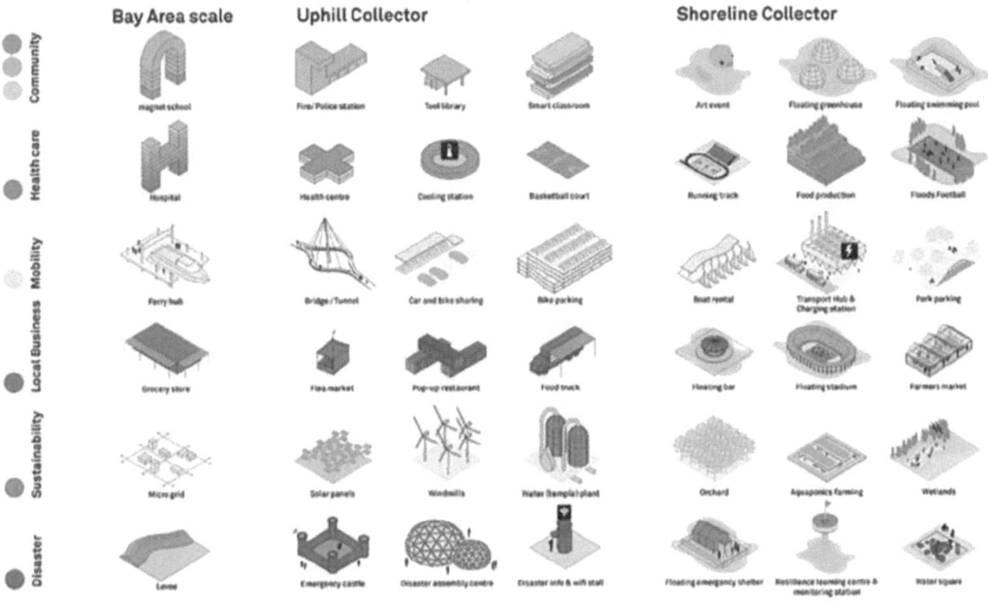

FIGURE 22.8 AR app collage. Resilient by Design, MVRDV, 2018

FIGURE 22.9 AR app collage. Resilient by Design, MVRDV, 2018

23

THE DIGITAL ARCHIVE

Eva Castro

The Digital Archive '3 Iterations'

The project(s) explore(s) the 'generic', a building type without a specific site and time, as a means of challenging preconceived cultural conditions, the 'known' and the 'appropriate', to create experimental *prototypes* whose specificity does not emerge from the regulative condition of a specific place but from the environmental fictions they are subjected to. The building's temporality is that of a desired future, and, as such, the consistency of a narrative was prioritized over the 'real' constraints of a specific environment. The 'time' in which our prototype sits is understood not as mere actuality but as an experimental field in which questions are prompted and onto which designs can be explored without the stifling weight of actual parameters. Hence, designing the 'time' in which the building exists requires understanding 'time' as a history to be made, in which we, as designers and as world-makers, must be active participants. We confront (pre)existing typologies in order to embark on the adventure of inventing new configurations and cater for new building-forms with digital/analogue (co)existence. The programme is to organize in space and time, through a crafted narrative, a series of interfaces, material or otherwise, between analogue atmospheres and digital environments.

Crafting Digital Tools: VR

Within the projects, a sensitiveness was fostered, much like that of an artisan, stemming from the utilization of specific tools and developed by crafting skills combined with end-pieces (Figures 23.1–23.3). The final work is therefore a synthesis of the relationship between design agency, future experience, and the employment-integration of such tools in the design process. The work presents an exploration of what is essentially the creative potential of such tools and their capacities to make us envision rather than visualize other experiences. Hence, the students were introduced to VR as a means of production, not taken directly as a means of phenomenological representation (not only), but as a new tool through which design can challenge aprioristic notions of place, type, and narrative, which therefore involved questioning the linear accumulation of commodified experiences of spaces, in time. Within this hyperreal context, the relationship between what we call 'material' and 'digital' is readdressed and thus becomes the main driving forces for the projects.

DOI: 10.4324/9781003183105-31

FIGURE 23.1 The proto-cemetery "THE TRANSITION"

Source: Grace Teo (supervisor Prof. Federico Ruberto)

Along the project(s) we discussed and explored solutions based on several initial questions.

How can new models be crafted that neither denigrate the virtual nor obliterate the sublime possibility of physical experience?

What does it mean to design a space that will cater for deep interaction between analogue and digital experiences?

What material spatial articulation is needed to engage-mediate with the digital organization or archives of 'memory'?

What is the role of VR and the architect's tool in such creative mediation?

How do we position ourselves as designers in the face of such developments?

Is the physical dematerialization of space experience exponential throughout our contemporary world, and would any act of resistance to this trend be puerile?

If so, what constructive alternative to the so-called disappearance of physical agency could we offer?

How will we employ VR-AR to craft new narratives and spaces that resist pure consumption?

FIGURE 23.2 The future theatre "ATLAS"

Source: Ashley Chen (supervisor Prof. Calvin Chua)

Acknowledgements

The author wishes to thank Calvin Chuan, Jason Lim, Federico Ruberto, Deniz Manisali (Studios Leads), Daril Ho (TA), and the IRL team (VR/AR).

FIGURE 23.3 The museum of memory "STORIES FROM THE ANTHROPOCENE"

Source: Megan Moktar (supervisor Prof. Denise Manisali)

24

SIRIUS GARDENS—THE BUILDING

Sean Pickersgill, Jason Semanic, and Chris Traianos

The Sirius Gardens project is a current exploration of design potential located in Sydney, Australia. The project concerns the adaptive re-use of an existing social housing complex, Sirius, originally completed in 1980. The building is sited in one of the most prominent locations within the Sydney Central Business District (CBD) in an area known colloquially as *The Rocks*. It is also in close proximity to well-known local icons such as the Sydney Harbour Bridge and, across Circular Quay, the Sydney Opera House.

Extreme developments in land value within the Sydney metropolitan area, and in the central city area, has made the Sirius building the subject of controversy. Considerable public backlash and political manoeuvring convinced local regulatory bodies to ensure that, in the event of a sale, the building would be protected from demolition by placing height restrictions on any new construction. Hence, the height of new work was limited to that of the approach apron of the Harbour Bridge. This limit was arrived at by artificially insisting that any new work must not impede the view of the Sydney Opera House from the Harbour Bridge pedestrian pathway.

Using the VR capabilities within the Oculus Rift, we have developed a project that employs the Oculus Rift headset for a fully immersive experience. The ability to reiteratively demonstrate the effect of design developments within the city context and to test the value of the viewing sightlines has been fundamental to the design process. The clients were concerned that the immersive experience accurately matched the expectations of the general public to be able to see the Opera House should any development of the Sirius Building be undertaken. As with most major projects that engage the general community, the ability to allow people to immerse themselves within the project encourages confidence in the design process overall.

While it was possible to create photorealistic renders that located the proposed development in its context and, by positioning the viewpoint, infer that no obstruction took place, we chose to employ the more immersive experience of VR, though with a diminished level of detail for the surrounding context (Figures 24.1–24.3 and 24.7). In this respect there was enhanced authenticity in demonstrating that the proposed development added to the skyline experience, without the distracting level of detail that photorealism brings. A 'clay' model of the Sydney Circular Quay and CBD area was employed to provide realistic scale of context, leaving detail to the proposed greenhouse structure to demonstrate transparency levels through the building (Figures 24.4–24.6).

Through the employment of VR technology, we were able to convince the clients of the viability of the proposal, and the non-standard approach to design compliance was only credible via the mediation of immersive technology.

DOI: 10.4324/9781003183105-32

FIGURE 24.1 General view, Circular Quay, Sydney, 2019

FIGURE 24.2 The rocks context, Circular Quay, 2019

FIGURE 24.3 Looking towards the Harbour Bridge, Circular Quay, 2019

FIGURE 24.4 Inside the Botanic Lantern 1, Sirius Building, Circular Quay, 2019

FIGURE 24.5 Inside the Botanic Lantern 2, Sirius Building, Circular Quay, 2019

FIGURE 24.6 Main Botanic Lantern Gallery, Sirius Building, Circular Quay, 2019

FIGURE 24.7 Looking across Sydney Harbour, Sirius Building in context, 2019

25

FORM AXIOMS

'The Politics of Mapping the Invisible'

Eva Castro

Our Testing Ground: The South China Sea

This studio follows our previous work's methodology taking on the challenging task of rethinking the area that circles around the *South China Sea* and its geopolitical and material ecology through the reconceptualization and design of large-scale infrastructures and localized-material assemblages. We seek areas of fragile ecologies, where the ocean's rising levels are beyond a hypothetical threat in the long term, but already an ongoing reality, and project possible and unforeseen futures.

To start thinking about how to devise strategies of cooperation and co-inhabitation in the South China Sea, one needs to shift from design taken as a process to deploy 'objects', to design as a process to fabricate processes—strategic/tactical, resilient in the short term, and directed in the long run. One must start thinking of the territory not as the material surface controlled once and for all (by national sovereignties and private agents) but as a recombinable network of agents, thinking how differences and diversities of 'earth' could/should be redistributed via the invention of new types of productions, of logistics, of inhabitation, by new models able to forward the idea of different futures.

This is a laboratory of ideas (narratives, stories, and shapes) that try to give form to alternative modes of being-together on the planet.

Terms Central to Our Methodology Are

Infrastructure

Rather than approach the question of infrastructure as a cosmetic problem in need of being concealed, we treat it as an opportunity to engage with the machinic processes ranged across its sites. The critical role played by infrastructure in the organization and management of the city is recognized as the basis from which its operation can be further developed beyond its tendency to fragment and divide toward other possibilities.

We pursue the formal and material articulation of infrastructure, coordinating its operations with the territorial processes, forms, and parameters identified in the site, developing its relation to the ground, and elaborating its architectural composition.

DOI: 10.4324/9781003183105-33

Hybrid Strategies

Specifically, we ask: What's autonomy in nowadays multi-layered capital liquidity? How does one sustain its particular territorial 'form of life'? Within this framework, and given it is a 'design studio', the student is supposed to unfold the delicate knot; define the relationship between bottom-up and top-down strategies; 'decide' how to design in a complex, vast multi-stratified territory that requires both interpolation of data and more defined—ideologically defined—interventions.

Speculative Approach (Meta-Fiction and Ecology)

The projects here presented, through the deployment of AR, read the (in)tangible lines drawn by geology, energy (resources), and politics and map the invisible, describe the submerged, uncover the concealed. In doing so, we design a future. Designers are in this course strategists, writers, conceptual and morphological explorers. To design in the course is to map and bring out layers of 'controversies', to form an alternative milieu whence a new reality could germinate. Such new realities deploy virtual reality as the medium to exist, adopting the digital as a new form of material; developing an aesthetic that re-describes at its core notions of time and belonging; generating the 'strange' as an alternative to our often-wasted vision of the real, proposing novel ways to (co)existing and inhabiting the planet.

What emerges at the end of the studio are works that are politicized at core, designs that have the courage to look onto post-hyper-anthropocentric scenarios and that give now hopes to one primary mission: liberating thought from the enslaving forces that make it a victim of its own incapacities, and with such liberation imaging new forms of living together on earth, and possibly in a future, in one of its distant horizons (Figures 25.1–25.5).

FIGURE 25.1 "The Marine Collective"

Source: Ryan Teo

FIGURE 25.2 "Prototypical Plastic Formations in the S.C.S"

Source: Yanhan Lim

FIGURE 25.3 "New Operaism: Post Material Futures"

Source: Ian Soon

The studio aims at implementing ecological infrastructures as the main vehicle to introduce new narratives within the territory's interstices, envisaging strategies that will dwell on issues of connectivity, political-geographical adjacencies, and temporal conditions.

We craft para-consistent fictions by tweaking some of the constitutive elements of a specific/given reality that is selected as study case.

FIGURE 25.4 "New Operaism: Post Material Futures"

Source: Ian Soon

FIGURE 25.5 "'Repolder-amming': The Discretization of Mammoth Infrastructure"

Source: Weng Whern

'A reality' is taken and analysed with political, environmental, social, and physical-material lenses to reconstruct a model of its constitutive cores oftentimes hiding in plain sight—too complex to be fully captured by a plain gaze, or too intrinsically part of the phenomenological framework of each thought.

Acknowledgements

The author wishes to thank Federico Ruberto, the IRL team (VR/AR), and Daryl Ho (TA).

26

OH AMBIENT DEMONS

Ringlets of Kronos + Coronis 2020, Decoded

Marcos Novak

Inescapably, 2020.

How might *virtual aesthetics*—or the *aesthetics of virtuality*—inform our understanding of a year when, quite suddenly, billons of people were forced to Zoom into virtuality by a global pandemic that struck in the midst of massive social, political, and economic upheaval, unfolding in circumstances so persistently bizarre as to embarrass fiction itself?

Partially, this is a limited account of the making of two paired multi-user VR/XR works that together inform how virtual works can become articulate in addressing current concerns in the languages of **<mediated worlds>** and **<literate media>**.

- *Ringlets of Kronos* builds a virtual refuge against a premonition of airborne menace
- *Coronis 2020 Decoded* confirms the premonition and responds with a reminder of a forgotten ancient warning

Significantly, the exhibition was shown at the *Reed Gallery* of the Peter Eisenman–designed *Aronoff Center for Design and Art* at the *University of Cincinnati*. The overall exhibition, and the VR/XR works themselves, took their initial inspiration from the specifics of the place and situation, both formally and thematically.

Initially, the development of these projects began with an invitation to present an exhibition of my work in relation to the theme of **Time**.

Eventually, the overall exhibition emerged as:

Oh Ambient Demons • Ringlets of Kronos
ArchiMusic XR | Sculpting in Spacetime | Found Forces

The exhibition statement read:

KIKKINOΣ = CINCINNUS = RINGLET

Using everything from humble found forces to evolving notions of quantum mechanical time, this installation explores the many flavours of designated spacetime, from fixity to becoming, from Ananke to the multiverse. Cincinnatus, the curly haired, shares

DOI: 10.4324/9781003183105-34

his ringlets with Kronos (not to be confused with Khronos). Cycles of time entangle like Borromean Rings. Near and far, then and now, East and West, past and future, once seemingly independent of each other, can nevertheless never be extricated from one another. Shaping time evolves into sculpting in spacetime, inviting Tarkovsky's cinema of rhythms into the trans-cinematic fusion of AR (augmented reality), MR (mixed reality), VR (virtual reality), and emerging SVR (social virtual reality), into the enigmatic XR (x-reality), come what may.

Tangibly, these paired projects began as multi-user **VR** worlds on the **Sansar** platform and were extended as **XR** installations. Through the multi-user technologies provided by **Sansar**, the worlds can be accessed by anyone with a powerful-enough computer and connection. The platform provides all the necessary means of shared co-presence: avatars, voice communication, gesture support, interactions with objects and other avatars, teleportation, three-dimensional sound, and more.

Socially, the immersive effect is compelling, especially under lockdown—in these virtual spaces, one encounters the avatars of others located anywhere on the planet and can directly speak to them as if they were co-present. This co-presence is, in fact, so effective that the invasion of personal space may become an issue—the remote other may be felt to be standing too close—but, by the same token, in the context of pandemic social-distancing, some comfort in closeness with others may also be felt.

Conceptually, these projects relate directly to our experience with *COVID-19* and all that has accompanied it. Combined, they modulate whatever expressive means are available and correlate the modulations with evocative references, blending percept with concept. For instance, the foggy atmosphere (thick, green, debris-filled, seemingly toxic, like the pandemic) morphs into *Blade Runner 2049*–like orange skies, resonant with those of the San Francisco fires of the summer of 2020. Everything perceptual also engages alternating layers of myth and fact, and the ultimate protagonist is the **architectural quality** of the space itself.

Formally, the projects are generated by the interplay of several *formal principles* against several *systems of signification*. The formal principles are derived from the generative rules of various **curled** and **helical** shapes, including:

1. the multi-layered formal logic of the Peter Eisenman building itself
2. the ringlets (curly hair, *cincinni* in Latin) of Lucius Quinctius Cincinnatus, for whom Cincinnati is named
3. the ringlets of Saturn (Kronos)
4. the turbulence of Jupiter (Khronos/Zeus)
5. plant morphology, especially the inflorescence pattern called *cincinnus*
6. elementary particle tracks, such as those seen in historical cloud, bubble, and, eventually, contemporary Hermetic particle detectors, such as those found at SLAC and CERN
7. Feynman diagrams
8. foliations of causal invariance hypergraphs (Wolfram Physics Project)
9. absolute and relative time

Computationally, the custom-written *Mathematica* code integrates the previously given principles into a recursive subdivision compositional algorithm, constrained to making optimal use of limited actual or virtual materials for maximal aesthetic effect. The 2D algorithm was used to generate a 63' x 13' site-specific composition for the longest gallery wall and was then extended to create equivalent 3D scattering compositions in virtual space. *Sansar scripting* provided interactive functionality for the VR worlds, while additional programming in *Max* provided algorithmically generated sound.

Architecturally, and very pointedly regarding the role of architectural expression in virtual space, the projects give highest priority to **space-as-medium**. The primary element of communication is the **architectonic quality** of space itself, not its nominal function or actual or virtual interactivity.

Aesthetically, the worlds both engage and challenge Baumgarten's notion of the '**aesthetic**', and also bring forward several notions of the 'virtual'. While every element of the worlds is aesthetically pleasing, narrow aesthetics as '**aesthesis**' (sensation) are shown to be severely limited. The projects augment narrow aesthetics with other means of signification and relevance, including the parallel and dialectical evocation of mythologies, sciences, and critical commentaries on difficult current events. Immersants are invited to explore the mythologies of **Time** and, especially, the myth of the Princess *Koronis*, astoundingly pertinent to our time when decoded. The elements of these myths are given tangible contemporary technological form in immersive VR/XR worlds that allow users to **feel** them before ever knowing the stories that they stem from. For the inquisitive, the stories lend depth that echoes through centuries of human experience.

May we find our own Chiron and come to trust our own Asclepius again. May our vaccines succeed.

FIGURE 26.1 Composite of generative principles derived from the figures of curled ringlets ("cincinni," κίκιννοι), relative and absolute time, branching patterns, biological inflorescence, turbulence, particle detector tracks, history and mythology, with references to Kronos, Khronos, Koronis, and Cincinnatus, among others

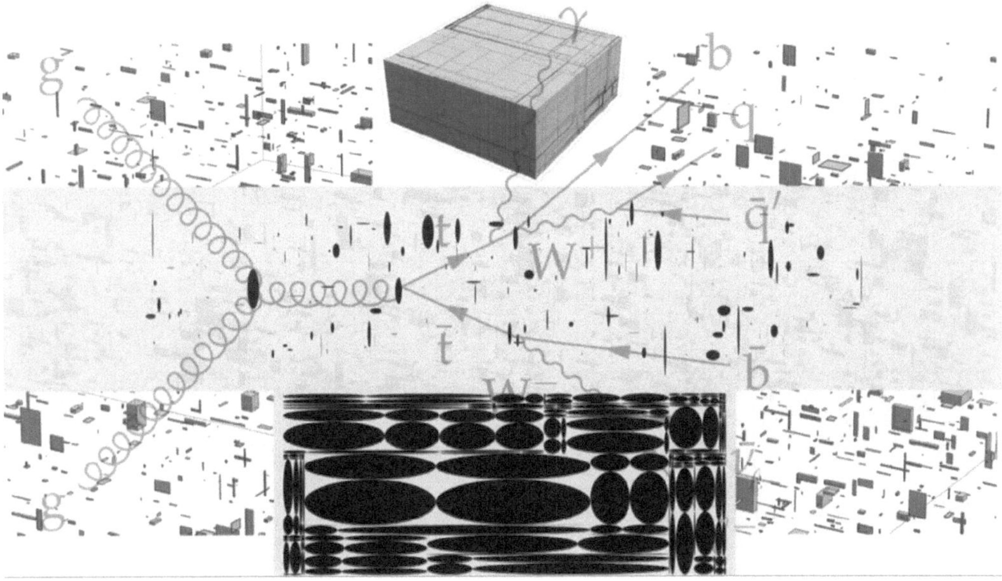

FIGURE 26.2 Composite of generative algorithms for composition of "divisive" mural and VR airborne pathogen debris field

FIGURE 26.3 View of 63' x 13' algorithmically composed mural, based on the same principles as those used in the 3D VR world

FIGURE 26.4 Composite view of local, remote, and online co-presence in multi-user virtual world

FIGURE 26.5 World view with avatar—from Kronos to Koronis: premonition of toxic atmosphere

FIGURE 26.6 World view with avatar

6.3

Enhancing Space

27

SKY GAZING TOWER

Kyriaki Goti and Christopher Morse

Sky Gazing Tower is an installation that aims to provide personal space for people who live in crowded urban environments and face everyday challenges such as social anxiety, stress, and agoraphobia (Figures 27.1 and 27.2). In parallel with the physical structure, a VR environment with a User Interface was developed that allows users to design their own structure (Figure 27.3). In this project, VR is used as a democratized tool for empowerment that encourages users to explore their needs for personal space and enables them to design a structure they feel comfortable in for themselves.

The physical structure gives each individual space and time to stare at the sky alone, whilst surrounded by a hanging translucent orange membrane that diffuses the light and creates a soothing environment. It is a low-cost, lightweight structure that can be easily assembled and transported, consisting of a white steel frame and vinyl orange membrane strips that hang loosely from the top ring. The membrane strips cover the upper part of the visitor's body, leaving the lower part visible to the public, clearly indicating that the tower is occupied. The translucent membrane creates a subtle connection with the external environment, whilst also providing a place which serves as a retreat.

The VR environment and User Interface are developed in Unity, a cross-platform game engine. Using the HTC VIVE VR system, users can experience the installation in a simulated urban environment and have the opportunity to virtually modify the structure and define their own personal space according to their needs and preferences. The bespoke User Interface allows for intuitive interaction and guides the user during the design process. This process is broken down into steps, so that only one feature of the installation can be modified in each step. Thus, non-experienced users with no design background can easily and quickly customize their personal space.

Each user can change the size, colour, and materiality of the installation and experience the results of these actions in the virtual space. The various designed outcomes are saved in a design library that expresses the different tastes and personal needs of the users. The VR tool developed in this project embraces the diversity of citizens living in big cities by giving everyone access to an intuitive design process.

DOI: 10.4324/9781003183105-36

FIGURE 27.1 Sky Gazing Tower installed on site

Source: Photo by Paul Vu

FIGURE 27.2 Inner view of the tower

Source: Photo by Paul Vu

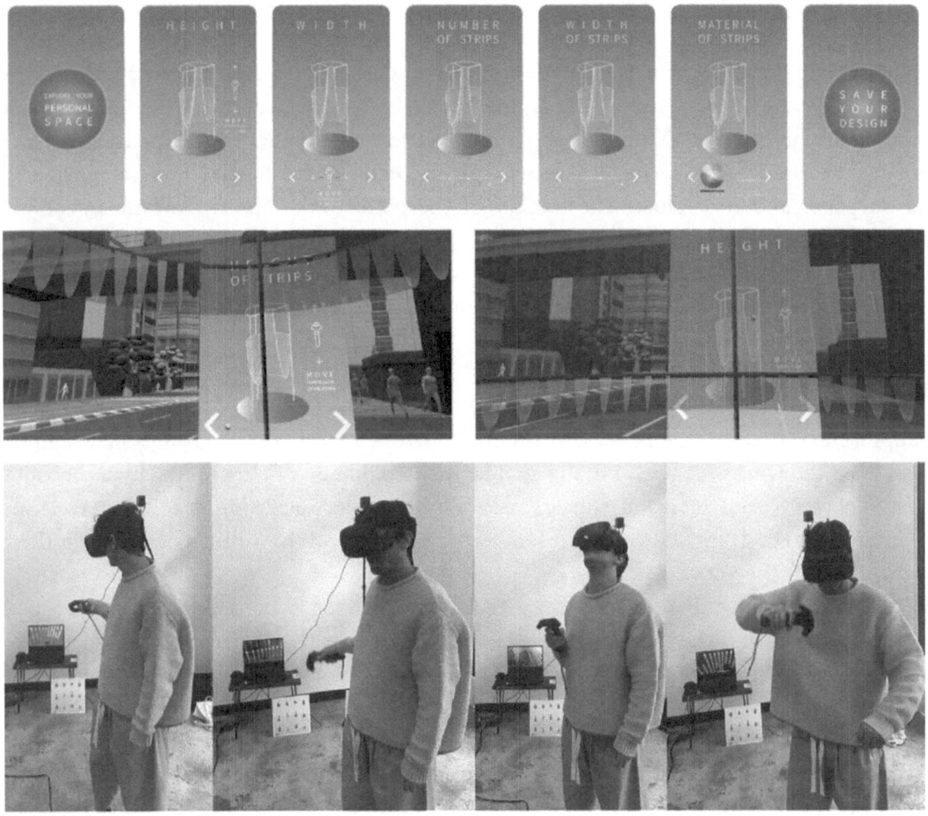

FIGURE 27.3 User Interface in virtual reality

Source: Photo by Paul Vu

28
IDENTITY

Rudolf Romero

The project IDENTITY was commissioned in 2018 by the Museum of Modern Art in Arnhem, a leading cultural institution in the Netherlands, for the development of a pilot version of a high-quality interactive virtual exhibition in WebVR. This virtual space needed to provide an alternative platform during a transitional period in which the museum was closed for renovation.

The WebVR Exhibition

For the pilot, we decided to focus on an exhibition of works on paper. The museum owns more than 9,000 drawings, prints, and collages, many of which have been forgotten during its long history and are hardly ever exhibited, partly due to the vulnerability of the medium.

During the renovation period, there was an opportunity to digitize and categorize these works on paper and re-evaluate the quality of the collection. One important aspect of the WebVR exhibition was that there was now an opportunity to make this process visible to the public and to show these works in a virtual world without the limitations of environmental factors such as light, which often makes it difficult to display such vulnerable works of art.

Design Plan

Our approach is based on the belief that the most critical aspect of any exhibition design is the way in which the works are contextualized. The added value of VR lies precisely in the fact that the design of the virtual environment can make a substantial contribution to the interrelation of the exhibited works. Both the works and the environment and the coherence between the two are significant for the general experience.

As a result, we formulated a conceptual framework that would develop the coherence between the works and the virtual environment, whilst also researching which aspects of the identity of a museum such as the one in Arnhem would remain when re-established a virtual form.

In the pilot exhibition, we decided that the concept of transitionality would provide us with a foundation for the design of the virtual space, since we believed there was a strong connection between the medium used for the works that would be exhibited (paper) and the current

DOI: 10.4324/9781003183105-37

conditions associated with the museum: both have the status of being in transition. Traditionally, a drawing or a sketch was a conceptual step between the initial brainstorming and the end result (such as a painting). Similarly, a museum without a building to display its collections is like an idea waiting to be conceptualized.

Development

A methodology was developed for sampling details from the etchings and drawings. The samples were used to create the virtual space and to refer to the works on display and the way in which they were conceived.

Part of our research into the translation of analogue techniques used in works produced on paper involved understanding of how simple lines, shadows, half-tone patterns, and watercolour techniques could be represented in a 3D environment (Figure 28.1). Eventually, exercises in perspective drawing (Figure 28.2), found in the Museum's collection, essentially provided us with a solution to bridge 2D and 3D, in order to contextualize the work within the environment.

UX

Visitors to the VR Museum can access the experience through a WebVR portal in their browser, either on a computer or a smartphone. They are able to navigate by focusing on arrow-shaped markers positioned throughout the environment. As can be seen in the images, the modules are two-dimensional at first and only expand to a 3D object, similar to an accordion, when the module is accessed (Figure 28.3).

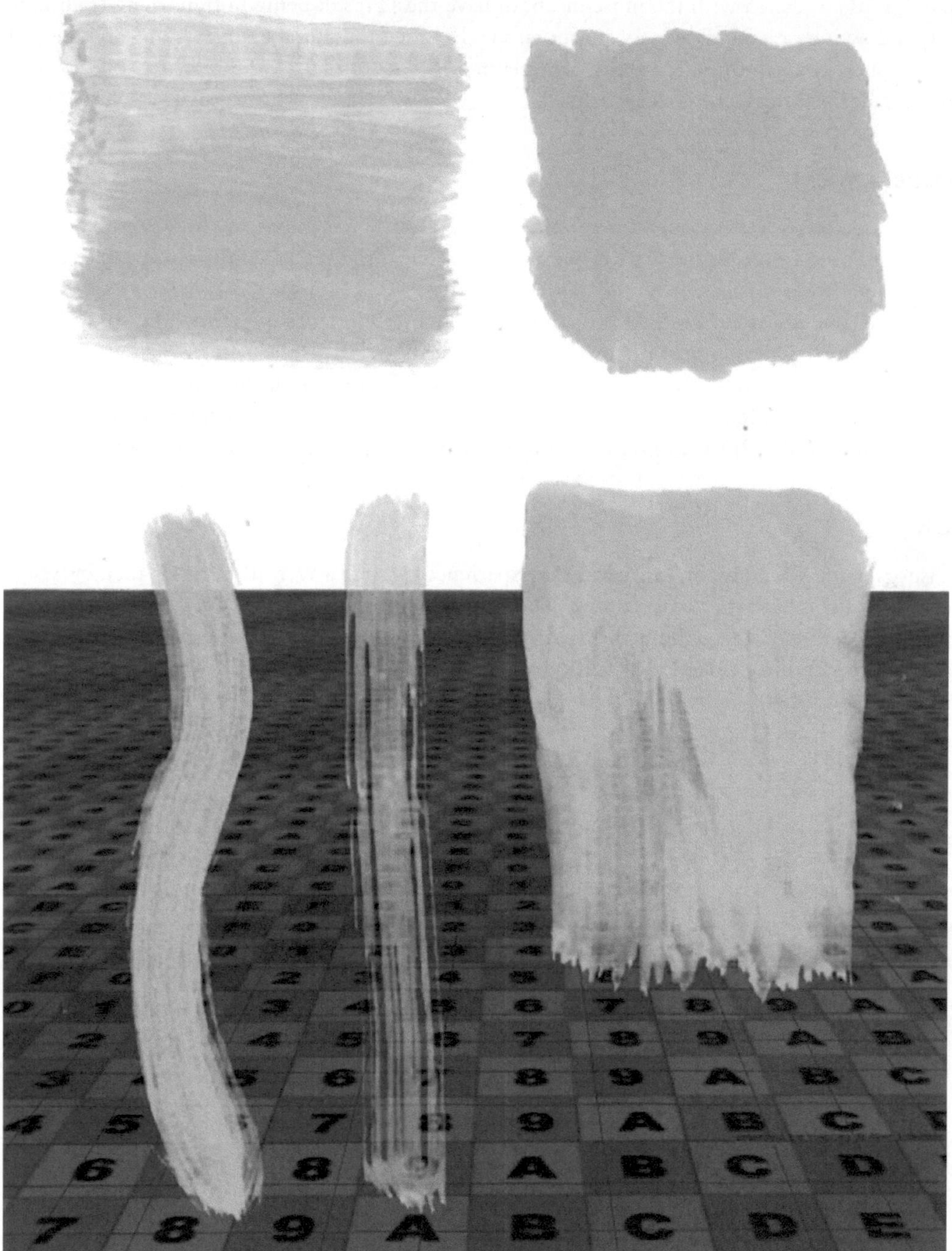

FIGURE 28.1 Sampling watercolour textures for testing in virtual space

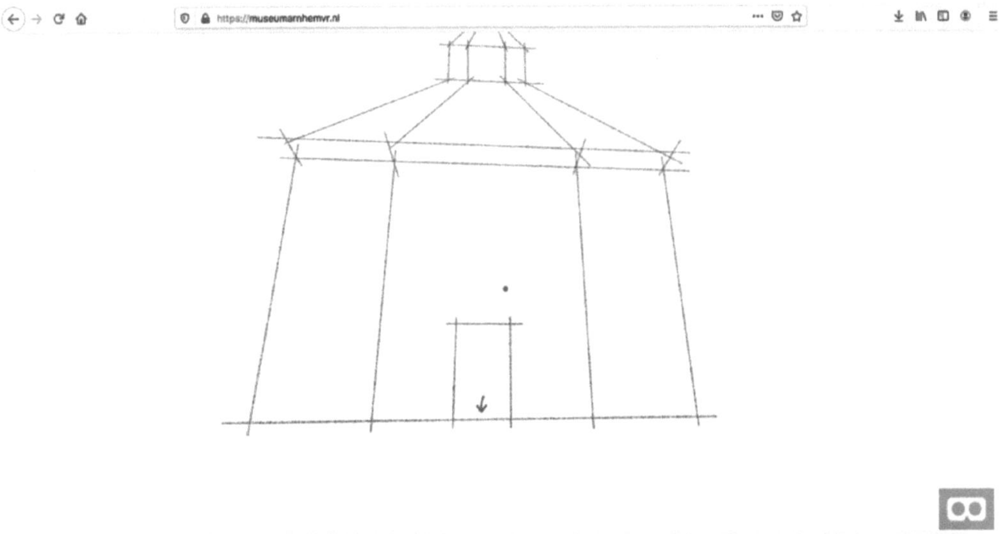

FIGURE 28.2 Users are able to access the virtual reality environment through their web browser, either on the computer or their smartphone.

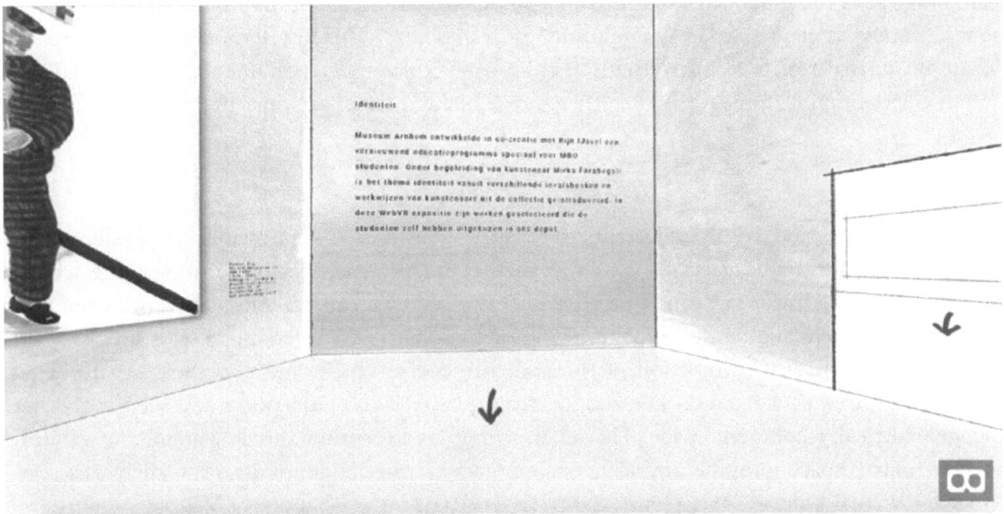

FIGURE 28.3 The arrow-shaped markers allow visitors to navigate freely in the virtual environment.

29

PERSPECTIVA VIRTUALIS

Julien Rippinger and Arthur Lachard

Introduction

The Perspectiva Virtualis installation explores the combination of perspective projection and architectural representation within the framework of augmented reality. Despite the ongoing technological developments, the significance of perspective in immersive architectural applications has not yet been regarded as a genuine research object. This installation contributes to the debate on virtual reality as an aesthetic medium by exploring a fundamental representational system and its implications in the specific context of augmented architectural representation.

Installation

Perspective projection is an underlying requisite of most AR applications implemented by smartphones, pads, or headsets. Their functionality usually arranges the observer, the screen, and the world in a linear fashion. The world is captured by a camera lens and transmitted on a screen, onto which 'augmented' imageries of virtual objects are overlapped. It is precisely the homologous perspective projection of the added imagery which connects the virtual objects with the captured background. The sought-after quality is the perception of a seemingly true and geometrically coherent space. However, while transforming the screen into a window opening onto a space lying behind it, the same space is also condemned to act solely as a container for virtual objects. As a counterpoint to this tendency, Perspectiva Virtualis focuses on space *per se* as the object being augmented, instead of the virtual object as an enhancement of space.

Perspectiva Virtualis proposes an AR application in which the core subject of augmentation is the interaction between a real space and a figurative space. Proposing the architectural section as an augmented spatial experience, we stress in a different manner the projective features of the previously highlighted elements—i.e., the observer's perception, the camera/screen coupling, and the augmenting imagery. The device itself acts as a digital mirror in which the screen becomes a reversed window opening towards the observer, hence overlapping the perspective projection depth with the space of the user's interactions (Figures 29.1 and 29.2). Moving towards or away from the screen, the user sees his reflection slicing through a virtual architectural space. The perspective sections are generated in real scale and calibrated to the camera's one-eyed central perspective (Figure 29.3).

DOI: 10.4324/9781003183105-38

FIGURE 29.1 Photograph of the Perspectiva Virtualis installation in the Artificial Realities exhibition: the performer, Aki Iwamoto, walks through the real-scale sections of the International Space Station visible on the mirroring screen in front of her. In addition to the software, the set-up consists of a computer, a webcam, and a projector.

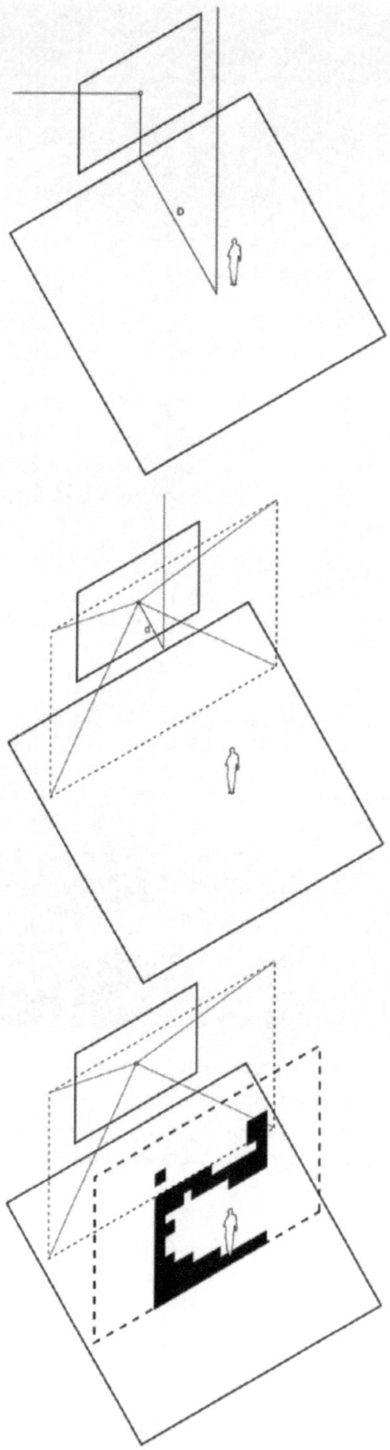

FIGURE 29.2 Axonometric scheme of the installation, showing the relationship between the screen and the user's perspective window

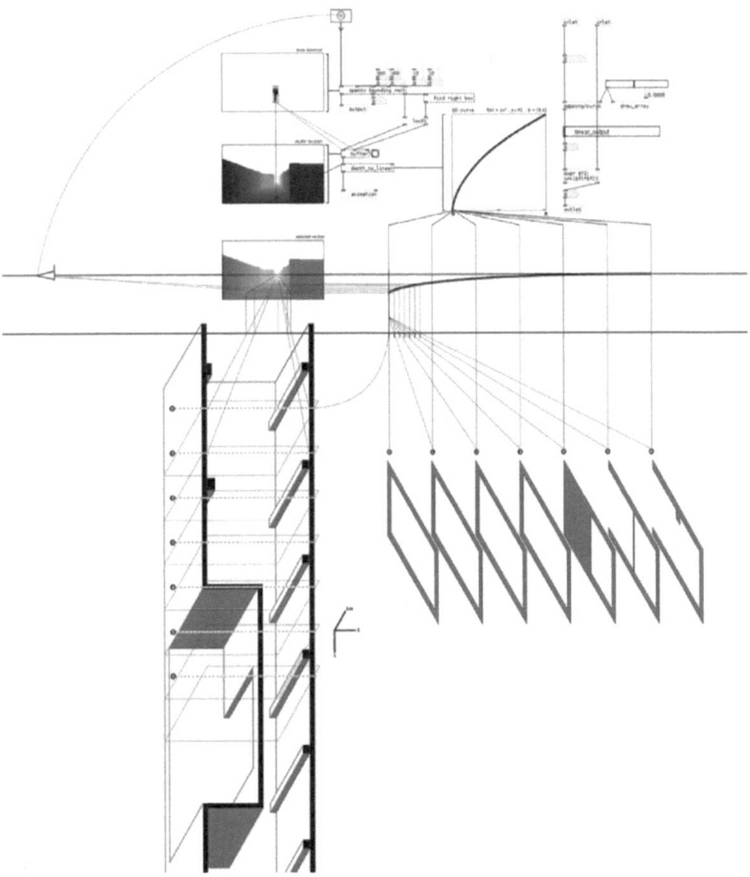

FIGURE 29.3 Diagram of the Perspectiva Virtualis software prototype, coded in 2016 in PureData with the OpenCV library. In brief, the software detects the depth position of the user and adds the corresponding perspective section to the camera's video stream. Nowadays, the software is written in Python, using the OpenCV, imutils, and scikit-image libraries.

Conclusion

The spatial augmentation takes shape at the threshold of the different projections overlapping into a single space. In addition to offering the unique gaze of a virtual space, the result is also an area of friction: firstly, between the observer's *perspectiva naturalis* and an instrumental mirror image captured by a single-eyed camera and, secondly, between the camera's recorded image and the calibration process which forces a *perspectiva artificialis* onto it. Furthermore, the act of sectioning introduces an orthographic projection in a space operated by depth.

Rather than harmonizing the different projections, the installation presents the inherent contradictions of AR with an appropriate space for their existence. The significance of the installation's augmentation therefore lies in the synthesis between the idealized perspective, the ocular perspective, and the orthographic projection. Consequently, Perspectiva Virtualis produces a spatial fiction composed of different projective layers, rather than an apparently coherent, immediate, and realistic architectural object.

30

HOLO-SENSORY MATERIALITY

Marcus Farr and Andrea Macruz

Holo-Sensory Materiality explores the overlapping relationships between augmented reality and human sensory experience. In order to do so, it employs Microsoft HoloLens technology as a primary decision-making tool in the design workflow, and wearable bio-sensors to evaluate the human experience (Figure 30.1). The exploration of these technological overlaps offers an expanded mode of inquiry relative to a host of architectural potentials, including the dialogue with augmentation and a deeper sense of conceptual development. The benefits include the real-time simulation of scale, form, colour, light, and shadow, and their manipulation as part of an ongoing decision-making process. The work is designed with Rhino, Houdini, Fologram, and HoloLens, which allow for an interchange of digital and physical processes that frame a very immersive architectural experience. With Fologram and HoloLens, users are immersed in an augmented environment that acts as a sensorial extension further activated by an iPhone app that allows the patterns to change colour and texture (Figures 30.2–30.4). To monitor and evaluate the reaction to the project, biodata is collected in real time and processed through a series of algorithms offering feedback in response to the sensorial qualities. The project uses Fologram to overlay a full-scale hologram in a physical artspace as a digital projection. Its purpose is to engage people with multi-sensory experiences that force humans to re-evaluate and re-perceive our material world. Additional sensory stimulations that can be experienced using the HoloLens headset enhance the experience. These experiences are subsequently monitored in real time using sensors that are designed to collect biodata from heart rate and contractions through a PPG sensor (photoplethysmogram) (Upmood sensors).[1] The sensors turn the data into analytics to generate an understanding of interactive stress levels, heart rate, and vitality levels that can lead to the identification of emotions.

The augmentation of the project provides a potential that merges the physical with the digital, the buildable with the not yet buildable, and the fabricated with the unfabricated. Given this potential, the project was interested in how people connected with these augmented experiences rather than those that were purely virtual, thus distinguishing between a computer-generated simulation and one that offered an augmented overlay of digital and physical experience. To connect with the physical, the human sensorium is brought into play with factors that arouse touch, scent, and sound. The project includes influences from the writings of Kant, and the *Reflexionenzur Anthropologie* (1882), Andy Clark and *Natural Born Cyborgs* (2003), Antonio Damasio and Gil Carvalho and *The Nature of Feelings: Evolutionary and Neurobiological*

DOI: 10.4324/9781003183105-39

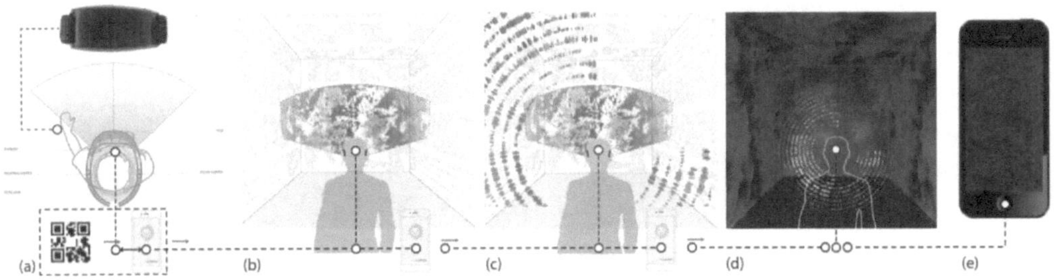

FIGURE 30.1 Process diagram depicting (1) the connection of HoloLens, iPhone, and UpMood wearable via QR-code, (2) digital overlay on physical gallery space, (3) presence of sound, (4) presence of affective memory and scent, (5) the iPhone as a tool for the experience

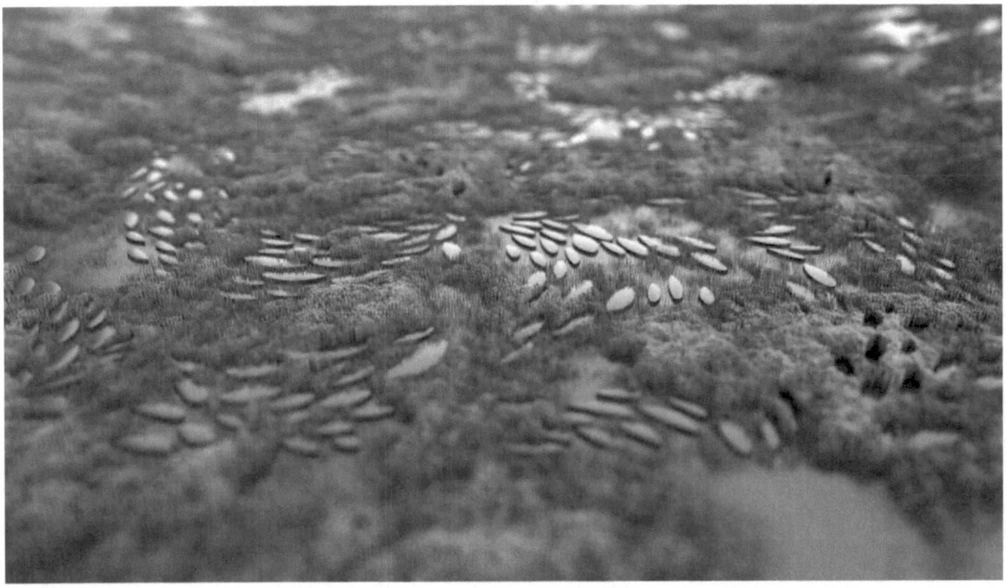

FIGURE 30.2 Digital surface materials experienced with HoloLens and iPhone referencing ongoing growth as a virtual overlay

Origins (2013), Anil Seth, Skywalker Sound (2019), Neal Leach and *Camouflage* (2006), and Juhani Pallasma (1996), who asks the far-reaching question of why, when there are five senses, one single sense, namely sight, has become so predominant in architectural culture and design.

The methodologies used in the project do not aim to provide solutions from the outset, but instead explore the use of the augmented design process and technology to inform solutions along the way, then attempt to evaluate the potential impact of a set of sensorial experiences. The aim was to build on the inherent theoretical underpinnings, whilst also informing best practices for how this process can contribute or be applied to future projects. The project positions itself as one that has an interest in looking to the future and creating a conversation about the potential of architecture in relation to technology and the sensorial experience of a given space. It has therefore evolved around the design and construction of a physical wall surface that became a room. The discussion of its material and sensorial qualities and its virtual

FIGURE 30.3 A composite of digital surface materials experienced with HoloLens and iPhone, referencing ongoing growth as a virtual overlay

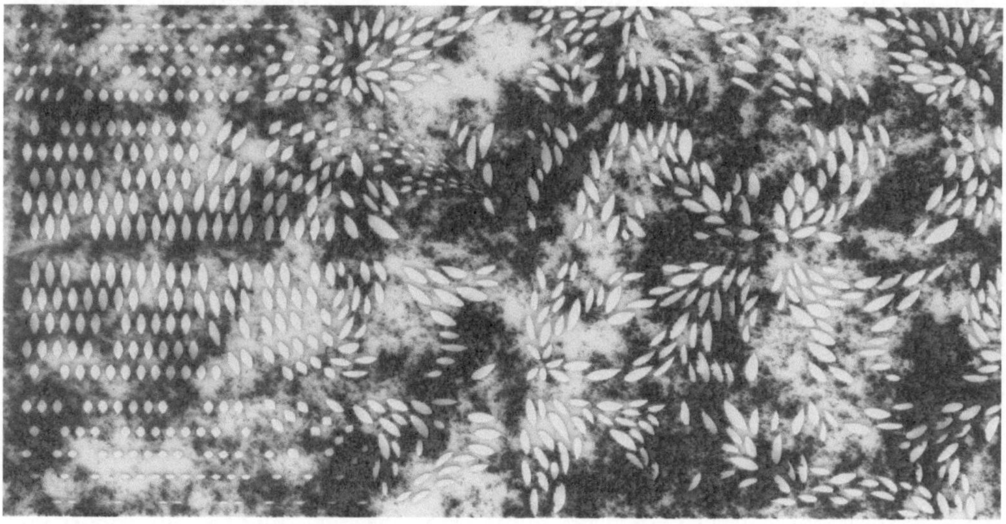

FIGURE 30.4 Digital surface materials experienced with HoloLens and iPhone, referencing ongoing growth as a virtual overlay

augmentation became a catalyst for new experiences. It employed the digital hologram to help build, perceive, and evaluate the overall experience and concludes that the methods used in the project work with the existing paradigms of architectural design, but also speculate on a new agenda for current processes, due to the vast possibilities of holograms in the design workflow. Hence, the project suggests a "re-centring" or new starting point for designers seeking to incorporate technologies into our design process, as well as in our understanding of what the design process can be. Rather than following the traditional path of design, followed by build, followed by experience, this project suggests that these activities have the potential to overlap more and inform each other in a real way throughout the course of a given design exercise, offering both quantitative and qualitative results.

Acknowledgement

The authors wish to thank Alina Sebastian and Ahmed Abdelnaby for their contributions.

Note

1. https://upmood.com/

References

Clark, A. (2003) *Natural Born Cyborgs: Minds, Technologies, and the Future of the Human Intelligence.* Oxford: Oxford University Press.

Damasio, A. and Carvalho, G. (2013) 'The Nature of Feelings: Evolutionary and Neurobiological OIrigins', *Nature Reviews Neuroscience*, 14, pp. 143–152.

Kant, I. (1882) *Reflexionen Kants zur kritischen Philosophie. 1.* London: Forgotten Books.

Leach, N. (2006) *Camouflage.* Cambridge, MA: MIT Press.

Pallasma, J. (1996) *The Eyes of the Skin.* New Jersey: Wiley.

Seth, A. (2019) 'Your Brain Hallucinates Your Conscious Reality', *Ted Talk.* Available at: www.youtube.com/watch?v=lyu7v7nWzfo (Accessed: 1 February 2021).

31

PORIFERA SUSPENDED TOPOLOGIES

Pablo Baquero, Effimia Giannopoulou, Ioanna Symeonidou, and Nuno Pereira da Silva

The Porifera Suspended Topologies installation is a large-scale biomorphic spatial structure that blends the boundaries between art, science, and technology. It is a *morphogenetic-morphodynamic* experiment developed through an interdisciplinary approach that implements generative design workflows to simulate physical and biological processes. Its form is inspired by the growth process of sponges and other porifera organisms, and it is further optimized with the use of computational algorithms. The study of the underlying mathematical logic of porifera (L-systems, Voronoi diagrams, natural patterns) led to the creation of the algorithmic design strategy, which involves the topological arrangement and subdivision of meshes that obtain their final curved form through dynamic relaxation, whilst also considering the material properties of the prototype and fabrication technique. A biological mechanism of stripe formations (known as Reaction-Diffusion after Alan Turing (1952)) is applied as the construction logic for the thin shell to create a characteristic pattern effect which often occurs in animals and, in parallel, to provide assembly efficiency and structural stability (Giannopoulou et al., 2019).

For the 3D modelling of the Porifera Suspended Topologies installation, a structure in static equilibrium with almost minimal surface properties was created through physics simulation, in a design process that instrumentalizes biomimetic principles to correspond to architectural requirements such as efficient structural behaviour and buildability. As in nature, economy of material leads to efficient forms that are optimized through several centuries of evolutionary development. As D'Arcy Thomson (1917) explains, "Form is a diagram of forces"; hence the Porifera Suspended Topologies installation is the outcome of the interplay between gravity, tension, and growth. The lightweight structure which is obtained is the result of the forces acting upon the system, and it is therefore structurally optimized and does not require an additional support system.

For the physical construction, the 3D geometry is discretized into stripes of planar sheet material which are digitally fabricated and assembled in situ. Thus, the computational model is segmented in the digital environment and reconnected in the physical world, using overlapping flaps (Figure 31.1). The 2D geometrical configurations of stripes, all different and systematically labelled, implement a specific cutting outline of star shapes that serve as openings to facilitate the assembling process and produce a lighting pattern effect. The material selected for the Porifera is translucent polypropylene, which can transmit light and create an immersive atmosphere.

DOI: 10.4324/9781003183105-40

The illuminated physical prototype resembled a hologram, as it was suspended in the middle of the exhibition space (Figures 31.2 and 31.3). The notion of gravity totally disappears, and the installation looks almost immaterial. This feature of dissolving materiality led to the idea of transferring the project to an augmented reality environment to experiment further with pattern growth, light, and visualization. The idea was to implement a process of algorithmic growth in the fabricated prototype in order to visualize it in AR and create a similar holographic experience in a different place through a visual augmented reality interface.

For the Artificial Realities Exhibition in *Lisbon Architecture Triennale 2019*, the Porifera Suspended Topologies installation was expanded and implemented in an augmented reality (AR) environment (Figure 34.1), thus challenging our perceptions of the boundaries between the natural and artificial, physical, and virtual. The Porifera Suspended Topologies installation examines the computational correlation between the artificial and the biological systems, how they both complement each other, and how the naturally occurring morphogenetic processes can be a source of inspiration that can be utilized in the algorithmic design process. The project seeks to position itself within the emerging field of biodigital architecture, merging ideas and implementing concepts taken from biology, architecture, computation, and design.

Technical Data of the Fabricated Prototype

Material: 64 laser-cut translucent Polypropylene (PP), 0.8mm thickness. Connectors: 1354 tie wraps. Lights: LED lights RGB (five lights). Dimensions: 1.5 (length) x 1.5 (width) x 3.00 (height).

FIGURE 31.1 Close-up of the Porifera Suspended Topologies installation

FIGURE 31.2 The Porifera Suspended Topologies installation in the 3rd Artecitya-Art Science Technology Festival: Visioning the City of Tomorrow at TIF, HELEXPO in 2018

FIGURE 31.3 The Porifera Suspended Topologies installation in the 3rd Artecitya-Art Science Technology Festival: Visioning the City of Tomorrow at TIF, HELEXPO in 2018

FIGURE 31.4 The Porifera installation in Artificial Realities: Virtual as an Aesthetic Medium in Architecture Ideation, Lisbon Architecture Triennale 2019.

Credits

Design and digital fabrication of Porifera Suspended Topologies by Pablo Baquero, Effimia Giannopoulou and Ioanna Symeonidou. Augmented reality implementation of Porifera Suspended Topologies by Nuno Pereira da Silva.

References

Giannopoulou, E. et al. (2019) 'Biological Pattern Based on Reaction-Diffusion Mechanism Employed as Fabrication Strategy for a Shell Structure', *IOP Conference Series: Materials Science and Engineering*, 471(10).

Thompson, W. A. (1917) *On Growth and Form*. Cambridge: Cambridge University Press.

Turing, A. (1952) 'The Chemical Basis of Morphogenesis', *Philosophical Transactions of the Royal Society of London*, Series B, Biological Sciences, 237(641), pp. 37–72.

AUTHOR BIOGRAPHIES

Henri Achten
[Czech Technical University in Prague, Czech Republic]
Achten is Professor of Architecture at the Czech Technical University in Prague. He graduated in 1992 (Technische Universiteit Eindhoven). He was the first diploma student in the Netherlands to present his diploma project in virtual reality, at the Institute Calibre. He obtained his PhD in 1997, after which he was a post-doc and later Assistant Professor in the TU/e Design Systems Group. Until 2010, he was active in the VR-DIS research programme, covering the design methodology section. He was appointed Assistant Professor at the Faculty of Architecture at the CTU in Prague (2005) and then in the Architectural Modelling Office, and obtained habilitation as Associate Professor (2008), followed by habilitation as Professor (2018). His research interest remains focused on the question of how the computer influences the design process and vice versa, namely how the design process should influence computers.

Turan Akman
[STG Design, United States of America]
Akman graduated from the University of Cincinnati with a master of architecture degree in May 2019. Akman currently works in the field of architecture in Austin, Texas. Before graduating from the University of Cincinnati, he received his bachelor of science degree in architecture from Kent State University. Throughout his academic career, he has received multiple design and research awards and recognitions, such as the first-place award at the Kent State Research Symposium, and an honourable mention at the Evolo Skyscraper Competition. His current research includes topics such as augmented reality and architecture, computational design, and the future of architecture.

Pablo Baquero
[Faberarium, Greece and Institute for Biodigital Architecture & Genetics (iBAG), Spain]
Baquero is an architect, artist, and computational designer whose main interest lies in innovative modelling systems related to emergence and biological procedures in teaching and research fields, and how natural systems and computer simulations are being used to improve the architecture of the future. He was born in Colombia and divides his time between Barcelona and Greece. He holds a PhD in genetic architecture from Esarq, Barcelona and an MSc in

advanced architectural design from Columbia University, and studied for his bachelor's degree in architecture at the U.P.C. Bogota. He has been co-teaching at the TU Delft Hyperbody interactive architecture studio and was also co-teaching and invited to participate as jury critic at GSAPP, Columbia University, the Pratt Institute, and Parsons University.

Mehmet Emin Bayraktar

[Istanbul Technical University, Turkey]

Bayraktar is an architect studying in the field of computational architecture. He graduated from the Faculty of Architecture at the Istanbul Technical University in 2007. Currently he is preparing his PhD thesis on the use of augmented reality in the early architectural design phase. He has been practicing as an architect in several offices, including his own studio mmnAD, for 12 years and has worked on different types of projects on multiple scales, including residential, commercial, and urban projects, primarily in Turkey.

Gülen Çağdaş

[Istanbul Technical University, Turkey]

Çağdaş is a graduate of the Faculty of Architecture at Istanbul Technical University, where she also began working as teaching assistant in 1981. She was awarded a PhD in architectural design from the same university in 1986. She became an Associate Professor in 1989 and Professor in 1997. She served as Vice Dean of Faculty of Architecture between 1997 and 2000, was the Head of Architectural Design Chair between 2004 and 2007, and was also Department Head of Architecture between 2008 and 2012. She was the Department Head of Informatics at the Institute of Science, Engineering and Technology, ITU from 2006 to 2018. Her main research area is architectural design computing.

Eva Castro

[Architecture & sustainable design/SUTD (Singapore University of Technology and Design), Singapore]

Castro is a Professor of Practice at AS+D—SUTD, where she currently is the coordinator of core studio 2. The work of core studio 2 has been ground onto the development of new narratives and the deployment of immersive realities to articulate possible futures. Castro is co-founder of the FormAxioms lab operating at the intersection of art, technology, and territorial design for academic research purposes, operating from within SUTD. FormAxioms has co-curated Negentropic Fields at the National Gallery of Singapore. She was the director of the Landscape Urbanism Program at the AA in London and at Tsinghua University in Beijing. She also held positions as Visiting Professor at HKU, Hong Kong, and as Honorary Professor at X'ian UAT.

Spyridoula Dedemadi

[Aristotle University of Thessaloniki, Greece]

Dedemadi graduated from the Aristotle University of Thessaloniki [A.U.Th.], Greece, and has been working as an independent architect since 2018. She has participated in competitions, exhibitions, and several workshops. Her work focuses on the applications of virtual reality and game design in architecture, and the digitalization and enhancement of historical heritage.

Luís Santos Dias

[Instituto Universitário de Lisboa (ISCTE-IUL), ISTAR, Portugal]

Dias holds a BSc in chemical engineering from the Instituto Superior Técnico and a postgraduate degree in sanitary engineering from the Faculty of Science and Technology at the New

University of Lisbon. He has worked at the ADETTI-IUL research centre on projects related to several areas, ranging from simulation of cloth behaviour to image compression using JPEG2000 and the processing of cardiac biometric data. He also has experience in the private sector, where he worked for companies in the banking and telecommunication sectors, engaged in software development. He is currently a researcher in ISTAR, where his main interests and activities lie in ambient assisted-living projects, virtual reality, and augmented reality.

Marcus Farr

[American University of Sharjah, United Arab Emirates]

Farr is a US Fulbright Scholar in Architecture, researching tectonics throughout China. He is the principal of the Material Artifact studio. His teaching and research focus on materials, new methods, and contemporary practice. He studied architecture at Rice University, and has had practical experience throughout the United States, Europe, the Middle East, and Asia. Relevant publications include contributions to the *Landscape Architecture Magazine*, *Architectural Record*, *Architect* and *New York Times*. He is Assistant Professor of Architecture at the American University of Sharjah in the United Arab Emirates.

Miloš Florián

[Czech Technical University in Prague, Czech Republic]

Florián, Doc. Ing. arch., PhD, architect, university lecturer (1983 FA CTU, 2005 PhD, 2011 Associate Professor of Architecture) has since 1995 been FA CTU, Department of Design II, Professor Assistant, and collaborated on the studio instruction and exercises for health and sport buildings. During 2002–2003, he was a researcher at the Institute of History of Art and Architecture. Since 2003, he has been a Professor Assistant and Associate Professor at the Department of Civil Engineering I. Since 2015, he has been Associate Professor at the Department of Architectural Modelling MOLAB, with studio teaching leadership and expertise. His specializations include structures of free forms, intelligent façade buildings, glass as a construction material, smart materials and systems, nanotechnology, additive architectural manufacturing, robotics architectural systems and structures, holistic planning, and Internet of Everything. In 2004, he founded and leads Studio Glass/FreeForm Architecture, since 2010 under the name FLO/W.

James Forren

[Dalhousie University, Canada]

Forren is an Assistant Professor of architecture in design and technology and Director of the Material, Body, and Environment Lab at Dalhousie University. He utilizes computational and fine arts methods in the study of new materials and material technologies in architectural contexts. His research focuses on the production of architectural components and assemblies, concrete and composite technologies, and people's experiences with materials in industrial, design, and public contexts.

Markéta Gebrian

[Czech Technical University in Prague, Czech Republic]

Gebrian is a Prague-based digital artist and architect for VR spaces. She started her studies at the Technical University in Liberec in the Czech Republic in 1999 and also studied at Rietveld Academy in Amsterdam, the Ecole Val-de-Seine in Paris, and La Sapienza University in Rome. She completed her master's degree in architecture in 2006 in Liberec. As an architect intern, she worked in Amsterdam at NL Architects, in Rotterdam at MAXWAN, in Paris at Jean Nouvel, and in London and Los Angeles at Steven Ehrlich Architects and Behnish Architects. She has exhibited her artwork in Basel, New York, Zürich, Miami, and Prague. Since 2015, she has been a PhD candidate at CTU Prague.

Effimia Giannopoulou

[Faberarium, Greece and Institute for Biodigital Architecture & Genetics (iBAG), Spain

Giannopoulou is founder of Faberarium: Fabrication Technologies for Architecture, holds an MSc in Biodigital Architecture from ESARQ, Barcelona, and a master's in architecture from the Aristotle University of Thessaloniki. She was awarded an Erasmus scholarship to study at the FAUP, Porto. As a freelance architect with an artistic background, she collaborated on several projects and exhibitions linking the relevance of biological paradigms to computational design and construction. She currently works as a research affiliate and visiting professor at the Institute for Biodigital Architecture & Genetics (iBAG) in Barcelona and is also engaged in finishing her PhD thesis and teaching, practicing, consulting, and writing about advanced modelling and fabrication techniques.

Joana Gomes

[Instituto Universitário de Lisboa (ISCTE-IUL), ISTAR, Portugal]

Gomes is an architect and MSc in architecture on the subject of "From Laser Scan to BIM Modelling: Experiences and Testimonials". She has worked in architecture, collaborating in initial design stages where point clouds and first BIM models are developed. She was a researcher at ISTAR, involved in a project on the efficient use of BIM in architect offices. Currently she works in an architectural office, using BIM during the later stages of design and construction.

Kyriaki Goti

[SomePeople, Pratt Institute School of Architecture, New York Institute of Technology (NYIT), United States of America]

Goti is the founder of the design and innovation studio SomePeople. She is a visiting assistant professor at the Pratt Institute School of Architecture and adjunct instructor at NYIT. She received her diploma in architecture from the Aristotle University of Thessaloniki and an MSc in integrative technologies and architectural design research from the Institute for Computational Design (ICD) at the University of Stuttgart. Her work has received several international awards, including the AZ Awards 2018, the Fast Company 2018 Innovation by Design Awards, and the MAD Travel Fellowship 2017. Her projects have been exhibited at ACADIA 2018, the Bangkok Design Week 2019, LA Design Festival 2019, and Tallinn Architecture Biennale 2019.

Alexander Grasser

[Graz University of Technology, Austria]

Grasser is an Austrian architect, designer, and researcher whose work focuses on computational architecture, collaborative objects, and elastic architecture. He is currently Assistant Professor at the Institute of Architecture and Media, Graz. Grasser has skills in computational architecture, robotic fabrication, and contemporary theory in architecture. In addition to his academic research, Grasser has had the opportunity to share his knowledge by teaching computational design courses as well as assisting architectural project courses in Innsbruck, Graz, and Vienna. He has also gained professional experience at Graft, Span, and CoopHimmelb(l)au, in addition to ongoing collaborations with Heron-Mazy and TeamA. Grasser's works have been widely published and received recognition in open architectural competitions.

Ramzi Hassan

[Norwegian University of Life Sciences (NMBU), Faculty of Landscape and Society (LANDSAM), Norway]

Hassan is an Associate Professor at the School of Landscape Architecture at the NMBU. He is the founder and leader of the Virtual Reality Lab. His research, teaching, and publications focus on digital applications for landscape and urban design. His current research involves interactive environments, exploring the potential for virtual technologies as a storytelling medium in the context of cultural heritage and historically important landscapes.

Brittney Holmes

[Cuningham Group Architecture Inc, United States of America]

Holmes is a designer and computational researcher in the architectural field in Los Angeles, California. Her work is focused on theme entertainment and mix-use commercial project types located both regional and internationally. She graduated from the Architectural Association School of Architecture in London with a master of science degree in emergent technologies and design. Since then, she has pursued ways to explore innovation through design with the use of computational design strategies. Her passion lies in telling stories that reflect and expose networks through analytics to inform design solutions, as well as design immersive environments that help connect people.

Helmut Kinzler

[Zaha Hadid Architects, United Kingdom]

Kinzler is Dipl Ing, Dipl Arch, BDA, Associate Director/Head of VR. Kinzler joined Zaha Hadid Architects in 1998 as a designer and project architect. He has subsequently worked on a series of important architectural projects, such as the Phaeno Science Centre in Wolfsburg, Germany. In addition to his work as a designer and project director, Kinzler founded the company's VR department in 2015, to research and develop the technology for applications in the practice's design and presentation workflow, and to develop a comprehensive understanding of emerging cybernetic space and culture. The group engages with multiple partners and has contributed projects to several public exhibitions showcasing VR technology and the practice's design work.

Arthur Lachard

[OXO Architects, France]

Lachard graduated from the Faculté d'Architecture La Cambre-Horta (ULB). During his studies, he specialized in architectural representation and procedural design as cognitive tools and completed an R&D internship in this field at the AlICe research laboratory (ULB), developing architectural augmented reality prototypes which subsequently became the topic of his master's thesis. After one year as assistant teacher, Lachard decided to go into professional architectural practice as computer designer, first at Barcode Architects in Rotterdam—experimenting with the resolution of complex geometries through scripts and procedural assets—and currently at OXO Architects in Paris.

Carla Leitão

[Rensselaer Polytechnic Institute School of Architecture, United States of America]

Leitão is an architect, professor, and writer. At RPI School of Architecture since 2010, Leitão's studios and seminars explore the intersection of architecture, urban systems, technology, ubiquitous cultures, and immersive VR. She is Co-Founder of AUM Studio and Spec.AE. Her interests include architectural design, curation, theory, scenarios, and interactive media; residential, installations, competitions in Europe and the US. Publications include relationships between technology, representation, and architectural and urban systems. She curated and organized "Portugal Now"/Cornell AAP Folio, an exhibition of 20+ Portuguese offices with conferences in Ithaca and NYC [2007]. She lives/works in New York, USA, and Lisbon, Portugal.

María López Calleja
[MVRDV, The Netherlands]
López studied architecture at the Technical University of Valencia and has worked for MVRDV since 2008. She has been involved in national and international projects of various scales and scopes. She oversaw the design process of the urban hybrid masterplan in Switzerland and has led the design teams of the Tianjin Binhai Library in Tianjin, China, and the Imprint in Seoul, South Korea. López is also responsible for the development and implementation of BIM as a design tool. "MVRDV gave me the opportunity to mature professionally surrounded by talented people, facing challenges on a worldwide level in many different types and scales of projects", she says.

Andrea Macruz
[Tongji University, China]
Andrea Macruz holds a BA in architecture from the Universidade Presbiteriana Mackenzie in São Paulo, a master's in biodigital architecture from the Universitat Internacional de Catalunya in Barcelona, and a master's in contemporary furniture design from the Istituto Marangoni in Milan. Currently, she is part of the DigitalFUTURES PhD programme at Tongji University in Shanghai. Andrea has exhibited in venues such as the Salone Satellite at the Milan Furniture Fair, the Piasa Auction in Paris, London Design Week, and the Architecture Beijing Biennale. In 2010, she founded a design studio focused on the study of nature and new technologies.

Christopher Morse
[SHoP Architects, United States of America]
Morse is an associate of interactive visualization at SHoP Architects. His research focuses on the integration of interactive visualization technologies such as VR and AR in all phases of the design process. He is collaborating with the Department of Architecture at Cornell University to use immersive VR tools as an integral part of an urban design studio. He received a master's degree in architecture from Cornell University and holds additional degrees in mathematics education and physics.

Ana Moural
[Norwegian University of Life Sciences (NMBU), Faculty of Landscape and Society (LANDSAM), Norway]
Moural holds a master's degree in architecture from Iscte—Lisbon University Institute. She is currently a PhD candidate at the Norwegian University of Life Sciences, working on mobile virtual reality as a tool to enhance stakeholder participation in the landscape design process. Her main research interests fall between 3D visualization tools, user experience, and public participation in landscape planning and design.

Marcos Novak
[transLAB, Media Arts and Technology Program, University of California Santa Barbara (UCSB), United States of America]
Novak is Founding Director of the transLAB (a transmodal/XR <worldmaking> lab exploring <transformation that leads to speciation, in fact, in fiction, in action>) at UCSB, affiliated with MAT, the AlloSphere, Art, and CNSI. He is an architect, artist, composer, theorist, pioneer of algorithmic design, and the originator of THEMAS, a <holistic, integrative, creative> model for research, practice, and pedagogy, beyond STEM and STEAM. In 2000, he was honoured to represent Greece at the Venice Biennale (to which he has since been invited numerous times). He lectures and exhibits at prominent venues worldwide.

Spiros I. Papadimitriou
[Aristotle University of Thessaloniki, Greece]
Papadimitriou is an Assistant Professor in architectural design and digital medium at the Architecture School of Aristotle University of Thessaloniki (Architect A.U.Th, March Architectural Association School, London (AA DRL)). He is a coordination and teaching member of the Postgraduate Program "Advanced Design, Innovation and Transdisciplinarity in Design". He practices architecture as an independent architect. He was curator of the exhibition digital_topographies and of the book under the same title. He was awarded the "Young Greek Architect Award" from the Greek Association of Architects (2011). The central square "Paramana" of the Municipality of Thermi was awarded by the Greek Institute of Architecture and was nominated for the Mies Van Der Rohe Awards 2011.

Nuno Pereira da Silva
[Instituto Universitário de Lisboa (ISCTE-IUL), ISTAR, Portugal]
Pereira da Silva is an architect, MSc in architecture on the subject of "Robotic Construction: The Use of Drones in Construction" and currently a PhD student at ISCTE and researcher at ISTAR Lisbon, investigating "Robotic Construction in Architecture: Design, Simulation, and Reality". Pereira da Silva's research topics are robotic construction, drones, building construction, robotic architecture, and virtual and augmented reality.

Elena Pérez Guembe
[RPI School of Architecture, United States of America]
Pérez Guembe is a B. Arch/MSc in urban planning (Universidad de Navarra, Spain), Licensed Architect 2002, MSc in advanced architectural design 2007, and Research 2008 (GSAPP Columbia University, NY, USA). She has worked at the Zaha-Hadid and Rafael Moneo studios as an architect designer and as a professor at the RPI School of Architecture in Troy, NY. Her research interests focus on the phenomenological, the intersection between art and architecture, and material experimentation. Her creative work has been published, won awards, and been exhibited internationally (including at the Cooper Union NY, Guggenheim Museum NY, and 2018 Venice Biennale). She is currently applying for the TU Delft A+BE PhD programme.

Sean Pickersgill
[University South Australia, Australia]
Pickersgill is a Senior Lecturer at the School of Art Architecture and Design at the University of South Australia, teaching courses based on contemporary theory, digital technologies, and design studio. He is also Chair of the Membership Committee for the Australian Research Centre for Interactive and Virtual Environments, a key research group linked with leading industry

organizations. He has published extensively on the intersection of philosophy, design theory, and architecture, focusing on the employment of digital technologies as a method for exploration and representation.

Makenzie Ramadan
[Dalhousie University, Canada]
Ramadan is a researcher at the Material, Body, and Environment Lab at the Dalhousie University School of Architecture. He received a diploma in architectural technology from the Southern Alberta Institute of Technology and later an undergraduate degree in environmental design from Dalhousie University, working for Ekistics Planning and Design in Dartmouth as part of a co-op. He currently is enrolled in the Master of Architecture program at Dal.

Ricardo Pontes Resende
[Instituto Universitário de Lisboa (ISCTE-IUL), ISTAR, Portugal]
Resende, Eng., MSc, PhD, is a structural engineer with a background in computational modelling. He is currently working on the digitalization of construction, combining building-information modelling, Internet of things, and mixed-reality tools to improve building sustainability over the whole lifecycle.

Julien Rippinger
[Université Libre de Bruxelles (ULB), Belgium]
Rippinger graduated from the Faculté d'Architecture La Cambre-Horta (ULB). Afterwards, he became a collaborator at the Fondazione La Biennale di Venezia for the 15th International Architecture Exhibition and for the 57th International Art Exhibition. He is currently a postgraduate student at the AlICe research laboratory (ULB). In his research, he studies historically and conceptually descriptive geometry and produces software prototypes which stress an alternative approach to computer-aided design. In general, his work focuses on architectural representation, history of science and technology, descriptive geometry, and computer graphics. His PhD is supported by the Fonds National de la Recherche Luxembourg.

Rudolf Romero
[01X, The Netherlands]
Romero studied artificial intelligence in Utrecht and graduated cum laude from the Artez Art Academy in 2012. He is shortlisted for many national and international awards and was selected by the Venice Biennale for their first VR college in 2017. Romero graduated from the renowned MA sculpture course at the Royal College of Art in London in 2017 and was selected best graduate in the UK. In 2015 Romero founded the research and development company 01X, a consultancy and speculative design platform with a strong focus on emerging technology and extended reality projects.

Ruth Ron
[University of Miami, United States of America]
Ron is an architect currently teaching at the University of Miami School of Architecture. Her work explores multiple aspects of digital design, focusing on the borders between architecture and technology, form, and media. Ruth received a bachelor of architecture degree from the Technion Israel Institute of Technology, a master's degree in advanced architectural design from Columbia University in New York, and a master's degree in interactive telecommunication

from New York University. She has worked for cutting-edge architectural firms in Israel and New York, including Asymptote and LOT-EK, taught at Arizona State University, the University of Florida, and Shenkar College (Israel), and exhibited her work in New York, Seattle, Boston, Georgia, Jerusalem, Florence, and Paris.

Federico Ruberto
[formAxioms, reMIX studio, Singapore University of Technology and Design, Singapore]
Ruberto is a writer and architect working in the area between philosophy and design. He holds a PhD in "Philosophy, Art and Critical Thought" from the European Graduate School, which focused on the concept of "contingency" in formal/natural languages. His texts connect metaphysical questions to the field of de-sign, examining the possibility of writing the open within the current computational paradigm. He is co-founder/partner of formAxioms, a Singapore-based research laboratory for speculative narratives, and reMIX Studio, an architectural office in Beijing. He currently leads design studios at the Singapore University of Technology and Design.

Rosana Rubio Hernández
[Tampere University, Finland]
Rubio Hernández has a PhD in architecture (2016, Escuela Técnica Superior de Arquitectura de Madrid, Universidad Politécnica de Madrid), an MSc in advanced architectural design and research (2008, GSAPP Columbia University), and an M.Arch (2000, ETSAM, UPM). She currently holds a post-doctorate research position at the Tampere University School of Architecture (Finland). She has taught and worked as a researcher in different universities since 2005, including the Schools of Architecture at the University of Virginia (USA), the UPM (Spain), and the Universidad Camilo José Cela (Spain). Her research interests centre on 'technified species of spaces', i.e. the interplay between new technologies and architectural design.

Sebastien Sarrazin
[Dalhousie University, Canada]
Sarrazin is a researcher in the Material, Body, and Environment Lab at the Dalhousie University School of Architecture. He received his undergraduate degree in architecture from Carleton University in Ottawa, Ontario, and has since collaborated in a variety of design practices internationally, including as an intern-in-residence at the Yestermorrow Design/Build school in Waitsfield, Vermont. He is currently enrolled in the Master of Architecture programme at Dal.

Dustin Schipper
[Cuningham Group Architecture Inc, United States of America]
Schipper is a researcher at Cuningham Group Architecture Inc. He is a recent graduate of the University of Minnesota's Master of Science in Research Practices programme. He has experience in applying computational thinking to design practice, academic projects, and research efforts. In his current role at Cuningham Group, he conducts and manages R&D projects with the aim of advancing design practice through technology, innovative methods, and the use of data to inform design.

Jason Semanic
[Space Laboratory, Australia]
Prior to founding the Space Laboratory, he graduated from the University of South Australia with a master's degree in architecture. He went on to gain significant experience within

some of Australia's leading architectural practices and was heavily involved with nationally and internationally recognized projects. He has furthered his own personal career as a designer by studying at Harvard University in Boston, where he is currently working as a tutor. With a focus on urban, infrastructure, and high-rise residential design, Semanic is passionate about achieving quality outcomes for his clients. He believes that by listening and facilitating good teamwork and communication between all parties, the design process often leads to unique and unexpected solutions.

Risa Tadauchi

[Zaha Hadid Architects, United Kingdom]

Tadauchi has a MArch. and BA. Tadauchi is a senior designer and virtual reality developer at Zaha Hadid Architects, and she has been part of the Zaha Hadid Virtual Reality Group since 2017. Tadauchi holds a master's of architecture degree from the Bartlett School of Architecture, UCL, and has experience in coordinating and leading research projects and VR projects using game engines. As a speaker and critic, she has given presentations at lectures and workshops in Europe and Japan.

Ming Tang

[University of Cincinnati, United States of America]

Tang, registered Architect, RA, NCARB, LEED AP (BD+C), is a tenured Associate Professor at the School of Architecture and Interior Design, College of Design, Architecture, Art, and Planning, University of Cincinnati. He has worked in the M.I.N.D Lab at the Michigan State University, the Institute for Creative Technologies at the University of Southern California, and the China Architecture Design & Research Group. His multidisciplinary research includes computational design, digital fabrication, BIM, performance driven design, virtual reality and augmented reality, eye-tracking, crowd simulation and wayfinding, and human-computer interaction.

Chris Traianos

[Realize Studio, Australia]

Traianos is the owner and director of Realize Studio in Adelaide, South Australia. He has considerable experience in the development of photorealistic digital rendering for both still, device-based, and VR applications and has pioneered the employment of game-engine software and the use of headsets for increased clarity in design decision-making. He has been at the forefront of developing VR technology as a standard tool within the property development and real estate industry. He has worked in partnership with academic research staff at the University of South Australia and the Australian Navy to develop the use of VR in spatial logistics calculations for naval vessel design and has taught at the University of South Australia.

Daria Zolotareva

[Zaha Hadid Architects, United Kingdom]

Zolotareva is a MArch. BA., senior architect. Zolotareva is an exhibition designer at Zaha Hadid Architects. Zolotareva holds a master's of architecture from Yale University and a bachelor of fine arts from the University of Pennsylvania and has experience working across a wide range of scales, from urban redevelopment projects to product design. She has been working with the ZHVR group to bring VR into the exhibition environment since 2016 and is collaborating with the team on current research into cross-disciplinary VR.

Renate Weissenböck

[Atelier Weissenböck/ Graz University of Technology, Austria]

Weissenböck is an architect with extensive experience in design and the realization of complex projects. She is currently teaching at Graz University of Technology (Austria). Her research explores the role of different digital media in the design process, such as industrial robots and augmented reality, working in the tension field between human, craft, and machine. Weissenböck holds a master's degree in architecture from the Academy of Fine Arts in Vienna, a master's degree in advanced architectural design from Columbia University in New York, and a PhD from Graz University of Technology. She has worked with the internationally recognized architecture firms Asymptote Architecture and Coop Himmelb(l)au and has taught and been involved in research at the Vienna University of Technology, University of Innsbruck, Art University Linz, University of Applied Sciences in Munich, and Kennesaw State University in the US.

INDEX

Page numbers in *italics* indicate a figure and page numbers in **bold** indicate a table on the corresponding page. Page numbers followed by 'n' indicate a note.